THE BOOK OF OFFICES AND SERVICES
OF THE ORDER OF SAINT LUKE

By Brothers and Sisters of the Order

Dwight W. Vogel, OSL, Editor and Compiler

Daniel T. Benedict, OSL, Abbot

Fourth Edition, 2012

The Book of
OFFICES AND SERVICES
of The Order of Saint Luke
(Fourth Edition)

Copyright © 1988, 1994, 2012
First Printing, October 2012
Second Printing, February, 2013
OSL Publications. All rights reserved.

ISBN-13: 978-1478391029
ISBN-10: 1478391022

Editorial Consultants
Cynthia Astle, OSL, Daniel Benedict, OSL, Robert Davis, OSL,
Jack Fahey, OSL, Anne Ferguson, OSL,
Heather Josselyn-Cranson, OSL, Sue Moore, OSL

Cynthia Astle, OSL, Production Editor

Contents not under copyright from other sources including all unattributed material and that bearing an OSL attribution may be reproduced by chapters and members of the Order or by local churches without further permission by including the following credit line and copyright notice:

"Reprinted from The Book of OFFICES and SERVICES of The Order of Saint Luke, copyright © 2012 by The Order of Saint Luke. Used by permission of OSL Publications."

TABLE OF CONTENTS

Chapter	Page
Preface by Dwight W. Vogel, OSL, Editor	i
Introduction by Daniel T. Benedict, OSL, Abbot	iii
Words of Appreciation from the Editor	vii
Guidelines for Use	vii
The Story of the Winged Ox	viii

Offices and Services

  Word and Table

Lukan Liturgy of Word and Table	4
Great Thanksgiving One	12
Great Thanksgiving Two	15
Great Thanksgiving Three	18
Great Thanksgiving Four	22

  The Daily Office

Morning Prayer or *Lauds*	27
The Diurnal Offices	34
Mid-morning Prayer or *Terce*	34
Mid-Day Prayer or *Sext*	36
Mid-afternoon Prayer or *None*	38
Evening Prayer, *Vespers* or *Evensong*	41
Compline	48
Vigil	56
Daily Office (brief form) *tan card rite*	63

  Pastoral Services

Service of Prayer for Healing	67
Service of Prayer for Reconciliation	72
Rite of Reconciliation for Individuals	78
Transitus	81

  Services of The Order of Saint Luke

Profession of Vows	87
Investiture of Officers	94

Worship Resources

Item	Number
Service Music	
Invitations to Silence	1-2
Kyrie Eleison	3-7
The Lord's Prayer	8-12
Gospel Acclamations	13-18
Agnus Dei	19-22
Word and Table	
Gathering Songs	23-32
Presentation of the Gifts	34-36
Communion	37-45
Sending Forth	46-51
Morning Prayer	
Opening of Morning Prayer	52-54
Canticle of Zechariah	55-56
Morning Hymns	57-62
Evening Prayer	
Opening of Evening Prayer	63-64
Phos hilaron	65-66
Evening Prayer Canticle	67-69
Canticle of Mary	70-73
Evening Hymns	74-78
Compline	
Night Hymns	79-87
Canticle of Simeon	88-91
Pastoral Services	
Healing	92-98
Reconciliation	99-104
Transitus	105-107
Times and Seasons	
Advent	108-111
Christmas	112-114
Epiphany	115-117
Lent	118-121
The Great Fifty Days	122-126
Pentecost	127-130
Ordinary Time	131-133

Worship Resources (continued)

Item	Number
Saints	134-136
Mary, Mother of Jesus	137-139
Saint Luke the Evangelist	140-143
Lukan Eucharistic Music	144-149
Order of Saint Luke Resources	
Litany for the Order	150
Intercessions for the Order	151
Collect of the Order	152
Affirmation of Vows	153
Prayers of Awareness (Confession and Assurance)	154-161
Affirmations of Faith	162-165
Prayers of the People	166-173
Sending Forth: Blessings and Commissioning	174-182
The Great Litany	183
Canticles	184-201

	Page
Psalter	293–313
Rule of Life and Service	314

Acknowledgements and Indices

Metrical Index	318
Index of Tune Names	319
Author and Composer	321
Topical Index	325
Index of First Lines and Common Titles	328
Acknowledgements	334
Contributors	336

Preface

In his preface to the third edition of this book, Br. Timothy J. Crouch, OSL, wrote that the intent throughout the preparation of the first three editions of this book had remained the same:

> that we should, after careful experimentation and use, provide a book of worship materials that would assist members of the Order in their daily life and work. It is not intended to be a set of rules set in stone; rather, it is a living and evolving expression of our growing awareness of the call to sacramental life.[1]

That understanding also applies to the current volume. In it we seek to provide resources that will help us live into and out of our prayer in the collect for the Order "that we may proclaim the apostolic hope, magnify the sacraments, and embody Christ's healing grace for all creation." The sacramental life we seek to live is informed by a spirituality grounded in the writings of Luke the Evangelist, the characteristics of which are lifted up by our Abbot in what follows. It is our hope that these offices and services reflect, engender, and nourish a Lukan spirituality. We pray that in and through them, Luke's priorities will be internalized through the ongoing conversion and transformation of our lives, both individually and corporately. What we pray and observe and celebrate in these offices and services seeks both to glorify God and to open ourselves to Christ's healing grace for the life of the Church and for the sake of the world.

The earlier editions included daily offices, services of profession and investiture, and widely influential services of healing. To these we have added a Lukan Service of Word and Table to embody our commitment to magnifying the sacraments, services of prayer for reconciliation to address an overlooked part of our Christian liturgical heritage, and a Transitus service to share together as we stand in the presence of the transition through death to Life. Worship resources are provided for each of these.

Some of these services and the resources that support them can be used by individual members of the Order; that is especially true when the Daily Office is prayed alone. However, the primary context for this book is our communal life together such as:

---

[1] *The Book of Offices and Services After the Useage of The Order of Saint Luke* (Akron, OH: Order of Saint Luke Publications, 1994), 1. The original offering of offices and services for The Order of Saint Luke came in 1982. An edition of *The Book of Offices and Services After the Useage of The Order of Saint Luke* came six years later in 1988. The third edition came in 1994 after another eight years of use throughout the Order. All three were edited and compiled by Br. Timothy J. Crouch, Chaplain General of the Order.

- when "two or three" are gathered in Christ's name (as in the domestic church when partners or families pray together),
- when a few members of the Order and their friends gather for prayer (perhaps beside the bedside of one who is ill or in the presence of that great transition through death to Life),
- when a chapter or subchapter or association of the Order meets together, or
- when the general chapter or the general council of the Order meets.

If all you have in addition to this book is a Bible, you should have adequate resources for your prayer and worship together. It is all you need. However, it may not be all you want! Most often it will be supplemented by other materials.

Members of the Order of Saint Luke seek to be faithful to our calling to be stewards of the mysteries of God.[2] We are custodians of the liturgical heritage of the Church through the ages. We do this, not out of an antiquarian impulse to preserve and replicate the past, but rather because the depth dynamics of that heritage reflect both the mystery of the Transcendent and the incarnational embodiment of Christ's healing grace for and in all creation. As an Order, we are not constrained by demands for quantitative success, nor by desires for what is deemed attractive by the culture of the day. Rather the relevance to our common life reflected in these offices and services is found in the motifs of Lukan concerns for inclusivity, care for the dispossessed and marginalized, and commitment to the healing grace of God's reconciling love.

Our aim has not been to provide services which can or should be replicated in the worship life of local churches, although it is our hope that the resources provided may be used and adapted by liturgical leaders there in appropriate ways. Rather we have sought to provide resources for the Order when we meet, be we few or many when we do so. Here are core resources for our life of prayer and worship as members of the Order. We pray that the Holy Spirit will use them to form, enrich and deepen the Lukan spirituality we share, and will use us as leaven in the loaf in the worship of the Church and for the life of the world.

Dwight W. Vogel, OSL
Editor and Compiler
Feast of the Annunciation, 2012

---

2 See I Corinthians 4:1.

INTRODUCTION TO THE FOURTH EDITION

As an Order, we are evolving. This revision of *The Book of Offices and Services* comes out of my discernment, with the confirmation of the Council, that the needs and practices of members of the Order require a revised, single volume daily office accommodating a range of usages. Since the "ordinary" for daily prayer published in *The Book of Offices and Services* forms the template for the "propers" in The Daily Office, the Council decided that a revision of our offices and services had to come first.

In the six decades since the founding of The Order of Saint Luke, our community has been exploring and discovering a spirituality informed by Saint Luke the evangelist, author of the gospel that goes by his name and his subsequent narrative in the Acts of the Apostles. Through continuing reflection on his "orderly account" (Luke 1:1, 3) we have begun to glimpse his priorities and distinctive insights into "the events that have been fulfilled among us."

Since any attempt to summarize or systematize Luke's telling of the story risks distorting Luke's work, we approach this attempt to identify a Lukan spirituality with humility and joy, not mastery. This venture is both evangelical and apostolic, for we desire to be shaped by Jesus in the power of the Holy Spirit to proclaim and embody the good news of Jesus Christ. This is clear in our Rule of Life and Service: we affirm the apostolic hope, live for the church, seek the sacramental life, promote the corporate worship of the church, magnify the sacraments, and accept the call to service. Clearly, our Rule of Life and Service sees in Luke a profound attentiveness to the evangel seen through the eyes of a community rooted in common life, liturgy and hope. Luke's description of the nascent community in Acts 2: 42-47 could well be the pattern for our life together: "They devoted themselves to the apostles' teaching and fellowship, the breaking of bread and the prayers.... [They] had all things in common...distributing as any had need...spent much time together in the temple, broke bread...with glad and generous hearts, praising God . . . " (Acts 2:47b). I can't help but note that they left the results to God!

What then is the spirituality we seek to embody in our worship and life together?

First, Lukan spirituality is liturgical. It is grounded in worship and prayer, the sacraments and the hallowing of time. The daily office canticles are found in Luke—the songs of Zechariah, Mary, Simeon, and the angels (the Gloria in Excelsis). Luke lays out the "Word and Table" pattern of worship with his resurrection story of the two walking to Emmaus (Luke 24). In Acts we see a community together for praise, the sharing of meals (meals are always sacramental!), and always "gathering" and "being sent"—two profoundly liturgical acts. Lukan spirituality practices and rejoices in this liturgical life. Far from being perfunctory or sidebars, they are central to forming and sustaining evangelical and catholic prayer and service. As in earlier editions, the resources in this volume invite us as a community to rest on a solid liturgical and sacramental foundation. While here and there you will see deliberate references to Luke's casting of gospel and ecclesial life, these Lukan themes underlie the entire project.

Second, Lukan spirituality is charismatic. We acknowledge, without apology, our dependence on the Holy Spirit, breathing life into dry bones. In Luke, the Holy Spirit is central. We cannot imagine faithful discipleship apart from the Holy Spirit's promptings. From the annunciation in Luke 1 to Jesus' "you will be baptized by the Spirit" to the Day of Pentecost to the apostles' reliance upon the Holy Spirit in their actions, Luke-Acts portrays the Holy Spirit animating each and all in the community. Other than John 15 and 16, there is no more sustained emphasis and narrative of the Spirit's working in ordinary people to do extraordinary things. The Holy Spirit descends upon Jesus, leads him into the wilderness, sustains him in the face of temptation, births the church and empowers its proclaiming and embodying of the reign of God. The apostolic community is a sent and directed community—a charismatic community. In this sense, we understand that our baptismal charism (gift, grace) is the Holy Spirit sent from the Father and the Son to indwell us and direct our life and work. We seek to be self-consciously aware of grace as the immediate and ongoing work of the Spirit within us. We commend the resources of this volume to one another in that spirit: not as a law but as invitation and resource for the Spirit to prompt and inform our prayer. We trust the Spirit to make good use of it in the varied settings and occasions in which we gather. This spirited freedom and practicality is consistent with much of Christian history, including that of the Wesleys and the early Methodists.

Third, Lukan spirituality is oriented to the poor and those who live and suffer on the margins of daily life. The character of the Spirit who baptizes us is the character of Jesus, who associates and suffers with the poor, the hungry, and those who weep (Luke 6:20-23). We seek to grow in his character and to trust that the Spirit who animates us proclaims and embodies good news to those most in need. Lukan piety will always impel us to commitment to the poor and marginalized because Jesus is to be found with them. By way of confession, this may be the most challenging aspect of Lukan spirituality for us. In general, we have much work to do in orienting ourselves toward those with whom Jesus identified and spent time.

Fourth, Lukan spirituality is prophetic and countercultural. This prophetic posture is imaginative and poetic in ways that subvert entrenched power and privilege. From the God-initiated radical reversals in the canticle of Mary to Jesus' sermon proclaiming release to the captives at Nazareth (Luke 4:18-19) to the narrative of Paul's upsetting of the economy in Ephesus (Acts 19:21-31), Luke sets out a vision of the reign of God that was alarmingly revolutionary to both Jews and Romans. In that world created and maintained by a massive slave population, the Messiah's letting all of the oppressed "go free" invoked a colossal reversal for the establishment. Unlike the beatitudes in Matthew, Luke's casting of the beatitudes, and the addition of the woes, unequivocally reverse the prevailing social values, then and now (Luke 6:20-26). These cannot be toned down to be just pious individual virtues. The Book of Acts reports the many beatings and imprisonments of Paul. Those events did not occur because Paul was a heretic in a narrowly religious sense. Recalling the uproar in Ephesus, imagine your local chamber of commerce organizing a citywide rally against your congregation's upsetting the local economy!

The reality is that most of us in The Order of Saint Luke are privileged and powerful. We are invested in what *is* more than in what in God's justice *will be*. Hence, we are rather deaf and blind to this dimension of Lukan spirituality. The coming reign of God challenges us to a deeper and more imaginative reading of this dimension of Luke's work.

Fifth, Lukan spirituality is communal. With the early apostolic community that Luke describes, we seek to continue in the apostles' teaching and fellowship, the breaking of bread and the prayers, even to share a common life in diaspora! That is why praying the daily office, continuing formation in the baptismal covenant, and celebration of the Holy Eucharist gives us such hope—hope that in sharing these disciplines faithfully, we share a common life though separated by regions, even continents. In our dispersion, we yearn for and commit to live in community, sharing joys, bearing burdens, and holding one another and ourselves accountable to the Rule of Life and Service. The one specific practice the Rule specifies is praying the daily office. This volume gives us the full structure for daily prayer and the hallowing to time through the day. At the center of this communal life is the Holy Eucharist. Let us celebrate the sacrament whenever we gather, graciously and fully aware of the risen Christ who gives us his body that we may be for each other and the world the body of Christ, redeemed by his blood. Here you will find well-considered new settings (textual and musical) for Eucharistic celebration. As an order, we seek to live the good news of God's new humanity as Christ's new community of love and justice.

Finally, Lukan spirituality is apostolic. We are a community sent (Greek *apostolos*) by Christ to many places. Luke portrays Jesus and the apostles as itinerant for the sake of the gospel. While we may experience our dispersion around the world as a disadvantage, perhaps it is a gospel advantage. With Jesus, we intentionally embrace our dispersion. Of course, many of us would like to live in residence, as many monastic communities do. When we are together in retreat, we know how rich such communal life can be, and we are deeply renewed and sustained in such settings. Yet, we give ourselves to an itinerant proclamation in deeds and words for conversion and forming disciples. You may think I am alluding to the distinctive itinerancy of Methodist clergy. I am not. Rather, I am proposing that Luke gives us a picture of missionary people, over against our human tendency to settle or see ourselves choosing where to reside.

As with that earliest apostolic community, Christ sends us as witnesses from our Jerusalem to our Judea and Samaria, and the ends of the earth (Acts 1:8). As a community in diaspora, we have many Jerusalems. Christ, by the Spirit, places us where we are to live the sacramental life and proclaim the apostolic hope. Our rule is a commitment in common to life-long spiritual formation. However, this formation is not an end to itself. What if we understood apostolic witness as itinerant ministry, not only in geographical terms, but also in terms of attentive presence. What if we understood our vocation as journey into the depths of the very place or places in which we find ourselves. Jesus' instructions to the seventy merit continuing contemplation: "Remain in the same house…do not move about from house to house" in our transient world (Luke 10:7ff). We cannot generalize about the meaning of location and stability for each other. We can support each sister and brother in the call of God and the meaning of being winsome listeners and catalysts of conversion in the places to which the Spirit sends us. The traditional monastic virtue of "stability" for us may be in sustained attentiveness in the context where God plants us for the life of the world.

Our Lukan spirituality continues to emerge. Let us be a liturgical and apostolic community under the guidance of the Spirit, especially for the sake of the poor and those living on the margins of life, seeking Christ's justice and reconciliation in the diverse places where the Spirit plants us.

So, my sisters and brothers, I commend this revision of *The Book of Offices and Services* to you. Use it well and anticipate a new single volume of *The Daily Office* in the not too distant future. I am grateful for all who have worked diligently to birth this greatly expanded revision. I want to add to the list of those to whom gratitude is due, Br. Dwight Vogel, who serves as the general editor for this project. His knowledge, *joie de vivre* and disciplined oversight are evident throughout the work. May this volume be good soil in which the seed of liturgical prayer grows. As always, the way of prayer is the way of faith. Use, adapt and supplement these rites and resources as you pray and worship with your sisters and brothers.

Soli deo Gloria.
+Abbot Daniel T. Benedict, OSL
Easter Thursday, 2012

Words of Appreciation from the Editor

The title page lists brothers and sisters of The Order of Saint Luke as the primary authors of this volume. There is not a page that does not bear the marks of your contributions, critiques, suggestions and creative work. I am deeply grateful for the diligence and commitment of our production editor, Sr. Cynthia Astle, and for the sustaining work and wisdom of our editorial consultants: Br. Robert Davis, Br. Jack Fahey, Sr. Heather Josselyn-Cranson and Sr. Sue Moore. Time and time again I have turned to Br. Richard Miller for advice and counsel. His attention to both small details and crucial theological and liturgical concerns has been a great gift. He and Sr. Virginia Ford have gifted us with their painstaking and time-consuming proofreading. They have caught a number of errors and inconsistencies. Those that remain are the responsibility of the editor.

Our beloved Abbot Daniel T. Benedict has undergirded and graced our work from his first vision of the project, to his sustaining wisdom along the way, to his amazing gift for euchological language, to his affirmation of the end product. Allen Tuten, our music copyist, and Donald F. Chatfield, our chant copyist, have made significant contributions to this volume. Sr. Anne Ferguson, our chaplain general, has overseen the use of these offices and services at retreat and council meetings, providing the opportunity for us to engage in and reflect on their embodied practice in the life of the Order. To all who have been a part of this project, especially those who are not named here but whose emails, letters, phone calls and conversations have contributed to this work, we express the heartfelt thanks, not only of the editor but of the entire Order.

Guidelines for Use

Symbols used throughout the book instruct the reader as follows:

+ Those who are able physically and wish to do so are invited to stand.

[Parts of the office or service which are optional, depending on day or season, or when a simpler form is desirable, such as when prayed alone or in the domestic church.

[ ] Words or phrases which can be omitted, for example [Alleluia] in Lent.

Note: When the word "kingdom" appears, some of our members prefer to say "kin-dom" to emphasize the beloved community of God's rule of love, peace, and justice.

For an explanation of the authors' abbreviations throughout the book, see Contributors on page 336.

Directions for singing to psalm tones, including reference to the meaning of underlining and use of italics, are found on page 295.

THE STORY OF THE WINGED OX

Christianity has used symbols since its earliest times, often to impart the Gospels to illiterate multitudes in the same way that Jesus used imaginative parables to teach about God. Later, as in the eastern branch of the Church, symbols known as icons became a sacred art form intended as "windows into heaven," or guides to prayer and meditation. During the Dark Ages, Celtic monks and Christian artisans created "high crosses" in stone using Christian symbols to teach Bible stories to believers who couldn't read. These ancient art forms are being discovered anew as aids to spiritual practice in the highly visual 21st century.

The Winged Ox has been the traditional symbol of Saint Luke from early Christianity. Its origin can be traced to no single creator, but the image combines clearly identifiable cultural elements that historically represented sacrifice, service and strength. As with the symbols for Matthew, Mark and John, the figure's wings signify divine inspiration. Since an ox or a bull was a frequent sacrifice by many ancient religions including the Judaism of Jesus, the figure also symbolizes Jesus' sacrifice in his passion and crucifixion and his standing as the Christ, our high priest before God. Because the ox is a faithful servant, the figure also signifies the obedience of Mary of Nazareth, whose consent to give birth to Jesus put into motion God's plan for human salvation. The latter interpretation especially derives from Saint Luke, who puts the greatest emphasis on Mary of any of the Gospel writers.

The Winged Ox illustrations in this book are:

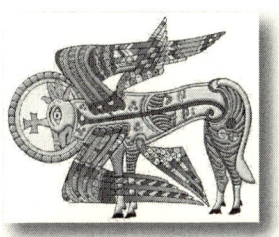

Cover, Title Page, Pastoral Services and Rule of Life and Service: The Winged Ox, Celtic artwork licensed to The Order of Saint Luke.

Offices and Services: The Four Evangelists from the Book of Kells, an illuminated manuscript Gospel book in Latin, created by Celtic monks ca. 800 or slightly earlier. The Winged Ox is in the lower left corner. Now housed at Trinity College, Dublin, Ireland. Public Domain Photo.

Word and Table: Contemporary Public Domain artwork from Internet Sacred Texts Archive, http://www.sacred-texts.com/cnote.htm

The Daily Office: Detail from an AD 12th century mosaic in the Saint Clement Basilica (San Clemente) in Rome. Public Domain Photo.

Services of The Order of Saint Luke: Badge of Saint Luke from *Alphabets & Numbers of the Middle Ages* by Henry Shaw, published in 1845. Public Domain.

Worship Resources: A depiction of Saint Luke and his symbol from The Lindisfarne Gospels, an illuminated manuscript produced on the island of Lindisfarne in Northumbria in the late 7th or early 8th century. The unique Lindisfarne style combined Anglo-Saxon and Celtic motifs. Now housed in the British Library. Public Domain Photo.

Other art used in this book was chosen from works that follow the Celtic style of the Winged Ox licensed to The Order of Saint Luke. All art or representations of artwork depicted herein are in the public domain.

Compiled by Cynthia Astle, OSL

WORD AND TABLE

A LUKAN LITURGY OF WORD AND TABLE

This liturgy seeks to reflect the themes and language of the writings of Luke the evangelist in his gospel and the Book of Acts. It is provided for use by the members of the Order of Saint Luke when they gather in order that they may be grounded in and formed by a Lukan spirituality as they celebrate Eucharist together. Hymns and prayers appropriate to the day or season should be selected. This service is not meant to be the only liturgy of Word and Table to be used by the Order, nor to replace the services and resources provided by the churches of which those belonging to the Order are members.

+ You are invited to stand as you are able.

GATHERING

GREETING
Blessed be God, who shepherds us and sets us free!
  May the dawn from on high break upon us
  to guide us into the way of peace.
With God's tender compassion,
  Christ walks with us,
  opening the scriptures,
  and making himself known to us in the breaking of bread.

[ADAPTED FROM LUKE 1:68, 78-79 AND 24:13-35]

+**HYMN** *(appropriate to the day or season; see Worship Resources 23-32, 108-143)*

+**PRAYER OF THE DAY**

The Holy One[1] be with you;
  and also with you.
Let us pray.

God of mystery and mercy:
You have created all things and called them good.
You breathe into us the breath of life
  and sustain us all our days.
When we are lost, you provide the way.

---
[1] Or "The Lord" or "God"

Come upon us in freedom and grace
that we may seek the lost, heal the sick, announce God's reign,
and delight that our hearts know you
as you walk with us on the Way. **Amen.**

[MJO'D AND DTB]

Following the prayer for the day, the "Gloria in Excelsis"(Luke 2:14; see Worship Resources 186-187) or another canticle (see Worship Resources 184-201) may be sung.

PROCLAMATION AND RESPONSE

PRAYER FOR ILLUMINATION
Mighty God,
  through whom we come to know the love
  and healing power of Jesus:
By the power of your Holy Spirit
open our minds and hearts
that we may hear what you have to say to us today. **Amen.**

[OSL DAILY OFFICE IV-B]

FIRST READING

PSALTER AND GLORIA

This or another psalm. This psalm reflects Lukan concerns. Omit "Alleluias" during Lent.

Psalm 146

Steven Elvey (1805-1860), alt.

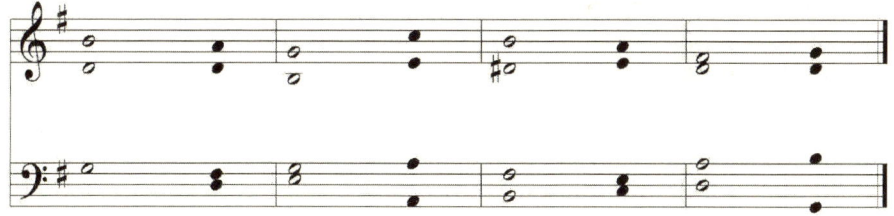

[Alleluia!] Praise God, O my *soul*!
I will praise God as long as I *live*;
I will sing praises to my *God*
  while I have *being*.

Put not your trust in rulers nor in any child of *earth*,
for there is no help in *them*.
When they breathe their last, they return to *earth*,
and in that day their thoughts *perish*.

Happy are they who have the God of Jacob for their help,
   whose hope is in their *God*;
who made heaven and earth, the seas and all that is *in them*,
whose promise abides for *ever*;
who gives justice to those who are oppressed
   and food to those who *hunger*.

God sets the prisoner *free*
and opens the eyes of the *blind*;
God lifts up *those*
who are bowed *down*.

God loves the righteous
   and cares for the *stranger*;
God sustains the orphan and widow
   and frustrates the way of the *wicked*.
[except in Lent:]
God shall reign for-*ever*,
your God, O Zion, throughout all generations. Alle-*luia*!
[in Lent:]
God shall reign for-*ever*,
your God, O Zion, throughout all gener-*ations*.

                                                      [OSH]

Glory be to *you*,
O Trinity most holy and *blessed*,
who is now, ever was, and ever shall *be*
unto endless ages, A–*men*.

(on holy days:)
Glory to God: Source of all, Eternal Word and Holy *Spirit*,
one God, holy and blessed *Trinity*,
who is now, ever was and ever shall *be*
      unto endless ages, A-*men*.

SECOND READING

+THE GOSPEL ACCLAMATION
(for Alleluias, see Worship Resources, 13-16; for Lenten Acclamation, see Worship Resources, 17-18)

+READING OF THE GOSPEL

+THE GOSPEL ACCLAMATION
(repeating the above acclamation)

HOMILY

+AFFIRMATION

(for affirmation of Lukan vows, see Worship Resources 153; for other affirmations, see Worship Resources 162-165).

The community is seated.

PRAYERS OF THE PEOPLE

The Holy One[1] be with you.
And also with you.

Let us pray.

(for other prayers, see Worship Resources 166-173)

Beginning and End of all things,
  we bless you for the present that is ever yielding
  to your new heaven and new earth.
We offer you our praise for all the means of grace
  and for every prompting of your Spirit,
  calling us to spurn sin and open ourselves
  to your presence and purpose.
Merciful God,
    Hear our prayer.

Here members of the community are invited to lift up thanksgivings and concerns, concluding each petition with "Merciful God," to which the community responds: "Hear our prayer."

We yield our concerns to your unceasing mercy:
    care for the sick and the suffering,
    touch the dying,
    claim the newborn,
    shelter the homeless,
    sing in the faithful,
    chasten the arrogant and powerful,
    lift up the lowly,
    center the Church,
    grant peace to every people,
    and shape our lives by the mystery of Christ.
  Merciful God,
    Hear our prayer.   [DTB]

---

[1] Or "The Lord" or "God"

PRAYERS OF SPECIAL INTENTION
(To be used only when the congregation is made up primarily of members of the Order)

[INTERCESSIONS FOR THE ORDER OF SAINT LUKE

Hear our prayer and let our cry come to you
  for *Brother/Sister (Name)*, our Abbot,
  for the officers of the General Chapter,
  for all who serve the Order of Saint Luke,
  for a sense of connectedness with others in the Order,
  for grace to live for you and with each other
    in faithfully keeping our Rule of Life and Service.
Merciful God,
  hear our prayer.

[COLLECT FOR THE ORDER OF SAINT LUKE

O Shepherd of us all,
  who inspired your servant Saint Luke the physician
  to set forth in the Gospel the love and healing power
    of Jesus:
Grant, we ask you, your Spirit to the Order of Saint Luke,
  that we may proclaim the Apostolic hope,
  magnify the Sacraments,
  and embody Christ's healing grace for all creation;
through Jesus Christ our Lord. Amen.

INVITATION

When we turn our feet toward home,
 God runs to us and embraces us, full of compassion,
 inviting us to eat at Christ's table and celebrate the joyful feast.
Trusting such boundless hospitality and steadfast love,
let us confess our sin before God and one another.

                                           [SEE LUKE 15:20-24; HJC]

CONFESSION AND PARDON
(see also Worship Resources 154-161)

    Loving and merciful God,
      we offer you all our personal and corporate sins,
      and those offenses in which we are complicit,
      knowingly and unknowingly.

                – silent confession –

Merciful God,
consume our sins with the fire of your love.

**Remove all the stains of sin,
and through your grace,
restore us mercifully with your kiss of peace.
We offer you all that is good in us,
in order that you may amend and sanctify it,
perfecting it more and more,
that we may live faithfully
in your loving presence.**

[Thomas a Kempis, 15th c., alt. see Luke 15:11-32]

THE KYRIE

(for sung versions, see Worship Resources 3–7)

Lord, have mercy.
   Christ, have mercy.
Lord, have mercy.

ASSURANCE OF PARDON

Hear the good news:
In the name of Jesus Christ,
through God's boundless love
you are forgiven in good measure, pressed down,
shaken together, and running over!

[HJC, see Luke 6:38]

   (in unison)
   **In the name of Jesus Christ, you are forgiven!
   Glory to God! Amen!**

THE PEACE

The peace of Christ be with you all!
   And also with you.
Let us share signs of reconciliation and peace with one another.

THANKSGIVING AND COMMUNION

Let us offer ourselves and our gifts to God.

+THE PRESENTATION OF THE GIFTS: TAKING THE BREAD AND CUP

(see Worship Resources 34-36 and 38)

+THE GREAT THANKSGIVING
(see Great Thanksgiving One (p. 12), Two (p. 15), Three (p. 18), and Four (p. 22)

THE LORD'S PRAYER *(see Worship Resources 8-12 for sung versions)*

And now with the confidence of those invited by Christ to his table, we pray as he taught us.

> **Our Father in heaven,**
> **hallowed be your name.**
> **Your kingdom come,**
> **your will be done,**
>   **on earth as in heaven.**
> **Give us today our daily bread.**
> **Forgive us our sins**
> **as we forgive those who sin against us.**
> **Save us from the time of trial,**
> **and deliver us from evil,**
> **for the kingdom, the power, and the glory are yours,**
> **now and forever. Amen.**

BREAKING THE BREAD

Because there is one loaf,
we, who are many, are one body, for we all partake of the one loaf.
The bread which we break, is it not a sharing in the body of Christ?
> **It is!**

The cup over which we give thanks, is it not a sharing in the blood of Christ?
> **It is!**

Come from the East and the West, from the North and the South and share in the bread and the wine made holy.
(see also Worship Resources, 33)

[THE AGNUS DEI *(see Worship Resources 19 - 22)*

SHARING THE BREAD AND CUP
(silence, instrumental music or see Worship Resources 37-45)

PRAYER AFTER RECEIVING

Let us pray.
> **Lord, you have now set your servant free**
> **to go in peace as you have promised;**

> for these eyes of mine have seen the Savior,
> whom you have prepared for all the world to see,
> a Light to enlighten the nations,
> and the glory of your people Israel.

[LUKE 2:29-35; ICET]

SENDING FORTH

+HYMN
(see Worship Resources 46-52 or "Life and Service" 143)

+ABBOT'S COMMENDATION AND BLESSING
If the abbot of the Order is not present, the commendation may be given by a prior abbot, one of the general officers, or the prior of the chapter beginning with the words "And now, on behalf of Abbot (first name of current abbot). I commend you to God . . . ."

> And now I commend you to God
>   and to the word of God's grace
> which is able to build you up
> and to give you an inheritance with all the saints.

[ACTS 20:32]

> The grace of our Lord Jesus Christ, and the love of God,
>   and the aid and comfort of the Holy Spirit be with you all.
>   **Amen.**

[II CORINTHIANS 13:14 ALT.]

The community may be seated for a time of reflection guided by music. If there is no music, the community remains standing for the commission.

COMMISSION
(see also Worship Resources 59, 88, 177-178, 180-182)

> You are witnesses of these things,
> sent forth, clothed with power from on high,
> Glorify God in all things,
>   heal the sick,
>   eat with the hungry and the outcast,
>   love the earth.

[SEE LUKE 24:48-49]

> Let us bless the Lord!
>   **Thanks be to God!**

When the Eucharist accompanies a Service of Profession of Vows, the last two lines above are replaced by "The peace of the Lord be always with you. And also with you," followed by the passing of the peace.

GREAT THANKSGIVING ONE[1]

The Risen Christ be with you.
>**And also with you.**

Lift up your hearts.
>**We lift them up to the Lord.**

Let us give thanks to the God of mercy and grace.
>**It is right to give our thanks and praise.**

Our souls outburst in praise to you, God of Israel,
 architect of galaxies, earth sculptor, life breather.
In you is the dawning of our hope.
In you is the life of the world.
In you are witnesses and servants of the Word.
In you are the songs of old men and young women.
In you is table and home for sinners and outcasts.
In you is the mercy promised to our ancestors.
In you is the unseating of the arrogant
and the raising up of the poor.

And so,
with Mary and Martha,
with Levi and Zacchaeus,
with the forgiven woman with her tears and her perfume,
with all earth's returning prodigals
and with all whose feet want to dance but cannot.
we join all creation in heaven's unending song:

---

[1] Text: DTB; Music: William J. Beasley, OSL ©OSL 2009

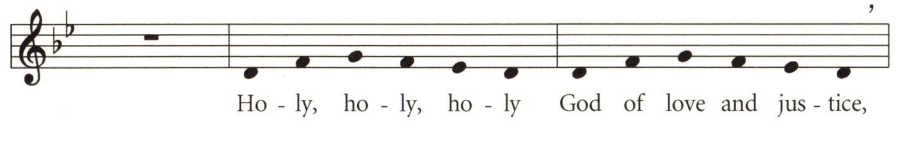

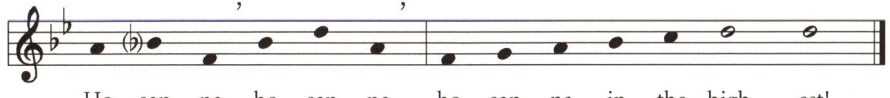

WORDS: Adapted from traditional sources
MUSIC: William J. Beasley, OSL, 2009
Music © 2009 Order of Saint Luke

Holy and blessed is the mighty savior you raised up for us,
Jesus, Mary's child,
who opens the way of salvation,
leading us home to your loving arms.

Healing the sick, feeding the hungry and eating with sinners.
he crossed boundaries
proclaiming your reign among us.
By the mystery of his incarnation, death and resurrection
he has continued with the Church
in the apostle's teaching and fellowship,
in the breaking of the bread, and the prayers.

At Pentecost your Spirit unleashed
a song-singing, story-telling, table-sharing people
from Jerusalem to the ends of the earth.

On the night he gave himself up for us,
he took bread, gave thanks to you,
broke the bread and said: "This is my body given for you."

[SEE LUKE 22:14-20]

And he took a cup, gave thanks to you and said:
"This cup is the new covenant in my blood.
 Do this, as often as you drink it, in remembrance of me."

[SEE I CORINTHIANS 11:25-26]

In this meal of hope
liberate us by your Spirit's anointing
to embody good news to the poor,
to declare release to captives and recovery of sight to the blind,
to set free the disheartened and the abused,
as we proclaim the mystery of faith
until Christ rules in love's final victory.

Christ's death, O God, we pro-claim. Christ's res-ur-rec-tion we de-clare. Christ's com-ing we a-wait. Glo-ry be to you, O God.

WORDS: Adapted from traditional sources
MUSIC: William J. Beasley, OSL, 2009
Music © 2009 Order of Saint Luke

Pour out your Holy Spirit on us gathered here,
and on these gifts of bread and wine.
Let them be for us the body and blood of Christ,
that we may be for the world the body of Christ
in service, justice, and compassion.

[SEE LUKE 22:24-28 AND 7:11-17 AND 2:46-55]

Blessing and glory are yours, Mighty God,
here and everywhere,
now and forever!

A - men, a - men, a - men, a - men.

WORDS: Trad.
MUSIC: William J. Beasley, OSL, 2009
Music © 2009 Order of Saint Luke

GREAT THANKSGIVING TWO[1]

The Lord be with you.
And also with you.
Lift up your hearts.
We lift them up to the Lord.
Let us give thanks to the Lord our God.
It is right to give our thanks and praise.

It is right, and a good and joyful thing
  always and everywhere to give thanks to you,
    Almighty God, Creator of heaven and earth.
> Our souls proclaim your greatness, O Lord. Our spirits rejoice in you, our Savior. For you, the Almighty, have done great things for us, and holy is your name. Your mercy reaches from age to age for those who fear you. You have shown strength with your arm. You have scattered the proud in their conceit. You have deposed the mighty from their seats of power and raised the lowly to high places.

[SEE LUKE 1: 46–56]

And so, with your people on earth
  and all the company of heaven,
we praise your name and join their unending hymn:

---

[1] Adapted by MJO'D from the Word and Table pattern of *The United Methodist Hymnal*. Portions of the prayer from that source are used with permission of The United Methodist Publishing House. Music: George R. Crisp, OSL ©2009 George R. Crisp; All rights reserved.

WORDS: English Language Liturgical Consultation (ELLC)
MUSIC: George R. Crisp, OSL, 2010
Words © 1988 English Language Liturgical Consultation (ELLC). Music © 2010 George R. Crisp.

Holy are you, and blessed is your Son Jesus Christ,
your Beloved, with whom you are well pleased.

[SEE LUKE 3:22]

Your Spirit anointed him
  to preach good news to the poor,
  to proclaim release to the captives and
  recovering of sight to the blind,
  to set at liberty those who are oppressed, and
  to announce that the time had come when you would save your people.
He sought the lost and welcomed home the wayward.
He healed the sick, fed the hungry and ate with sinners,
that there might be joy in the presence of your angels
over each sinner who repents.

[SEE LUKE 15:3-9; 19:10; 15:11-32; 15:10]

By the baptism of his suffering, death, and resurrection,
> you gave birth to your church,
>> delivered us from slavery to sin and death,
>> and made with us a new covenant
>> by water and the Spirit.

On the night in which he gave himself up for us
> he took bread, gave thanks to you, broke the bread,
> gave it to his disciples, and said,

"Take, eat; this is my body which is given for you.
Do this in remembrance of me."

When the supper was over he took the cup,
> gave thanks to you, gave it to his disciples, and said,

"Drink from this, all of you; this is my blood of the
> new covenant poured out for you and for many
>> for the forgiveness of sins.

Do this as often as you drink it,
> in remembrance of me."

And so, in remembrance of these your mighty acts in Jesus Christ,
we offer ourselves in praise and thanksgiving
> as a holy and living sacrifice,
> in union with Christ's offering for us,

as we proclaim the mystery of faith.

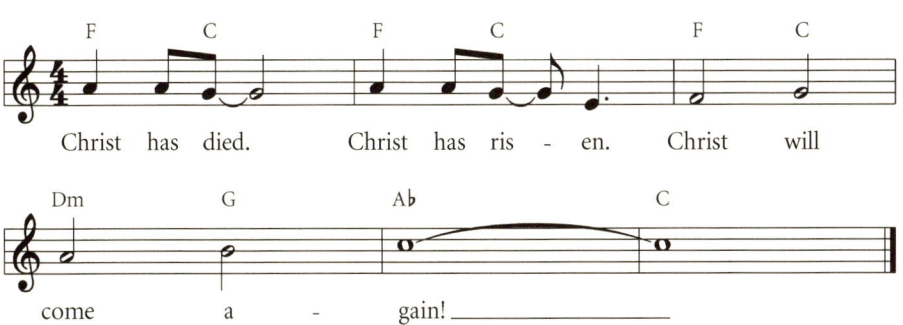

Christ has died. Christ has ris-en. Christ will come a-gain!

WORDS: English Language Liturgical Consultation (ELLC)
MUSIC: George R. Crisp, OSL, 2010
Words © 1988 English Language Liturgical Consultation (ELLC). Music © 2010 George R. Crisp.

Pour out your Holy Spirit on us gathered here,
    and on these gifts of bread and wine.
Make them be for us the body and blood of Christ,
that we may be for the world the body of Christ,
    redeemed by his blood.
Help us to hold these mysteries fast in our hearts
    and to bear fruit with patient endurance
that we might be neighbor
    to the least, the last, the little, and the lost.
        [SEE LUKE 8:15; 10:36-37; 9:45; 14:13-14,21; 16:25; 21:3-4; 13:30;
        22:24-27; 9:47; 17:2; 18:16-17; 15:1-32; 19:10]

By your Spirit make us one with Christ,
    one with each other and
    one in ministry to all the world,
until Christ comes in final victory and
    we feast at the heavenly banquet.

Through your Son Jesus Christ,
with the Holy Spirit in your holy church,
all honor and glory is yours, almighty God,
    now and for ever.

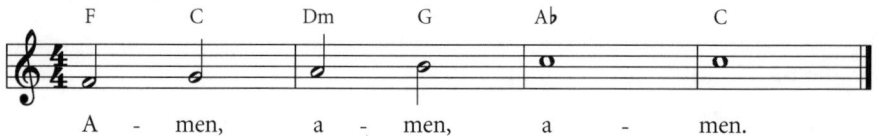

WORDS: Trad.
MUSIC: George R. Crisp, OSL, 2010
Music © 2010 George R. Crisp

GREAT THANKSGIVING THREE[1]

The Risen Christ be with you.
    And also with you.
Lift up your hearts.
    We lift them up to the Lord.
Let us give thanks to the God of mercy and grace.
    It is right to give our thanks and praise.
Blessed are You, God of song and healing;
all creation praises your holy name.

---

[1] Text: DES; Music: DIVINUM MYSTERIUM, arr. DWV © 2011, OSL

On earth Mary, Zachariah and old Simon
lead us in singing praise;
in heaven, the angel hosts cry out
  "glory in the highest."
For you came to us in human form
to teach and to heal,
to walk our Emmaus roads,
and to take our life in your hands
forgiving, restoring, and raising us to new life.

So we join with the chorus of stars
and with all creatures on earth and in heaven,
Singing:

WORDS: Adapt. from traditional responses
MUSIC: Adapt. from 11th cent. *Sanctus* trope, DIVINUM MYSTERIUM;
       arr. Dwight W. Vogel, OSL, 2011
Arr. © 2011 Order of Saint Luke

Blessing and honor and praise are yours
through Jesus Christ your child, our brother.
You gather a people from every race and nation
and speak beatitude to all who listen,
inviting us in Jesus to the table of grace,
pouring your love out like precious oil,
washing us with water and Spirit,
reconciling us with a cross-born glory.

On the night in which he was abandoned
and handed over to suffering by friends,
when they were at table, Jesus took bread,
blessed it, broke it and gave it to his disciples, saying:
"Take, eat, this is my body given for you and for many.
Do this for my remembrance."
After supper he took the cup,
and when he had given thanks
he gave it to them saying,
"Drink from this all of you,
for this is my blood of the New Covenant,
poured out for you and for all.
Do this as often as you drink it,
for my remembrance."
So we offer you praise and thanksgiving
in company with Luke the physician
and witness from the ends of the earth.
Remembering all that has been revealed to the world,
we proclaim the mystery of faith:

Dy-ing you de-stroyed our death. Ris-ing you re-stored our life.

Come Lord Je-sus Christ, come in res-ur-rec-tion glo-ry!

WORDS: Adapt. from traditional responses
MUSIC: Adapt. from 11th cent. *Sanctus* trope, DIVINUM MYSTERIUM;
arr. Dwight W. Vogel, OSL, 2011
Arr. © 2011 Order of Saint Luke

You open wide your arms to embrace
old and young, rich and poor, women and men,
promising never to abandon us,
and sending your Holy Spirit to strengthen and to cheer us.

Come Holy Spirit on us gathered out of love for you.
   Come, Holy Spirit!
Come Holy Spirit upon these gifts of bread and wine;
making them to be for us the body and blood of Christ.
   Come Holy Spirit!
Come Holy Spirit, enlivening us in gratitude and service,
   Come Holy Spirit.
Look with mercy on the world's infirmities and suffering.
Draw strength from our weakness,
making us a community of justice and peace.
Unite us in love for all people,
and hasten the day when all shall be well
and all manner of things shall be well.

In, with and through Jesus Christ our Light,
our Bread, our Wine, our Way, our Truth,
and our Life in your blessed triune glory.

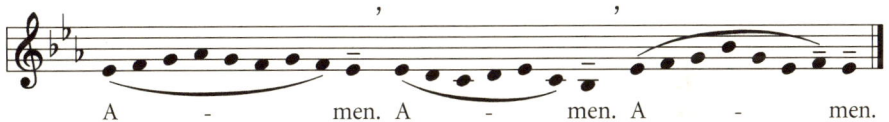

A - men. A - men. A - men.

WORDS: Trad.
MUSIC: Adapt. from 11th cent. *Sanctus* trope, DIVINUM MYSTERIUM;
   arr. Dwight W. Vogel, OSL, 2011
Arr. © 2011 Order of Saint Luke

GREAT THANKSGIVING FOUR[1]

God be with you.
God is with us! We are not alone.
Christ be with you.
Christ is with us!
The Risen One has met us,
blessed and fed us
on the road that leads us home.
What is the promise?
Be we few or many, the Comforter will come.
Then lift up your hearts!
Our hearts with rapture thrill!
Here we assemble as your family.
We are your people and you are our God.
Your love makes us friends;
your blood makes us kin.
Holy One, Trinity of grace and power:
it is good; it is right; it is a joyful thing to give you thanks,
Maker and Mother, Beloved and Lover, Father and Friend.
You are ever the father who gives us bread, not stones.
You are the mother who never forgets we're her own.
From the beginning of life to the closing of time,
you are the One who is with us to the end.
And so we sing:

> **Salvation, glory and power to God**
> **for Jesus our redeemer reigns;**
> **The mountains, hills, and valleys sing**
> **as angels, saints, and heav'ns proclaim:**
> **Hallelujah, Hallelujah, Halle, Halle, Hallelujah!**
> **Salvation, glory and power to God**
> **for Jesus our redeemer reigns.**

SUGGESTED TUNE: CANDLER; SEE WORSHIP RESOURCES 147

---

[1] Adapted from an Appalachian Lord's Supper from the Open Source Liturgy Project of the General Board of Discipleship of The United Methodist Church. and a Lukan Great Thanksgiving by HME. As with the other Great Thanksgivings in this book, it follows the classic Antiochene pattern for the prayer.

Holy are you and blessed is your Beloved, Jesus, meek and wild.
By his birth, his baptism into life, death and glory,
Christ redeemed us from sin, and restored creation's story.
> **Truly human, whole and holy, he gave us grace,**
> **showed us truth, and taught us what forgiveness means.**

We remember the night when Jesus gave himself to us.
> **We remember, we will never forget.**

He took bread and gave thanks.
> **We remember, we will never forget.**

He gave it to his friends:
This is my body.
Take. Eat. Share. Remember.
> **We remember, we will never forget.**

He took the cup and gave thanks.
> **We remember, we will never forget.**

He gave it to his friends:
This is my blood, given for you.
Take. Drink. Live. Remember.
> **Oh, how we remember!**

We remember the Gift you've given,
> **and offer ourselves to you as Christ offers himself to us,**
> **a whole and holy sacrifice of prayer and praise.**

In the name of your Beloved, we proclaim the mystery of faith:

> **What wondrous love is this, O my soul, O my soul,**
> **what wondrous love is this, O my soul!**
> **What wondrous love is this that caused the Lord of life**
> **to lay aside his crown for my soul, for my soul,**
> **to lay aside his crown for my soul.**
>
> **To God and to the Lamb I will sing, I will sing,**
> **to God and to the Lamb I will sing!**
> **To God and to the Lamb who is the great I AM,**
> **while millions join the theme I will sing, I will sing,**
> **while millions join the theme I will sing!**

TUNE: WONDROUS LOVE, SEE WORSHIP RESOURCES 148

Breathe, Holy Spirit!
> **Breathe, Holy Spirit!**
Breathe on this bread and cup.
> **Breathe on us gathered here,**
> **and all in your keeping.**
Breathe peace, Jesus.
> **Breathe, Holy Spirit!**

By your Spirit, make us one with Christ,
> **one with each other,**
> **and one in ministry to all the world,**
> **until Christ comes again in grace and glory,**

Then lost in wonder, love, and praise,
we and all creation sing for joy:

> > **Praise God from whom all blessings flow.**
> > **Praise God, all creatures here below.**
> > **Praise God, blest holy Trinity**
> > **both now and for eternity. Amen.**
> >   Tune: OLD 100th, see worship resources 149

THE DAILY OFFICE

MORNING PRAYER
(Lauds)

Each morning we celebrate God's new creation and the resurrection of Jesus from the dead, even as waking itself is a new creation, a resurrection after the night's sleep. We ask God to open our lips, for even when I pray this office alone, I remember that I am part of a community praying the Church's prayer. As Martin Luther remembered his baptism when he washed his face each morning, so we celebrate our new life in Christ, touching the water when we are alone, or hearing and seeing it poured or sprinkled when in community.

After the Morning Hymn and Prayer, the Psalter and the Gloria, we hear God's word to us in scripture. Then our attention is focused on a brief part of that scripture, a practice that comes to us from the tradition of Count Nicholas von Zinzendorf who would provide a "watchword" for his flock, a practice that continues among the Moravians to this day. These "heart words" serve to guide but not restrict our time of silent meditation.

We then join the Church through the ages and around the world in the morning canticle, the song of Zechariah. A brief reading from historic or contemporary spiritual classics may follow, after which we lift up our prayers of thanksgiving and supplication, our traditional morning collects, the Lord's prayer, and a concluding collect. We join our voices in a hymn, followed by a blessing. Strengthened by God's grace, we go forth to live a sacramental life in the day ahead.

OPENING

CALL TO PRAISE AND PRAYER
(see Worship Resources 53 for a sung version)

    O God, open our lips,
        and our mouths shall proclaim your praise.
    From the rising of the sun to its setting,
        we praise your name, O God.

                      [ADAPTED FROM PSALM 51:15 AND 113:3]

REMEMBRANCE OF BAPTISM
(Water may be touched, poured or sprinkled.)

    By Word and water
    God renews us this day
    in the living fountain of God's grace,

and raises us with Christ Jesus
to live a new life in the Spirit.
**Satisfy us in the morning
   with your steadfast love, O God,
that we may sing for joy
   and be glad all our days.**

[PSALM 90:14]

+MORNING HYMN OR CANTICLE
(See Worship Resources 195-201 for other canticles and 57-62 for Morning Hymns. The Venite Exultemus which follows is commonly sung to psalm tone three or spoken in unison.)

Come, let us sing to the <u>Ho</u>-ly *One*;*
let us shout for joy to the Rock of <u>our</u> sal-*vation*.
Let us come before God's presence <u>with</u> thanks-*giving*,*
and raise a loud <u>shout</u> with *psalms*.
For you, O God, are <u>a</u> great *God*,*
you are great a-<u>bove</u> all *gods*.
In your hand are the <u>caverns</u> of the *earth*,*
and the heights of the <u>hills are</u> yours *also*.
The sea is yours, <u>for</u> you *made* it,*
and your hands have molded <u>the</u> dry *land*.
Come, let us bow down and <u>bend</u> the *knee*,*
and kneel before <u>God</u>, our *Maker*.
For you are our God,
   and we are the people of your pasture
   and the sheep <u>of</u> your *hand*.*
Oh, that today we would hearken <u>to</u> your *voice*!

[PSALM 95:1-7 (OSH PSALTER)]

+MORNING PRAYER
(When prayed in community:

The Holy One* be with you;
And also with you.
Let us pray:)
   (one of the following or another morning prayer)

Dawn from on high,
your light illumines all our days.
Awaken us to your visitations throughout this day.
Be merciful in us for the sake of others.

---

* Or "The Lord" or "God"

Make us fearless when confronting injustice and need,
that we may give you glory in the power of the Spirit. **Amen**
[DTB]

New every morning is your love, great God of light,
and all day long you are working for good in the world.
Stir up in us desire to serve you,
to live peacefully with our neighbors,
and to devote each day to your Son,
our Savior, Jesus Christ the Lord. **Amen**.
[PRESBYTERIAN WORSHIPBOOK, USA., 20TH C. USED BY PERMISSION.]

PSALMODY

PSALTER AND GLORIA
(see pp 294-313)

> *Antiphon*
>
> *Psalm(s)*
>
> *Gloria:*
>
> Glory to you, O Trinity most <u>ho</u>ly and *blessed,*
> one God, now and for-<u>ev</u>er, A – *men.*
>
> *(on holy days:)*
> Glory to God: Source of all, Eternal Word and <u>Ho</u>-ly *Spirit,*
> one God, holy and <u>bless</u>-ed *Trinity,*
> who is now, ever was and <u>ev</u>er shall *be*
> > unto endless <u>ag</u>es, A-*men.*
>
> *Antiphon*
>
> *Silence*

WORD

SCRIPTURE[2]
 After the reading(s), the reader says
> Holy wisdom, holy word.
> **Thanks be to God!**

---

[1] For recommended psalms, see *The Daily Office of The Order of Saint Luke.* For the Revised Common Lectionary psalms for Daily Prayer, see
http://www.commontexts.org/publications/index.html

[2] For the Revised Common Lectionary readings for Daily Prayer, see
http://www.commontexts.org/publications/index.html

Hear what the Spirit is saying:
> *Here one or two verses of the preceding scripture*
> *or a part thereof, may be reiterated.*

SILENCE FOR REFLECTION

+CANTICLE OF ZECHARIAH *(The Benedictus)*
(may be said or sung antiphonally to psalm tone three, with the second voice taking the indented lines, or be sung in unison; see Worship Resources 55,56, 188, 189 for other versions)

> We bless you, Adonai, God of *Israel*,
> for you come to visit us and ransom us from *bondage*.
> You have brought forth a strong De-*liverer*
> in the house of your child *David*.
>
> > This is what your holy prophets an-*nounced*:
> > deliverance from enemies and from the hand of all who *hate us*;
> > mercy a-mong our *ancestors*,
> > and remembrance of your ho-ly *covenant*.
>
> This is the promise you swore to our an-cestor, *Abraham*,
> to make us un-a-*fraid*,
> to rescue us from our *enemies*,
> to serve before you, holy and just,
>   all the days of our *lives*.
>
> > And this, my little child, shall be called prophet of the Most *High*,
> > going before you, Adonai, to pre-pare your *paths*,
> > making your people know de-*liverance*
> > by the forgiveness of their *sins*.
>
> *[Unison]*
> Through your merciful compassions, God our *God*,
> the dawn from on high shall *visit us*,
> to shine on those kept in dungeons and the shadows of *death*
> and to guide our feet onto the path of *peace*.
>
> [LUKE 1:68-79; TBE, ALT., OSL]
>
> Glory to you, O Trinity, most holy and *blessed*,
> one God, now and for-ever, A-*men*.

[A READING FOR MEDITATION AND REFLECTION]

Prayers

(When prayed in community:

>The Holy One[3] be with you,
>**and also with you.**
>
>Let us pray:)

Silent Prayer

Prayers of Thanksgiving and Supplication
Give thanks and pray for the coming day and the needs of the world, then pray one or usually more of the following collects.

>God of abundance,
>by your Spirit call us anew this day
>to hold lightly our goods and possessions,
>so that the poor and outcast may find in us generous friends,
>through Jesus Christ, our Lord. **Amen.**
>
>>[DTB]
>
>Mighty God,
>from whom all thoughts of truth and peace do come:
>pour into the hearts of all people, we pray,
>the true love of peace,
>and guide with your wisdom
>those who take counsel for the nations of the earth,
>that in tranquility your work may go forward
>until the world is filled with the knowledge of your love;
>through Jesus Christ our Lord. **Amen.**
>
>>[Bishop Francis Paget, 1851-1911, alt TJC]
>
>O God, by whom we are guided in judgment,
>and who raises up for us light in the darkness:
>grant us, in all our doubts and uncertainties,
>the grace to ask what you would have us to do;
>that your Spirit of Wisdom may save us from all false choices,
>and in your straight path we may not stumble;
>through Jesus Christ our Lord. **Amen.**
>
>>[John W. Sutter, Jr., inspired by Is. 30:15 and Ps. 46:11; from Services for Trial Use: Series Three, 1973, of the Church of England; alt TJC]

---

[3] Or "The Lord" or "God

Prayers of Special Intention

Collect of Commemoration[4]

Collect for the Order of Saint Luke[*]

O Shepherd of us all, who inspired your servant Saint Luke the physician to set forth in the Gospel the love and healing power of Jesus: Grant, we ask you, your Spirit to the Order of Saint Luke, that we may proclaim the Apostolic hope, magnify the sacraments, and embody Christ's healing grace for all creation, through Jesus Christ our Lord. Amen.

The Lord's Prayer
(See Worship Resources 8–12 for sung versions)

**Our Father in heaven,
 hallowed be your name,
 your kingdom come,
 your will be done, on earth as in heaven.
Give us today our daily bread.
Forgive us our sins
 as we forgive those who sin against us.
Save us from the time of trial
 and deliver us from evil.
For the kingdom, the power, and the glory are yours
 now and forever. Amen.**

(after which a concluding collect such as the following is prayed)

Mighty and everlasting God,
who has safely brought us to the beginning of this day:
defend us with your mighty power,
and grant that this day we fall into no sin,
 neither run into any kind of danger,
but that all our doings, ordered by your governance,
may be always pleasing in your sight,
through Jesus Christ our Lord. **Amen.**

[Book of Common Prayer]

---

[*] *May be preceded by Intercessions for the Order of Saint Luke (see Worship Resources 152)*

[4] See the sanctoral cycle in FOR ALL THE SAINTS or another resource.

+Hymn *(see Worship Resources 57-62, 108-143)*

+Blessing
(see also Worship Resources 174-182)
> May the God of hope
> fill us with all joy and peace in believing,
> so that by the power of the Holy Spirit,
> we may abound in hope. **Amen.**
>
> [Adapted from Romans 15:13]

The community may be seated for a time of reflection guided by music.

The grace of the Lord Jesus Christ be with us.

THE DIURNAL OFFICES

These brief diurnal or daytime offices punctuate the day with prayer. They are prayed in the setting in which we find ourselves, whether at work, as a community gathered for learning and fellowship, or on retreat. While the traditional times for these are at the third, sixth, and ninth hours (that is, at 9:00 am, noon, and 3:00 pm), the exact time for each is variable according to the context of the settings in which we pray them.

A diurnal office may be replaced by a Service of Word and Table or a Service of Healing or Reconciliation. When one of the diurnal offices is used to open a gathering, hymns may be inserted between the opening sentences and the first prayer, and between the concluding prayer and the closing dialog. A time of shared petitions and intercessions may be added to the time of silent prayer. On Wednesdays or Fridays, the Great Litany (Worship Resources 183) may replace one of the diurnal offices.

The beginning and ending of the period of silence that begins each of these offices may be marked by the ringing of a bell or meditation bowl. See Worship Resources 1-2 for sung Invitations to Silence.

MID-MORNING PRAYER (Terce)

At the hour when the Holy Spirit came upon the Church at Pentecost we pray.

SILENCE

Be still, aware of God's presence within and around.

OPENING SENTENCES

> O God, come to our assistance.
> **O Lord, hasten to help us.**
> Glory to the holy and blessed Trinity,
> **one God now and forever. Amen.**

PRAYER

(When prayed in community:

> The Holy One[1] be with you;
> **And also with you.**

Let us pray:)

> Holy Spirit,
> come upon us this hour without delay;
> pour out your graces on our souls.

---

[1] Or "The Lord" or "God"

Let tongue and soul and mind and strength proclaim your
    praise.
Set our love aflame by the fire of your love,
and may its warmth enkindle love in our neighbors.
Empower us with your presence
    in the name of Christ. **Amen.**

[FROM THE HYMN FOR THIS HOUR ATTRIBUTED TO ST. AMBROSE, 340-397, ALT,]

PSALTER *(commonly sung to psalm tone three or said in unison)*
Praise God, <u>all</u> you *nations*,
    laud the Most High, <u>all</u> you *peoples*.

(except during Lent)

For God's loving-kindness toward <u>us</u> is *great*,
    and the faithfulness of God endures forever.
<u>Al</u>-le-*luia*!

(during Lent:)

For God's loving-kindness toward <u>us</u> is *great*,
    and the faithfulness of God en-<u>dures</u> for-*ever*.

[PSALM 117, OSH PSALTER]

Glory to you, O Trinity, most <u>holy</u> and *blessed*,
one God, now and for-<u>ever</u>, A-*men*.

THE LITTLE CHAPTER
God says to us:
I will draw you from far and near,
        gather you from your exile
        and bring you home.
    I will wash you with fresh water,
        and make you clean from all that defiles you.

I will give you a new heart,
    and breathe a new spirit into you.
    I will take away your heart of stone,
    and give you a faithful spirit,
        my own spirit to lead you,
    so that you may walk faithfully in my ways.
    You will be my people
    and I will be your God.

[A CANTICLE PARAPHRASED FROM EZEKIEL 36:24-28, OSL]

– a brief time of silent prayer –

THE LORD'S PRAYER

Our Father in heaven,
hallowed be your name,
your kingdom come,
your will be done, on earth as in heaven.
Give us today our daily bread.
Forgive us our sins
as we forgive those who sin against us.
Save us from the time of trial
and deliver us from evil.
For the kingdom, the power, and the glory are yours
now and forever. Amen.

CONCLUDING PRAYER

Living God, in whom we live and move and have our being,
guide and govern us by your Holy Spirit,
so that in all the cares and occupations of our life
  we may not forget you,
but remember that we are ever walking in your sight;
through Jesus Christ our Lord. **Amen.**

[BCP, ALT]

Let us bless the Lord!
Thanks be to God!

MID-DAY PRAYER (Sext)

At the hour when Jesus was placed on the cross, we pray.

SILENCE

Be still, aware of God's presence within and around.

OPENING SENTENCES

O God, come to our assistance.
O Lord, hasten to help us.
Glory to the holy and blessed Trinity,
one God now and forever. Amen.

PRAYER

(When prayed in community:

The Holy One[2] be with you;
and also with you.

---

[2] Or "The Lord" or "God"

Let us pray:)

Risen Savior,
at this hour you hung upon the cross,
stretching out your loving arms:
Send your Holy Spirit into our hearts,
to direct us in your way,
to comfort us in our afflictions,
and to lead us into all truth;
through Jesus Christ our Lord. **Amen.**

[BCP, ALT]

PSALTER   *(commonly sung to psalm tone three or said in unison)*
Give praise, you <u>servants</u> of *God.**
Praise the name of <u>the</u> Most *High.*
Let God's <u>name</u> be *blessed**
from this time forth for <u>ev</u>-er *more.*
From the rising of the sun to its <u>go</u>-ing *down.**
let God's holy <u>name</u> be *praised*!

[PSALM 113: 1-3 OSH PSALTER]

Glory to you, O Trinity, most <u>holy</u> and *blessed*,
one God, now and for-<u>ever</u>, A-*men.*

THE LITTLE CHAPTER

Even the young may grow weak and fall exhausted,
but those who trust in God for help will find their strength renewed.
They will rise on wings like eagles.
They will run and not be weary;
when they walk, they will not grow weak.

[A CANTICLE PARAPHRASED FROM ISAIAH 40:30-31, OSL]

– a brief time of silent prayer –

THE LORD'S PRAYER

Our Father in heaven,
hallowed be your name,
your kingdom come,
your will be done, on earth as in heaven.
Give us today our daily bread.
Forgive us our sins
as we forgive those who sin against us.

Save us from the time of trial
   and deliver us from evil.
**For the kingdom, the power, and the glory are yours
   now and forever. Amen.**

CONCLUDING PRAYER

Holy Wisdom, in your loving kindness you created us.
restoring us when we were lost.
Inspire us with your truth,
that we may love you with our whole minds
  and run to you with open hearts,
through Christ our Savior. **Amen.**

[ALCUIN OF YORK, 8TH C.]

Send forth your Spirit, Lord.
   Renew the face of the earth.
Creator Spirit, come.
   Inflame our waiting hearts.
Lord, hear our prayer,
   and let our cry come to You.
Bless the Lord!
   Thanks be to God!

MID-AFTERNOON PRAYER (NONE)

At the hour when Jesus died on the cross, we pray.

SILENCE

Be still, aware of God's presence within and around.

OPENING SENTENCES

O God, come to our assistance.
   O Lord, hasten to help us.
Glory to the holy and blessed Trinity,
   one God, now and forever. Amen.

PRAYER

(When prayed in community:

The Holy One[3] be with you;
   And also with you.
Let us pray:*)*

---

[3] Or "The Lord" or "God"

Living, loving God,
through your wisdom the hours of the day move on,
and there is yet much to do.
Keep us in your care and renew us with your strength
   so that we may not forget you
nor be unaware of your love towards those around us,
   in the name of Christ
who lives and reigns with you and the Holy Spirit. **Amen.**

[DWV]

PSALTER *(commonly sung to psalm tone five or said in unison)*

Happy are they who have not walked
   in the <u>coun</u>sel of the *wicked*,*
nor lingered in the way of sinners,
   nor sat in the <u>seats</u> of the *scornful*!
Their delight is in the law of the <u>Ho</u>-ly *One*,*
and they meditate on [God's] law <u>day</u> and *night*.
They are like trees planted by streams of water,
   bearing fruit in due season,
   with leaves that <u>do</u> not *wither*,*
everything they <u>do</u> shall *prosper*.
It is not so <u>with</u> the *wicked*;*
they are like chaff which the wind <u>blows</u> a-*way*.
Therefore the wicked shall not stand upright
   when <u>judg</u>-ment *comes**
nor the sinner in the council <u>of</u> the *righteous*;
For the Holy One knows the <u>way</u> of the *righteous*,*
but the way of the <u>wicked</u> is *doomed*.

[PSALM 1, OSH PSALTER. ALT.]

Glory to you, O Trinity, most <u>holy</u> and *blessed*,
one God, now and for-<u>ever</u>. A-*men*.

THE LITTLE CHAPTER

Let each of us look out for the interests of one another,
having the attitude that Christ Jesus had
who, having the nature of God,
did not seek to exploit equality with God,
but emptied himself,
taking the nature of a servant,
becoming like us in human form,

humbly walking the path of obedience
all the way to death on the cross.

Therefore, God lifted him high,
giving him a name above all names,
    that at the name of Jesus
our knees should bend and our tongues proclaim
to the glory of God Most High:
"Jesus Christ is Lord."

                  [A CANTICLE PARAPHRASED FROM PHILIPPIANS 2:6-11 [OSL]

– a brief time of silent prayer –

THE LORD'S PRAYER
  Our Father in heaven,
    hallowed be your name,
    your kingdom come,
    your will be done, on earth as in heaven.
  Give us today our daily bread.
  Forgive us our sins
    as we forgive those who sin against us.
  Save us from the time of trial
    and deliver us from evil.
  For the kingdom, the power, and the glory are yours
    now and forever. Amen.

CONCLUDING PRAYER
  Lord Jesus Christ, who came to set us free:
  let the shadow of your cross fall upon us in this hour
  that we may wonder at the gift of your redeeming love,
  and be empowered by your Spirit
  to take up our own cross daily and follow you. **Amen.**

                                                       [DWV]

Show us, O God, your mercy,
    and grant us your salvation.
Bless the Lord!
    Thanks be to God!

EVENING PRAYER

*(with references for use at Vespers on holy days
and for Festive Vespers or Evensong on major feasts)*

With the lighting of a solitary candle or oil lamp, we share in the ancient practice of opening Evening Prayer with a service of light. A dialog from scripture reminds us that evening prayer is prayer to Christ, the light of the world. We sing the oldest non-scriptural hymn still in use and give thanks for the Light of the paschal mystery through which we are incorporated into Christ's incarnation, life, death, resurrection and coming again. As we look back on the past day we pray for awareness of our own shortcomings before God and one another. After the psalter and gloria, we hear God's word to us in scripture. Then our attention is focused on a brief part of that scripture, "heart words" that serve to guide but not restrict our time of silent meditation.

In response, we join the Church through the ages and around the world in the evening canticle, the Song of Mary. A brief reading from historic or contemporary spiritual classics may follow, after which we lift up our prayers. We join our voices in a hymn, and entrusting ourselves to God's grace, receive the assurance of God's blessing.

Festive Vespers or Evensong replaces Evening Prayer and Compline on the evening before major feasts. Elements peculiar to holy days or major feasts are noted below.

OPENING[1]

Entrance of the Light
(See Worship Resources 63 for a sung version)

> Jesus Christ, you are the Light of the World,
> **the light no darkness can overcome.**
> Stay with us, for it is evening,
> **and the day is nearly over.**
> For with you is the fountain of life,
> **and in your light do we see light.**
>
> [Adapted from John 8:12, Luke 24:29, Psalm 35:9]

(The proper for major feasts may be added.)

---

[1] When Evening Prayer is prayed alone or in the domestic church, the Thanksgiving for the Light and the Evening Prayer Canticle may be omitted. The Prayer of Awareness is a model for recollection of the day and may be abbreviated or recast, so long as a time of recollection and silence for awareness is observed.

+Hymn of Light *(The Phos Hilaron)*
((See also Worship Resources 65, 66 for alternative settings. This form is commonly sung in unison to psalm tone one)

>O gra-cious *Light*,*
>pure brightness of our everlasting God in *heaven.*
>O Je-sus *Christ*,*
>ho-ly and *blessed.*
>Now as we come to the setting of the *sun*,*
>and our eyes behold the ves-per *light,*
>we sing your praises, O *God*,*
>most holy and bless-ed *Trinity.*
>You are worthy at all *times,* *
>to be praised by hap-py *voices,*
>O Son of God, O Giver of *Life*,*
>and to be glorified through all the *worlds.*

>><small>[Phos hilaron, late 3rd/early 4th c.;
>>adapted by Timothy J. Crouch
>>from the work of Charles Mortimer Gulbert]</small>

[+Thanksgiving for Light]

(Always included in Festive Vespers or Evensong; see also Worship Resource 64; for Marian feasts, see Worship Resource 137).

(When prayed in community:

>The Holy One[2] be with you,
>**and also with you.**
>Let us pray:)

>God of life and light,
>who has been with us throughout this day,
>we give you thanks for Christ our Light.
>As evening falls,
>let your grace shine upon us.
>so that, with all your people,
>we may live in the light of your love
>now and through eternity. **Amen.**   [DWV]

>>*The community is seated.*

[Evening Prayer Canticle
(see Worship Resources 67–69, may be accompanied by the lighting of incense; always included in Festive Vespers or Evensong)

---

[2] Or "The Lord" or "God"

PRAYER OF AWARENESS[3]

>As we come before the Holy One,
>we come as we are,
>wounded or well,
>sick, sinful or sorrowful,
>seeking the grace of Christ
>which is sufficient for all our needs.
>
>*– a time of silent reflection –*
>
>Let us pray.
>**Triune God,**
>**Giver of grace,**
>**Christ of compassion,**
>**Saving Spirit,**
>**we open ourselves to you.**
>**Frail creatures, we fail, we sin,**
>**we eat forbidden fruit.**
>**We suffer wrongs that others have done to us.**
>**Holy God,**
>**transform us from glory to glory**
>**   into the image of Christ,**
>**that we may do justice,**
>**love mercy, walk humbly with you,**
>**and forgive as you have forgiven us,**
>**through your Spirit who is able to make all things new.**
>**Amen.**

WORDS OF ASSURANCE:

Hear the good news:
   The God of new beginnings
      wipes every tear from our eyes,
   forgives us and frees us,
   for former things have passed away
      through the grace of Christ
      and the power of the Holy Spirit.
         Amen! Thanks be to God!!

[RUTH DUCK, C. 2010]

---

[3] Other prayers of awareness or prayers of confession and assurance may also be used; see *Worship Resources* 154–161.

PSALMODY

PSALTER AND GLORIA

> *Antiphon*
>
> *Psalm(s)*
>
> *Gloria*
>
> a) Glory to you, O Trinity most <u>ho</u>ly and *blessed*
> one God, now and for-<u>ev</u>er, A – *men*.
>
> b) +(*On holy days the following form of the Gloria is used:*)
> Glory to God: <u>Source</u> of *all*,
> Eternal Word and <u>Ho</u>-ly *Spirit*,
> One God, holy and <u>bless</u>-ed *Trinity*,
> Who is now, ever was and ever shall be
>   for endless <u>ag</u>es, A-*men*.
>
> c) +(*For Festive Vespers or Evensong, the following form of the Gloria is used:*)
> Glory to God, Love abounding be-<u>fore</u> all *ages*;
> Glory to God, Love shown forth
>   in the self-emptying of <u>Je</u>-sus *Christ*;
> Glory to God, Love poured out through the gift of the Spirit,
>   who fashions and renews the <u>face</u> of the *earth*;
> Glory to the holy and <u>bless</u>-ed *Trinity*!
> All things a-<u>biding</u> in *Love*;
> Love abiding <u>in</u> all *things*,
> as it is now, <u>ev</u>-er *was*,
> and ever shall be for endless <u>ag</u>es, A–*men*.   [DAVID N. POWER]

ANTIPHON

SILENCE

WORD

SCRIPTURE[4]

After the reading(s), the reader says:

> Holy wisdom, holy word.
> **Thanks be to God!**
> Hear what the Spirit is saying:
>> *Here one or two verses of the preceding scripture, or a part thereof, may be reiterated.*

SILENCE FOR REFLECTION

---

[4] For the Revised Common Lectionary psalms for Daily Prayer, see http://www.commontexts.org/publications/index.html

CANTICLE OF MARY *(The Magnificat; Luke 1:39-56)*
(See Worship Resources 70-71, 73 and 190-191 for sung versions. This form is commonly sung to psalm tone two).

My soul proclaims your great-ness, *Lord*;
my spirit rejoices in you, my *Savior*;
For you have looked with favor on your low-ly *servant*,
from this day all generations will call me *blessed*.

> You the Almighty have done great things for *me*,
> and Holy is your *Name*.
> You have mercy on those who fear *you*
> in every gen-er-*ation*.

You have shown the strength of your *arm*;
you have scattered the proud in their con-*ceit*.
You have cast the mighty from their *thrones*;
you have lifted up the *lowly*.

> You have filled the hungry with good *things*;
> and the rich have been sent a-way *empty*.
> You have come to the help of your ser-vant *Israel*,
> for you have remembered your promise of *mercy*,
> the promise you made to our *forebears*,
> to Abraham and his children for *ever*.

[TJC, OSL]

(unison)
> Glory to you, O Trinity, most holy and *blessed*;
> one God, now and for-ever, A-*men*.

[A READING FOR MEDITATION AND REFLECTION]

PRAYERS

(When prayed in community:
> The Holy One[5] be with you,
> **and also with you.**
> Let us pray:)

---

[5] Or "The Lord" or "God."

Silent Prayer

Pray for the life of the church and the world and the concerns of the heart.

[Prayers of Supplication and Intercession]
(see Worship Resources 166-173 for possible texts; at Festive Vespers or Evensong The Great Litany may be used, see Worship Resources 183).

Collects

One and usually more of the following collects.

> God of tender compassion,
> you shine on those who live in darkness
>   and under the shadow of death:
> Keep us mindful of Lazarus hungry at the gate
>   and bold to confront the powers that keep him there,
> through Christ, our Lord. **Amen.** [DTB]

> Most holy God,
> the source of all good desires,
> all right judgments, and all just works;
> give to us, your servants, that peace which the world cannot give,
> so that our minds may be fixed on the doing of your will,
> and the fear of our enemies having been removed,
> we may pass our time in rest and quietness;
> through the mercies of Jesus Christ our Savior. **Amen.**
> [Gelasian Sacramentary, 8th century, alt. TJC]

> O God,
> the life of all who live, the light of the faithful,
> the strength of those who labor,
> and the repose of the dead,
> we thank you for the blessings of the day that is past
> and humbly ask for your protection through the coming night.
> Bring us in safety to the morning hours;
> through him who died and rose again for us,
> our Savior Jesus Christ. **Amen.**
> [Mozarabic Sacramentary, 6th century]

Prayers of Special Intention

Collect of Commemoration

Proper collects for holy days and major feasts

Intercessions for the Order of Saint Luke[6]
Hear our prayer and let our cry come to you
for *Brother/Sister (first name)* our abbot,
for the officers of the General Chapter,
    Brother/Sister (first names),
for our priors,
    or: for Brother/Sister (first name), our prior,
for our brothers and sisters in the Order (*especially . . .*),
for a sense of community with others in the Order,
for grace to live for you and with each other
    in faithfully living our Rule of Life and Service.
Merciful God,
    hear our prayer.

The Lord's Prayer *(see Worship Resources 8–12 for sung versions)*
Our Father in heaven,
    hallowed be your name,
    your kingdom come,
    your will be done, on earth as in heaven.
Give us today our daily bread.
Forgive us our sins
    as we forgive those who sin against us.
Save us from the time of trial
    and deliver us from evil.
For the kingdom, the power, and the glory are yours
    now and forever. Amen.

(after which a concluding collect such as the following is prayed)

O God,
in your servants
you manifest the signs of your presence.
Send forth upon us the Spirit of love,
that in companionship with one another
your abounding grace may increase among us;
through Jesus Christ, our Lord. **Amen.**   [BCP, ALT.]

---

[6] At the conclusion of these intercessions, the collect for The Order of Saint Luke may be prayed (see *Worship Resources* 151).

Hymn

(see Worship Resources 74–78 for Evening Hymns; see Worship Resources headings for hymns appropriate to the day or season)

For Festive Vespers or Evensong or when Compline is not prayed later in the evening, the commendation and Song of Simeon may be included here (see Worship Resources 89-90, 192).

Blessing

May God bless us and keep us.
May God's face shine upon us
  and be gracious to us.
May God lift up the divine countenance upon us,
  and give us peace. **Amen.**   [Adapted from Numbers 6:24-26]

(The community may be seated for a time of reflection guided by music.)

The grace of the Lord Jesus Christ be with us.
Let us bless the Lord![7]
  Thanks be to God!

COMPLINE

Compline is the office that "completes" the day. It has been called the "bedtime prayer of the Church." It opens with a significant time of silence. The mood of the entire office is one of peace and tranquility. Both speaking and singing are done quietly. The community remains seated throughout. The beginning and ending of times of silence may be marked by the sound of a bell or meditation bowl. The service ends in silence.

SILENCE*

Be still, aware of God's presence within and around.

Call to Prayer

O God, come to our assistance.
  O Lord, hasten to help us.
The Holy One grant us a restful night,
and peace at the last.
  Amen.

---

[7] On holy days and at Festive Vespers or Evensong, this invitation is replaced with: "Together with XXX and all the saints, let us bless the Lord!" (or another appropriate invitation).

* For a sung "Invitation to Silence," see *Worship Resources* 1–2

NIGHT HYMN
- Advent and Christmas: "Creator of the Stars of Night" *(Worship Resources 79)*
- Ordinary Time after Epiphany: "All Praise to Thee, My God, This Night" *(Worship Resources 81)*
- Lent: "Fast Falls the Night" *(Worship Resources 82)*
- Great Fifty Days: "Come Down, O Love Divine," *(Worship Resources 84)*
- Ordinary Time After Pentecost: "The Beauteous Day Now Closes," *(Worship Resources 85)*
- Ordinary Time Before Advent: "Now God Be With Us," *(Worship Resources* 86)

CONFESSION AND ASSURANCE

O most Holy and Beloved,
our Companion, our Guide upon the way,
our bright evening star:
We repent the wrongs we have done.
We have wounded your love.
O God, heal us.
We stumble in the darkness.
Light of the world transfigure us.
We forget that we are your home.
Spirit of God, dwell in us.

Eternal Spirit, living God,
in whom we live and move and have our being,
all that we are, have been, and shall be
is known to you,
   to the very secrets of our hearts
and all that rises to trouble us.
Living flame, burn into us,
cleansing wind, blow through us,
fountain of water, well up within us,
that we may love and praise in deed and in truth.

[JIM COTTER, *PRAYER AT NIGHT*;
CAIRNS PUBLICATIONS, 1991. USED BY PERMISSION.]

a time of silence

We are a forgiven people!
Thanks be to God!

Psalter and Gloria

> Our help is in the name of the Lord;
> **who made heaven and earth.**

(One or more of the following psalms followed by the Gloria. Also see Psalter Psalm 23).

Psalm 4
(May be spoken quietly by one voice or sung softly and prayerfully in unison)

> Answer me when I call, O God,
>   defender <u>of</u> my *cause*;*
> you set me free when I am hard-pressed;
>   have mercy on me and <u>hear</u> my *prayer*.
> You mortals, how long will you dis-<u>honor</u> my *glory*;*
> how long will you worship dumb idols
>   and run <u>after</u> false *gods*?
>
> Know that God does wonders <u>for</u> the *faithful*;*
> when I call, <u>God</u> will *hear me*.
> Tremble, then, and <u>do</u> not *sin*;*
> speak to your heart in silence up-<u>on</u> your *bed*.
>
> Offer the ap-<u>poin</u>-ted *sacrifices*,*
> and put your trust in <u>the</u> Most *High*.
> Many are saying,
> "Oh, that we might <u>see</u> better *times*!"*
> Lift up the light of your countenance upon <u>us</u>, O *God*.
>
> You have put gladness <u>in</u> my *heart*, *
> more than when grain and wine and <u>oil</u> in-*crease*.
> I lie down in peace; at once I <u>fall</u> a-*sleep*;*
> for only you, God, make me <u>dwell</u> in *safety*.

[OSH Psalter]

Psalm 134
(May be chanted or spoken softly and prayerfully in unison)

> Behold now, bless God, all you <u>servants</u> of *God*,*
> you that stand by night in the <u>house</u> of *God*.
> Lift up your hands in the holy place <u>and</u> bless *God*;*
> God who made heaven and earth <u>bless you</u> from *Zion*.

[OSH Psalter]

Psalm 139:1-11

(May be chanted or spoken softly and prayerfully in unison)

O God, you have searched me <u>out</u> and known *me;**
you know my sitting down and my rising up;
   you discern my thoughts <u>from</u> a-*far.*
You trace my journeys and my <u>rest</u>-ing *places,**
and are acquainted with <u>all</u> my *ways.*

Indeed, there is not a word <u>on</u> my *lips,**
But you, O God, know it <u>al</u>-to-*gether.*
You press upon me behind <u>and</u> be-*fore,**
and lay your <u>hand</u> up-*on me.*

Such knowledge is too wonder-<u>ful</u> for *me;**
it is so high that I can-<u>not</u> at-*tain it.*
Where can I go then <u>from</u> your *Spirit,**
Where can I flee <u>from</u> your *presence*?

If I climb up to heaven, <u>you</u> are *there;**
if I make the grave my bed, you <u>are</u> there *also.*
If I take the wings <u>of</u> the *morning**
and dwell in the uttermost parts <u>of</u> the *sea,*
even there your <u>hand</u> will *lead me,**
and your right hand <u>hold</u> me *fast.*

If I say, "Surely the darkness will <u>co</u>-ver *me,**
and the light around me <u>turn</u> to *night,"*
darkness is not dark to you;
  the night is as bright <u>as</u> the *day,**
darkness and light to you are <u>both</u> a-*like.*

                                        [OSH Psalter]

Glory to the holy and <u>bless</u>-ed *Trinity,*
one God, now and for-<u>ever</u>. A-*men.*

Silence

The Little Chapter *(a brief passage of scripture such as one of the following)*

Advent/Christmas/Epiphany

The God who said: "Let light shine out of darkness" is the God who shines in our hearts with light, bringing us the radiance of the knowledge of the glory of God in the face of Jesus Christ. We have this treasure in common earthenware so that the incomparable power is clearly from God and not from us.   II Corinthians 4:6-7, OSL

Lent
> Out of the rich treasures of divine glory, may God strengthen you inwardly with power through the Holy Spirit, and may Christ dwell in your hearts through faith, and as you are rooted and grounded in love, may you, with all the saints, be able to grasp and to know the breadth and length and height and depth of Christ's love that goes beyond all human understanding, so that you might be filled with all the fullness of God.   EPHESIANS 3:16-19, OSL

The Great Fifty Days
> The God of peace, who brought again from the dead that great shepherd of the sheep, our Lord Jesus, in the blood of the eternal covenant, make you complete in every good thing so you might do God's will, as God works in you what is well pleasing in God's sight through Jesus Christ, to whom be glory unto ages of ages. Amen.
>   HEBREWS 13:20-21, OSL

Ordinary Time (the following or one of the above)
> Come to me, all who labor and carry heavy burdens and I will give you rest. Take my yoke upon you and learn from me, for I am gentle and humble in heart, and you will find rest for your souls, for my yoke is easy and my burden is light.   MATTHEW 11:28-30, OSL

> Holy wisdom, holy word!
> **Thanks be to God!**

– silence for reflection –

PRAYERS

(When prayed in community:
> The Holy One[1] be with you,
> **and also with you.**
> Let us pray:)

THE KYRIE

Lord, have mercy.	*or*	Kyrie, eleison.
Christ, have mercy.		**Christe, eleison,**
Lord, have mercy.		Kyrie, eleison.

SILENT PRAYER

NIGHT PRAYERS

---

[1] Or "The Lord" or "God"

(Selected from among the following)

Day dies away,
yet your light shines on in the darkness.
As we pray at the ending of the day,
bring our work to a close,
and prepare us for rest and peace at the last. **Amen.**

[DTB]

Be present, Spirit of God,
within us, your dwelling place and home,
that here all darkness may be penetrated by your light,
all troubles calmed by your peace,
all evil redeemed by your love,
all pain transformed in your suffering,
and all dying glorified in your risen life. **Amen.**

[ANZPB-HKMOA, ALT.]

Keep watch, dear Lord,
with those who work or watch or weep this night,
and give your angels charge over those who sleep.
Tend the sick, give rest to the weary, bless the dying,
soothe the suffering, comfort the afflicted, shield the joyous,
and all for your love's sake. **Amen.**

[BCP]

O Lord,
support us all the day long of this troublous life,
until the shadows lengthen and the evening comes,
and the busy world is hushed,
and the fever of life is over, and our work is done.
Then in your mercy grant us a safe lodging,
and a holy rest, and peace at the last. **Amen.**

[JOHN HENRY NEWMAN, 1801-1890]

Visit this place, O Lord,
and deliver us from every snare of the enemy.
May your angels be round about us
   to guard us in peace,
and let your blessing be upon us always;
through Christ our Lord. **Amen.**

[ADAPTED FROM THE ROMAN BREVIARY]

CONCLUDING PRAYER[2]

>Eternal Spirit,
>Life Giver, Pain Bearer, Love Maker,
>Source of all that is and that shall be,
>Father and Mother of us all,
>Loving God, in whom is heaven:
>
>The hallowing of your name
>   echo through the universe!
>The way of your justice
>   be followed by the peoples of the world!
>Your heavenly will be done by all created beings!
>Your commonwealth of peace and freedom
>   sustain our hope and come on earth.
>
>With the bread we need for today, feed us.
>In the hurts we absorb from one another, forgive us.
>In times of temptation and test, strengthen us.
>From trials too great to endure, spare us.
>From the grip of all that is evil, free us.
>
>For you reign in the glory of the power that is love,
>   now and for ever. Amen.

[JIM COTTER, *PRAYER AT NIGHT*;
CAIRNS PUBLICATIONS, 1991. USED BY PERMISSION.]

HYMN *(see Worship Resources, 87)* [84.84.888.4; TUNE: AR HYD Y NOS, UMH 688]

>God who made the earth and heaven, darkness and light,
>who the day for toil has given, for rest the night.
>May thine angel guards defend us,
>slumber sweet thy mercy send us,
>holy dreams and hopes attend us
>this live-long night.
>
>When the constant sun returning unseals our eyes,
>may we born anew like morning, to labor rise.
>Gird us for the task that calls us,
>let not ease and self enthrall us,
>strong through thee whate'er befall us,
>O God most wise!

[REGINALD HEBER, 1783-1826]

---

[2] The Lord's Prayer may be said or sung instead of this prayer or in addition to it.

COMMENDATION

In peace we will lie down and sleep.
> **In the Lord alone we safely rest.**

Guide us waking, O Lord, and guard us sleeping,
> **that awake we may watch with Christ,**
> **and asleep we may rest in peace.**

May the divine help remain with us always.
> **and with those who are absent from us.**

silence

Into your hands, O Lord, I commend my spirit,
> **For you have redeemed me, O Lord,**
> **O God of Truth.**

[SARUM BREVIARY, PS. 4:8 AND 30:5, ADAPTED]

CANTICLE OF SIMEON *(The Nunc Dimittas)*
(Commonly sung in unison to psalm tone one; see Worship Resources 90)

Lord, you have now set your ser-vant *free*
to go in peace as you have *promised*;
for these eyes of mine have seen the *Savior*,
whom you have prepared for all the world to *see*:
a Light to en-lighten the *nations*,
  and the glory of your peo-ple *Israel*.

[LUKE 2:29-32; ICET]

Glory to you, O Trinity, most holy and *blessed*;
one God, now and for ever. A-*men*.

BLESSING

May the holy and blessed Trinity guard and bless us.
Let us bless the Lord.
> **Thanks be to God!**

Members of the community continue in prayer,
and then depart in silence, one by one.

VIGIL

(Resurrection Vigil on Saturday evenings or a night-time office)

Vigils are times of watching and waiting, trusting the resurrection light that breaks forth within the mystery of darkness. They are "wombs of silence" in which we are called to "loving listening." [1] *We take time to sense the music of the spheres, the "song the morning stars began," and join with all creation, the heavenly host, and the Church through the ages in singing the praise of God.*

This Vigil office may be prayed in two ways: 1) On Saturday evenings, a Resurrection Vigil supersedes Evening Prayer and Compline. The service below primarily reflects this use. Those parts of the service specific to a Resurrection Vigil are marked [R]. 2) It may serve as a night-time office in its own right as one of the seven Lukan hours of the Daily Office, traditionally prayed near midnight. In such a night-time office vigil, the service begins with a time of silence after which the following dialogue is spoken:

> O God, open our lips,
> **and our mouths shall proclaim your praise.**
> O God, come to our assistance.
> **O Lord, hasten to help us.**
> Glory to you, O Trinity, most holy and blessed,
> **one God, now and for ever. Amen.**

A night-time office vigil then moves directly to the Canticle of Praise to God (the Venite Exultemus on page 59).

An office vigil begins and ends in silence. A Resurrection Vigil may begin with music, but ends in silence.

---

[1] David Steindel-Rast and Sharon Lebell, *Music of Silence* (Berkley, CA: Seastone, 2002), p20.

OPENING

[R] ENTRANCE OF THE LIGHT[2]

(see Worship Resources 63 for a sung version)

> Risen Christ, you are the light of the world,
> **the light no darkness can overcome.**
> Stay with us, for it is evening,
> **and the day is nearly over.**
> With you is the fountain of life,
> **and in your light do we see light.**
>
> [ADAPTED FROM JOHN 8:12, LUKE 24:29, PSALM 35:9]

[R] +CANTICLE OF THE RESURRECTION *(The Paschu Nostrum)*

(During Lent: spoken in unison, omitting the alleluias; otherwise commonly sung in unison to psalm tone three or spoken in unison. See Worship Resources 193 for another sung version.)

> [Alleluia!] Christ our Passover is sacri-<u>ficed</u> for *us*;*
> therefore let us <u>keep</u> the *feast*,
> not with the old leaven of <u>malice</u> and *evil*,*
> but with the unleavened bread of sin-<u>cerity</u> and *truth*.
>
> Christ being raised from the dead
>   will never <u>die</u> a-*gain*;*
> death no longer has dominion <u>o</u>-ver *him*.
> The death he died, he died to sin, <u>once</u> for *all*,*
> but the life he lives, he <u>lives</u> to *God*.
>
> So consider yourselves <u>dead</u> to *sin**
> and alive to God in Jesus <u>Christ</u> our *Lord*.
> For as in <u>Adam</u> all *die*,*
> so also in Christ shall all be made alive. [Al-le-*luia*!]
>
> [I CORINTHIANS 5:7-8 AND ROMANS 6:9-11,
> TEXT ADAPTED FROM BCP, DTB, DWV]

[R] +PRAYER

(When prayed in community:

> The Holy One[3] be with you,
> **and also with you.**
> Let us pray:)

---

[2] From Evening Prayer page 39 or Worship Resources 60-65.
[3] Or "The Lord" or "God."

Dawn Treader,
as light fades
you come to us with the promise of dawn.
With the women who came to the tomb and found it empty,
stir up in us holy wonder
in the mystery of your resurrection,
so that asleep and awake
we adore you
and eagerly await your making all things new, Amen.

[DTB]

OR

Blessed are you, O Holy One.
As we walk with you on the way,
you continue to recreate and form us with the light of your love.
In this weekly memorial of Christ's death and rising,
we rejoice to have been born from the font,
the womb of your Church,
and give thanks that your light continues to shine in the darkness.
All glory be to you through Jesus our risen Lord,
in the light of the life-giving love of the Holy Spirit ,
this evening, and unto ages of ages. **Amen.**

[BY PERMISSION OF ALLELUIA PRESS. ALT.]

[R] [EVENING PRAYER CANTICLE[4]]

(see Worship Resources 67–69; may be accompanied by the lighting of incense)

[R] A TIME OF SILENT CONFESSION

[R] ASSURANCE

May God who said, "Let light shine out of darkness," shine in our hearts to give us the light of the knowledge of the glory of God in the face of Jesus Christ.

[ADAPTED FROM II CORINTHIANS 4:6]

We are a forgiven people. Let us give thanks!

---

[4] When prayed alone or in the domestic church, the Evening Prayer Canticle may be omitted.

+CANTICLE OF PRAISE TO GOD *(The Venite Exultemus)*
(commonly sung to psalm tone one or spoken in unison; see Worship Resources 197 for a another version)

> Come, let us sing to the Ho-ly *One*;*
> let us shout for joy to the Rock of our sal-*vation*.
> Let us come before God's presence with thanks-*giving*,*
> and raise a loud shout with *psalms*.
> For you, O God, are a great *God*,*
> you are great a-bove all *gods*.
> In your hand are the caverns of the *earth*,*
> and the heights of the hills are yours *also*.
> The sea is yours, for you *made it*,*
> and your hands have molded the dry *land*.
> Come, let us bow down and bend the *knee*,*
> and kneel before God, our *Maker*.
> For you are our God,
>   and we are the people of your pasture
>   and the sheep of your *hand*.*
> Oh, that today we would hearken to your *voice*!
>
> [PSALM 95:1-7 (OSH PSALTER)]

THE BLESSING

> Lord, grant us your blessing.
>
> *– a brief time of silence –*
>
> Kindle in our hearts, O God,
> the flame of that love which never ceases,
> that it may burn in us, giving light to others.
> May we shine forever in your temple,
> set on fire with your eternal light,
> even your Son Jesus Christ,
> our Savior and our Redeemer. **Amen.**
>
> [ST. COLUMBA, 6TH C.]

WORD AND RESPONSE

SCRIPTURE

At a resurrection vigil, the lections for the following day[5] may be read, with the first lesson followed by the appointed psalm. Each reading is followed by a time of silence, after which an appropriate selection of music may be heard or sung. In a night-time office vigil, from one to seven lessons may be selected. The last reading (or the only reading if

---

[5] For the Revised Common Lectionary readings for the Lord's Day, see http://www.commontexts.org/publications/index.html

a single reading is used) should be the Gospel reading for the morrow, calling forth the prayer of the Church in one of the following canticles.

+CANTICLE
    Advent: Second Canticle of Isaiah [*Isaiah 55:6-11*]
        (*Worship Resources 198*).
    Christmastide: Canticle of God's Glory [*Gloria in Excelsis*]
        (*Worship Resources 187*).
    Lent: Canticle of Redemption [*De Profundis*]
        (*Worship Resources 194*)
    The Great Fifty Days: Canticle of the Holy Trinity [*Te Deum Laudamus*]
        (*Worship Resources 185*)
    Ordinary Time after Pentecost: Canticle of Joy [*Jubilate Deo*]
        (*Worship Resources 199*)
    Ordinary Time before Advent: Canticle of Thanksgiving [*Bonum Est*]
        (*Worship Resources 196*)

PRAYERS

(When prayed in community:

    The Holy One[6] be with you,
    and also with you.
    Let us pray:)

SILENT PRAYER

[R] PRAYERS OF SUPPLICATION AND INTERCESSION[7]
    Let us pray for
    those who suffer or are in trouble...
    the concerns of this local community...
    the world, its peoples and leaders...
    the life and mission of the Church...
    the earth and all its creatures...
    the concerns of our hearts…
    and the communion of the saints...

Intercessions for The Order of Saint Luke and the Collect for The Order of Saint Luke (Worship Resources 151-152) may be prayed here.

---

[6] Or "The Lord" or "God"
[7] In an office Vigil THE GREAT LITANY (*Worship Resources 183*) or selected sections thereof replaces this prayer.

THE LORD'S PRAYER *(said or sung; for musical versions see Worship Resources 8-12)*
> **Our Father in heaven,**
>> **hallowed be your name,**
>> **your kingdom come,**
>> **your will be done, on earth as in heaven.**
>
> **Give us today our daily bread.**
> **Forgive us our sins**
>> **as we forgive those who sin against us.**
>
> **Save us from the time of trial**
>> **and deliver us from evil.**
>
> **For the kingdom, the power, and the glory are yours**
>> **now and forever. Amen.**

> *In a night-time office vigil, when Compline was observed earlier,*
> *the service moves directly to the concluding prayer.*

[R] COMMENDATION
> In peace we will lie down and sleep.
>> **In the Lord alone we safely rest.**
>
> Guide us waking, O Lord, and guard us sleeping,
>> **that awake we may watch with Christ,**
>> **and asleep we may rest in peace.**
>
> May the divine help remain with us always.
>> **And with those who are absent from us.**
>>> *silence*
>
> Into your hands, O Lord, I commend my spirit.
>> **For you have redeemed me, O Lord, O God of truth.**

>> [SARUM BREVIARY; PSALM 4:8 AND 30:5 ADAPT.]

[R] CANTICLE OF SIMEON *(The Nunc Dimittas)*
(commonly spoken in unison or sung to psalm tone one)
> Lord, you have now set your <u>ser</u>-vant *free**
> to go in peace as <u>you</u> have *promised*;
> for these eyes of mine have <u>seen</u> the *Savior**
> whom you have prepared for all the <u>world</u> to *see*,
> a Light to en-<u>lighten</u> the *nations*,*
> and the glory of your <u>peo</u>-ple *Israel*.

>>>> [ICET]

> Glory to you, O Trinity, most <u>holy</u> and *blessed*:*
> one God, now and for-<u>ever</u>. A-*men*.

Concluding Prayer

(at a Resurrection Vigil:)

> Risen Son,
> day dies away,
> yet your light shines on in the darkness.
> Our hearts burn within us for you come to us
>   in the unfolding of the scriptures,
>   in the breaking of bread, and the prayers.
> Incorporate us anew into your dying and rising again,
> that by the power of the Holy Spirit,
> we may live in grace and peace. **Amen.**
>
> [DTB]

(In Advent or at a night-time office vigil:)

> Bridegroom of Creation,
> so trim our lamps and fill our hearts
>   with the oil of gladness,
> that whether you come at midnight or cockcrow,
> we are prepared to rise and join your procession. **Amen.**
>
> [DTB]

O God, hear our prayer,
> **and let our cry come to you.**

Listen to the prayers of your servants;
> **have mercy on us, Lord Jesus Christ.**

Let us bless the Lord!
> **Thanks be to God!**

May the souls of the faithful departed,
through the mercy of God, rest in peace.
> **Amen.**

*No music follows; the community remains in prayer
and then departs in silence, one by one.*

Daily Office[1]
(A brief portable office)

O God, open our lips,
   and our mouths shall proclaim your praise.
Glory to you, O Trinity most holy and blessed,
   who is now, ever was, and ever shall be
   unto endless ages. Amen.

[HYMN; PSALM AND GLORIA; LESSON(S)]

MORNING CANTICLE

We bless you, ADONAI, God of *Israel*,
for you come to visit us and ransom us from *bondage*.
You have brought forth a strong De-*liverer*
   in the house of your child *David*.

   This is what your holy prophets an-*nounced*:
   deliverance from enemies and from the hand of all who *hate us;*
   mercy a-mong our *ancestors*,
   and remembrance of your ho-ly *covenant*.

This is the promise you swore to our an-cestor, *Abraham*,
to make us un-a-*fraid*,
to rescue us from our *enemies*,
to serve before you, holy and just, all the days of our *lives*.

   And this, my little child, shall be called prophet of the Most *High*,
   going before you, ADONAI, to pre-pare your *paths*,
   making your people know de-*liverance*
   by the forgiveness of their *sins*.

Through your merciful compassions, God our *God*,
the dawn from on high shall *visit us*,
to shine on those kept in dungeons and the shadows of *death*
and to guide our feet onto the path of *peace*.

   Glory to you, O Trinity, most holy and *blessed*:
   one God, now and for ever. A-*men*.
                              [LUKE 1: 68-79; TBE, ALT.]

[

EVENING CANTICLE:
My soul proclaims your great-ness, *Lord*;
my spirit rejoices in you, my *Savior*;
For you have looked with favor on your low-ly *servant*,
from this day all generations will call me *blessed*.

---

1 Commonly known as the "Tan Card Rite" which replaced the "Green Card Rite" used in the early life of the Order.

You the Almighty have done great things for *me*,
and Holy is your *Name*.
You have mercy on those who *fear you*
in every gen-er-*ation*.

You have shown the strength of your *arm*;
you have scattered the proud in their con-*ceit*.
You have cast the mighty from their *thrones*;
you have lifted up the *lowly*.

You have filled the hungry with good *things*;
and the rich have been sent a-way *empty*.
You have come to the help of your ser-vant *Israel*,
for you have remembered your promise of *mercy*,
the promise you made to our *forebears*,
to Abraham and his children for *ever*.

Glory to you, O Trinity, most holy and *blessed*:
one God, now and for ever. A-*men*. [LUKE 1:39-56; TJC, OSL]

PRAYERS

Kyrie eleison, Christe eleison, Kyrie eleison.
(Lord, have mercy; Christ, have mercy; Lord, have mercy)

Give thanks and pray for the world, the Church, and the concerns of the heart, followed by The Lord's Prayer, *and concluding with the collect for the Order.*

O Shepherd of us all, who inspired your servant Saint Luke the Physician to set forth in the gospel the love and healing power of Jesus: Grant, we ask you, your Spirit to the Order of Saint Luke, that we may proclaim the Apostolic hope, magnify the Sacraments, and embody Christ's healing grace for all creation; through Jesus Christ our Lord. Amen.

GOING FORTH:

Lord, you have now set your ser-vant free
to go in peace as you have *promised*;
for these eyes of mine have seen the Savior,
whom you have prepared for all the world to *see*.
a Light to en-lighten the nations,
and the glory of your peo-ple *Israel*.

[LUKE 2:29-32; ICET]

Glory to you, O Trinity, most holy and *blessed*;
one God, now and for-ever. A-*men*.

The grace of our Lord Jesus Christ, the love of God and the sustaining community of the Holy Spirit be with us today and always.

[ADAPTED FROM II CORINTHIANS 13:14]

Let us bless the Lord. **Thanks be to God.**

PASTORAL SERVICES

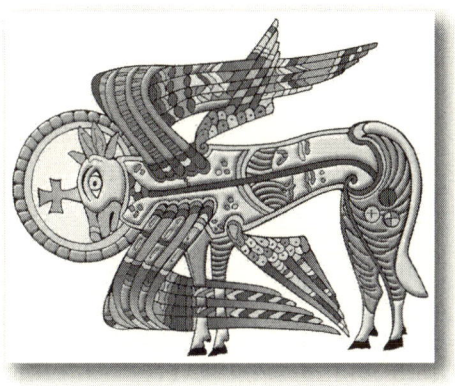

Service of Prayer for Healing

Since 1980, the Order of Saint Luke has been providing resources for healing rites, and our work has been used by the United Church of Christ, the Presbyterian Church (USA) and the United Methodist Church in their books of worship. As the Church we are called to offer God's healing to persons who are living in brokenness; broken in body, mind, spirit and relationships. This service engages the senses of hearing, sight, touch and smell, and, when celebration of the Eucharist is included, the sense of taste as well. In the tangible, we are touched by the Transcendent. Through the gentle, soothing, healing touch of another in the laying on of hands, God's nearness and love may be recognized and affirmed.[1]

In a private service, at least two persons, in addition to the person for whom prayers for healing will be offered, should be present, with the person(s) other than the presider representing the community and taking their lines. In a corporate service of healing, sections marked with "[ ]" brackets may be included.

GREETING
Grace to you and peace from God
  who is, and who was, and who is to come.
    Amen.
Bless the Holy One, O my soul,
  and all that is within me, bless God's holy Name.
Bless the Holy One, O my soul,
  and forget not all the gifts of God.
O God, you forgive all our sins,
  and you heal all our infirmities;
You redeem our life from the grave
  and crown us with mercy and loving-kindness;
You satisfy us with good things,
  and our youth is renewed like an eagle's.

[ADAPTED FROM PSALM 103:1-4, OSL]

[+HYMN]
(See Worship Resources 92–97 for appropriate hymns)

---

[1] Adapted from the preface to the Rite of Anointing by Br. Timothy J. Crouch, OSL found in earlier editions of this book.

+OPENING PRAYER

The Holy One[2] be with you.
   And also with you.
Let us pray:
   (one of the following)
All loving and all caring God,
source of life and wholeness:
we come to you this day,
each one of us broken in our own way.
You know our struggles; you know our pain.
With your Spirit, open us to your loving touch
 that we may be made whole
   through Jesus Christ the Healer, we pray. **Amen.**

[MJO'D, ALT.]

or

Living God,
make us conscious now of your healing nearness.
Touch our eyes that we may see you;
open our ears that we may hear your voice;
enter our hearts that we might know your love.
Overshadow our souls and bodies with your presence,
that we might partake of your strength, your love, and your healing life; in the Name of Jesus our Lord. **Amen.**

[TJC]

[A Prayer for Illumination, Scripture Lessons, appropriate music and a brief homily may be included here.]

CONFESSION AND PARDON

Hear these words of Scripture:
"If we say we have no sin, we deceive ourselves, and the truth is not in us. But if we confess our sins, God, who is faithful and just, will forgive our sins and cleanse us from all unrighteousness."

[I JOHN 1:8-9, NRSV, ALT.]

Let us confess our sin before God.
   Most merciful God, we confess that we have sinned against you in thought, word, and deed by what we have done, and by what we have left undone. We have not loved you with our whole heart; we have not loved our neighbors as ourselves; and we are

---

[2] Or "The Lord" of "God"

diminished in soul and body. We are truly sorry and we humbly repent. For the sake of our Lord Jesus Christ, have mercy on us and forgive us, so that we may delight in your will, and walk in your ways giving glory to your holy name. Amen.

[BCP, ALT.]

- silent confession -

Hear the good news:
Christ died for us while we were yet sinners;
that proves God's love toward us.

[ADAPTED FROM ROMANS 6:8]

In the name of Jesus Christ, I declare to you:
you are forgiven.
  In the name of Jesus Christ, you are forgiven!
  Glory to God! Amen!

INVITATION TO THE ANOINTING RITE

We come to lift up [our brothers and sisters or [our brother Name/our sister Name] before God as we recall these words of scripture: "Are any among you suffering? Let them pray. Are any cheerful? Let them sing a hymn of praise. Are any among you sick? ... Pray over them, anointing them with oil in the name of the Lord."

[ADAPTED FROM JAMES 5:13-14]

THANKSGIVING OVER THE OIL

Let us pray.
  Loving God,
  you come to us with healing in your wings.
  You prepare a table before us and anoint us with oil.
  We thank you for this oil,
  a sign of your grace and favor.
  Send your Holy Spirit on us and on this gift
  that through this anointing,
  we may know the healing that comes from you. **Amen.**

PASTORAL LITURGIES AND PRAYERS FOR SPECIAL OCCASIONS
© 1990, DIVISION OF MISSION IN CANADA, UNITED CHURCH OF CANADA.
USED BY PERMISSION.

[In a corporate service of healing, persons are invited to come to a prayer station and briefly share their request, saying "I come for the healing of physical pain," . . . "for the healing of memories," . . . "for the healing of a broken relationship," . . . " for the healing of my church" or "my nation" or "my world" or a similar request. Or a person may say "I come on behalf of another for . . . ." The healing team is cautioned not to treat this as an opportunity for counseling which should be carried out at another time and place, but to allow the Holy Spirit to fill this anointing and the words that accompany it with significance beyond our human understanding. During this time the congregation may share in prayers for healing by singing quietly and meditatively].

ANOINTING

Name, the Holy Spirit anoint you with the healing power of God, (+) in the name of the holy and blessed Trinity.

PRAYERS FOR HEALING AND WHOLENESS WITH THE LAYING ON OF HANDS

Name, these hands are laid on you in the name of Jesus Christ, our Savior and Healer, for the healing of . . . *(the prayer may be adapted to the specific situation).* May our loving Creator grant you the inward anointing of the Holy Spirit. May the love of Jesus, who also suffered, flow through your mind and body, bringing you peace and strength. **Amen.**

>   ADAPTED FROM *HEALING FROM THE HEART* BY ROCHELLE GRAHAM, FLORA LITT AND WAYNE IRWIN. COPYRIGHT (C) 2008 ROCHELLE GRAHAMA, FLORA LITT AND WAYNE IRWIN, WOOD LAKE PUBLISHING INC. USED BY PERMISSION.

or, in the case of one who comes on behalf of another:

Name, these hands are laid on you in the name of Jesus Christ, our Savior and Healer, with the prayer that you may be an instrument of healing in the life (lives) of _____. May the power of God's indwelling presence bring him/her/them wholeness, that he/she/they may serve God with a loving heart. **Amen.**

PRAYER AFTER ANOINTING

>   Merciful God,
>   we pray that all our brothers and sisters everywhere
>   may be comforted in their suffering and made whole.
>   Give strength to the weary,
>   comfort to the sad,
>   relief to those in pain
>   and help to those in tribulation.
>   [ADAPTED FROM THE 9TH C. AMBROSIAN SACRAMENTARY]

> In the name of Jesus the Great Physician
> who rose with healing in his wings
> *[if Eucharist is to be celebrated:* we pray. **Amen**.
> *[if Eucharist is not celebrated:* and taught us to pray:

[EUCHARIST *(beginning with the Presentation of the Gifts on p. 9)]*, OR

[THE LORD'S PRAYER *(see sung versions in Worship Resources 8-12)*]

CLOSING PRAYER
> Mighty and merciful God,
> your healing presence has been with us.
> As we wait in hope for the coming of that day
> when crying and pain shall be no more,
> help us by your Holy Spirit
> to receive your grace in our lives
> trusting in your eternal love,
> through Jesus Christ our Savior. **Amen**.

+[HYMN] *(see Worship Resources 46-52)*

+BLESSING AND COMMISSION
> The Holy One who heals all your iniquity bless and keep you;
> the face of the One who heals all your afflictions
> shine upon you and be gracious to you;
> the light of the countenance of the One who redeems your life
> be lifted upon you and give you peace. **Amen**.

[ADAPTED FROM NUMBERS 6:24-26, OSL]

The community may be seated for a time of reflection guided by music.

Go in peace. Love and serve Christ and one another.

Let us bless the Lord.
Thanks be to God!

Service of Prayer for Reconciliation

The focus of this service is deepening our friendship with God. It is concerned with more than recognizing that we have done what we ought not to have done, and have not done what we ought to have done. It is about the restoration of relationship with God, others, and ourselves. Sin is relational and our individual sins manifest deep ruptures not only in ourselves, but in the systems of which we are a part. We are complicit in ruptures of which we may be unaware, and often feel powerless to control. Sin is part of the fabric of our lives, but the focus of this service is not our unworthiness, but the forgiving, caring, compassionate, welcoming love of God. It is because we do not want to mar our deep friendship with God that we seek reconciliation. The service may be used as a communal response to systemic evils.

The sacramental sign/act that seals our reconciliation with God and one another is water. Baptismal waters mark us as Christ's own people. Every day water cleanses us. We cannot live without water. When cool water refreshes us in the desert places of our lives, we receive grace upon grace. In this service we come to the cleansing flood of God's grace, grace that receives and accepts and forgives and reconciles us, marked by water and the Word as a sign of our continuing conversion.

Preparation

Prior to the service, a time needs to be set apart for a time of confession. The service cannot be expected to bear the burden of meeting the differing needs of its participants, nor can it provide the various avenues through which those needs may be most fruitfully addressed. The following are among the approaches which should be provided during this time of preparation.

- *Locations of confessors or spiritual guides who are ready to listen and respond should be announced.*
- *Places where persons can talk with mentors or soul friends should be provided.*
- *When there is a fractured relationship with another in the community, restoration of that relationship may be sought, usually in the presence of a confessor, soul guide, or soul friend.*
- *A place of solitude should also be provided for those who need space alone, not turning away from others so much as seeking a place freed from the distractions that other persons and talking sometimes engender. This can often be in the worship space itself*

where the deep, silent places of the soul may be nurtured.

- *For some, there is already a deep sense of assurance, a peace that passes human understanding, a feeling of reconciliation so real that the touch of the water is but a reflection of the magnitude of the mercy of the Holy One. Nothing is needed but being open to a sense of the promise of God.*
- *Some will not feel anything, no matter how hard we try. God is not made in the image of our emotions. God's acceptance of us is always amazing grace, a free gift not confined by thought or feeling, a mystery beyond our comprehending. And we will dare to come to the service anyway, confidant that God is greater than what we sense or feel, trusting that God does more than we can ask or even think.*

At the service itself, the lighted paschal candle stands near basin(s) and pitcher(s) of water.

GREETING

The grace of our Lord Jesus Christ,
and the love of God,
and the sustaining community of the Holy Spirit
be with you all.
    And also with you.

[ADAPTED FROM 2 CORINTHIANS 13:14]

Bless the Holy One, O my soul,
and all that is within me, bless God's holy name.
    Bless the Holy One, O my soul,
    and forget not all God's benefits,
who forgives all your iniquity,
and heals all your diseases,
    who redeems your life from the grave,
    and crowns you with steadfast love and mercy.

[ADAPTED FROM PSALM 103:1-4]

+GATHERING HYMN

(see Worship Resources 24, 31, 92-94, 96, 102, 103, 132, 133)

+COLLECT

The Holy One[1] be with you;
    and also with you.

---

[1] Or "The Lord" or "God."

Let us pray:

Almighty God, to whom all hearts are open, all desires known, and from whom no secrets are hid: Cleanse the thoughts of our hearts by the inspiration of your Holy Spirit, that we may perfectly love you and worthily magnify your holy name, through Jesus Christ our Lord. Amen.

[SARUM MISSAL; THOMAS CRANMER, TRANS. 1549]

SCRIPTURE

(such as Psalm 51:10-12, I John 1:5-9, II Corinthians 5:17-20, and Matthew 11:28-30)

[HOMILY]

EXAMINATION OF CONSCIENCE

Hear these words of our Savior Jesus Christ:
(see Worship Resources 99 for a sung version)

Blessed are you poor,
   for yours is God's commonwealth.
Blessed are you that hunger now,
   for you shall be satisfied.
Blessed are you that weep now,
   for you shall laugh.
Blessed are you when you are hated, excluded and reviled on account of me,
   for your reward is great in heaven.
Woe to you that are rich,
   for you have already received your consolation.
Woe to you that are full now,
   for you shall hunger.
Woe to you, when all speak well of you,
   for so their ancestors did to the false prophets.

[ADAPTED FROM LUKE 6:20B-26, OSL]

Christ, have mercy on us,
   and guide us in your way.

Examination of conscience in an extended period of silence

CALL TO CONFESSION

Brothers and Sisters in Christ:
God knows what we need before we ask,
and through the Holy Spirit is already working in us,

preparing us, so that, even in our asking,
we receive the gift of grace.
> **Breathe the healing grace of your Holy Spirit on us**
> **so that we may confess all that separates us**
> **from God and from our neighbor.**

THE KYRIE

A setting of the Kyrie is sung (see Worship Resources, 3-7) or the following is said:

> Lord, have mercy.
> **Lord, have mercy.**
> Lord, have mercy.

> Christ, have mercy.
> **Christ, have mercy.**
> Christ, have mercy.

> Lord, have mercy.
> **Lord, have mercy.**
> Lord, have mercy.

Let us come to the fountain of grace,
asking to be made aware of both our personal sins
and our corporate silence
in the face of the evil powers that infect us,
confessing what has wounded us
or harmed others knowingly or unknowingly.

May we receive God's mercy
and share with one another the ministry
of grace and reconciliation.

Let us pray:

PRAYER FOR FORGIVENESS

Members of the community may kneel or bow in prayer

> **Author of love,**
> **we are reluctant to set aside our hurt,**
> **our anger, our disappointment.**
> **Heal us with your tender touch,**
> **that we might be cleansed of all unclean thoughts and actions,**
> **freed from doubts that distract,**
> **released from memories that constrict.**

> **Forgive the sins done in our name,
> both the ones we know,
> and the ones of which we are unaware.**
>
> **Open our eyes to the power of your self-giving love
> on the cross of your Son, Jesus Christ,
> in whose name we pray. Amen.** [MJO'D]

Ritual Act of Cleansing[2]

As they are moved by the Spirit, persons come to one of the stations provided, holding their hands over a basin while water is poured from a pitcher by the companions stationed there, while one of them says:

> My sister (my brother),
> we are forgiven and reconciled to God.
> Let us remember our baptism that,
> cleansed by water and the Spirit,
> we may live faithfully as disciples of Jesus Christ,

with "Amen" as the response.[3]

Prayer of Healing
and Forgiveness: The Lord's Prayer[4]

(see Worship Resources 8–12 for sung versions)

With the confidence of the children of God, let us pray as Jesus taught us:
> **Our Father in heaven,
>   hallowed be your name,
>   your kingdom come,
>   your will be done, on earth as in heaven.
> Give us today our daily bread.
> Forgive us our sins
>   as we forgive those who sin against us.
> Save us from the time of trial
>   and deliver us from evil.
> For the kingdom, the power, and the glory are yours
>   now and forever. Amen.**

Assurance of Pardon

The steadfast grace of God is from everlasting to everlasting.

---

[2] This ritual act of cleansing may be accompanied by footwashing.
[3] This ritual act in a corporate rite of confession comes to us from the practice of the Society of Mary at Deepahalli, Bangalore, India.
[4] The use of the Lord's Prayer as a prayer of healing and forgiveness comes to us from the practice of the Benedictines of St. John's Abbey, Collegeville, Minnesota.

Hear the good news:
  Christ died for us while we were yet sinners;
  that proves God's love toward us. [SEE ROMANS 5:8]

In the name of Jesus Christ,
and as your *brother/sister* in the priesthood of all believers,
I declare to you: you are forgiven.
  In the name of Jesus Christ,
  and as your sisters and brothers,
  we declare to you: you are forgiven.

A moment of silence as the community stands

+ May the God of mercy, who forgives all our sins,
strengthen us in all goodness,
and by the power of the Holy Spirit,
transform us by the renewing of our minds
to live new lives in Jesus Christ,
that all may be well in our souls,
and we may be channels of God's grace
for healing and reconciliation in the world. [SEE ROMANS 12:2]

Thanks be to God! Amen!!

(see Worship Resources 149 or 186 for possible sung responses)

+PASSING THE PEACE

As forgiven and reconciled people,
let us share signs of reconciliation and love with one another.

(If Holy Eucharist is to be celebrated, it begins here with the Presentation of the Gifts, p. 9)

+HYMN *(a hymn of reconciliation; see Worship Resources 100-104)*

+BLESSING AND COMMISSION[5]

May the peace of God, which passes all understanding,
keep your hearts and minds in Christ Jesus,
so that the peace of Christ may abide with you in all you do.
[PHILIPPIANS 4:7, ADAPTED]

The community may be seated for a time of reflection guided by music
or remain standing for the Commission.

Bear witness to the love of God in this world,
so that those to whom love is a stranger
will find in you generous friends.[6]
Go in peace to love and serve the Lord. **Amen. Thanks be to God!**

---

[5] The blessing is given by the presider; the dismissal by another person.
[6] From "The Service of Christian Marriage" in The United Methodist Hymnal, p. 869.

Rite of Reconciliation for Individual Persons

This rite is an adaptation of the previous service for use with an individual or small group of persons. It provides a ritual component within a more informal service that should be adapted in each situation to the needs of the person or persons involved.

We are called to "bear one another's burdens" (Galatians 6:2) and share in the priesthood of all believers (I Peter 2:5,9). We use the traditional language of "confessor" for the one exercising this priesthood on behalf of the Church, and "penitent" for the person (or persons) coming to experience the liberating blessing that comes through confession and assurance. The confidentiality of the confessional must be honored, unless so doing puts someone(s) in danger.

A candle may be lighted and placed near a basin and pitcher of water.

Greeting
The grace of our Lord Jesus Christ,
and the love of God,
and the sustaining community of the Holy Spirit
be with you. [Adapted from II Corinthians 13:14]

 [*The penitent may respond:* **and also with you.**]

Hear the words of the psalmist:
  Bless the Holy One, O my soul,
  and all that is within me, bless God's holy name.
  Bless the Holy One, O my soul,
  and forget not all God's benefits.
  who forgives all your iniquity,
  and heals all your diseases,
  who redeems your life from the grave,
  and crowns you with steadfast love and mercy.

[Adapted from Psalm 103:1-4]

Collect
     The Holy One[1] be with you.
 [The penitent may respond: **and also with you.**]
Let us pray:

---
[1] Or "the Lord" or "God"

Almighty God, to whom all hearts are open, all desires known, and
from whom no secrets are hid: Cleanse the thoughts of our hearts by
the inspiration of your Holy Spirit, that we may perfectly love you and
worthily magnify your holy name, through Jesus Christ our Lord.
Amen. [Sarum Missal; Thomas Cranmer, trans. 1549]

My brother/sister in Christ:
God knows what we need before we ask,
and through the Holy Spirit is already working in us,
preparing us, so that, even in our asking,
we receive the gift of grace.

Pastoral Conversation

The confessor invites the penitent(s) to talk about what prompts them to seek forgiveness, offering understanding and support.

Confession

The penitent(s) may confess silently or aloud, and/or be prompted to repeat:

> Lord, have mercy.
> > **Lord, have mercy.**
> Christ, have mercy.
> > **Christ, have mercy.**
> Lord, have mercy.
> > **Lord, have mercy.**
> God be merciful to me.
> > **God be merciful to me.**

Ritual Act of Cleansing

Penitent(s) are invited to hold their hands over a basin while water is poured from a pitcher by the confessor who says:

> My sister (my brother),
> we are forgiven and reconciled to God.
> Let us remember our baptism that,
> cleansed by water and the Spirit,
> we may live faithfully as disciples of Jesus Christ.

Assurance of Pardon

The steadfast grace of God is from everlasting to everlasting.
Hear the good news:
  Christ died for us just as we are;
  that proves God's love toward us. [Adapted from Romans 5:8]

In the name of Jesus Christ,
and as your brother/sister in the priesthood of all believers,
I declare to you: you are forgiven.

BLESSING AND COMMISSION

The confessor raises a hand in blessing.

May the God of mercy, who forgives all our sins,
strengthen us in all goodness,
and by the power of the Holy Spirit,
transform us by the renewing of our minds
to live new lives in Jesus Christ,
that all may be well in our souls,
and we may be channels of God's grace
for healing and reconciliation in the world.

[SEE ROMANS 12:2]

The confessor lowers the hand and addresses the penitent(s):

Bear witness to the love of God in this world,
so that those to whom love is a stranger
will find in you (a) generous friend(s).[2]

Let us go in peace to love and serve the Lord.

The confessor, reading the situation, will help the penitent(s) transition from the ritual moment to sacramental life in the world beyond it. This may include a bow to the penitent(s) with a guiding gesture toward the exit from the space, communicating that the session is to end in silence. Or, it may include a gesture toward the exit and walking with the penitent(s) to an adjoining space for casual conversation.

---

[2] From "The Service of Christian Marriage" in *The United Methodist Hymnal*, p. 869.

The Transitus
A Service for the Time of Passage through Death to Life

We believe that death is not an end but a transition, a passage through death to Life, ritually marked by the Transitus rite. We prepare for this service every time we pray Compline. As in that office, this service is a marker on our pilgrimage, a journey we make in solidarity with our brothers and sisters. As John Wesley observed on his death bed, "The best of all is this: God is with us." To which we add: our brothers and sisters are with us, too. Thus, it is hoped that several members of the Order will share in any Transitus service.

This service may be used in three different ways:

(1) Prior to death as a sending forth (components of the service used only in this way are marked with a P),

(2) Just after the time of death as a committal of our brother or sister to God (components of the service relevant to this use are marked with a D), or

(3) By the chapter or general chapter when commemorating the death of a member or members of the Order (components of the service relevant to this use are marked with an M)

Those parts of the service which are not marked are included in all three of the options above.

When observed in connection with one of the daily offices, the opening dialogue is omitted and the Transitus part of the service begins with the words of scripture below which become the scripture for the service; this rite then replaces the prayers and remaining parts of the office.

Greeting
(a musical response may be sung; see Worship Resources 92, 107, 133, 135)

O God, come to our assistance.
> **O Lord, hasten to help us.**

Glory to the holy and blessed Trinity
who is now, ever was, and every shall be for endless ages.
> **Amen.**

Hear these words of Holy Scripture:
>Though I walk through the valley of the shadow of death,
>I will fear no evil for you are with me,
>Your rod and staff comfort me.
>You anoint my head with oil;
>My cup runs over.
>Surely goodness and mercy shall follow me all the days of my life,
>And I will dwell in the house of the Lord forever.

>If we live, we live to the Lord,
>and if we die, we die to the Lord.
>Whether therefore we live or die,
>we belong to the Lord.

>Blessed be the God of our Lord Jesus Christ,
>by whose great mercy we have been born anew to a living hope
>by the resurrection of Jesus Christ form the dead.[1]

PD [Here the sign of the cross with oil may be made on the forehead of the person with the words: "Remember that you were sealed by the Holy Spirit at your baptism and marked as Christ's own forever" or, in the case of one who has died: "You were sealed by the Holy Spirit at your baptism and marked as Christ's own forever]

[BCP alt.]

Prayers

The Holy One[2] be with you.
>**And also with you.**

Let us pray:

(See Worship Resources 19-22 for musical settings)
Jesus, Lamb of God,
>**have mercy on us.**

Jesus, Lamb of God,
>**have mercy on us.**

Jesus, redeemer of the world,
>**grant us your peace.**

---

[1] Adapted from Psalm 23, Romans 1:4-8, and I Peter 1:3 as used in ANZPB/NKMOA.
[2] Or "The Lord" or "God."

O Lord, support us all the day long of this troublous life, until the shadows lengthen and the evening comes, and the busy world is hushed, and the fever of life is over, and our work is done. Then in your mercy, grant us a safe lodging, and a holy rest, and peace at the last. **Amen.** [JOHN HENRY NEWMAN, 1801-1890]

P *[At the bedside of one who is dying, the reserved sacrament may be shared with all present, or a brief service of Holy Communion may take place.]*

M *[At a memorial celebration:*
Witness is given about each life whose transitus is being celebrated. After each time of witness, the presider says: "May his/her soul, and the souls of all the faithful departed, through the mercy of God, rest in peace," *to which the community responds:* **"Merciful God, we thank you for this witness of faith and service."**
At the conclusion of this time of naming, the presider says: "Blessed are the dead who die in the Lord and their works do follow them," *to which the community responds,* **"Amen."**

COMMENDATION

> In peace we will lie down and sleep.
> **In the Lord alone we safely rest.**
> Guide us waking, O Lord, and guard us sleeping,
> **that awake we may watch with Christ,**
> **and asleep we may rest in peace.**
> May the divine help remain with us always,
> **and with those who are absent from us.**

- silence -

> Into your hands, O Lord,
> we commend the spirit of our *Brother/Sister N* or *our Brother(s) and Sister(s)*
> **For you have redeemed us, O Lord,**
> **O God of Truth.**

[SARUM BREVIARY, PS. 4:8 AND 30:5, ADAPTED]

> Receive *him/her/them* into the arms of your mercy,
> into the blessed rest of eternal peace,
> and into the glorious company of the saints in light. **Amen.**

Canticle of Simeon *(The Nunc Dimittis; Luke 2:29-32)*

(spoken or sung in unison to psalm tone one)

Lord, you have now set your ser-vant *free*
   to go in peace as you have *promised*;
for these eyes of mine have seen the *Savior*,
   Whom you have prepared for all the world to *see*.
A Light to en-lighten the *nations*,
   And the glory of your peo-ple *Israel*.

[ICET]

Glory to you, O Trinity, most holy and *blessed*,
   One God, now and for-ever. A-*men*.

PD [Here the brother or sister whose transitus is being celebrated, or in the case of recent death, the body of the same, may be anointed with oil in the name of the holy and blessed Trinity, and the following benediction be accompanied with the laying on of hands.]

Benediction

PD The holy and blessed Trinity + bless you and keep you.
The face of God shine on you and be gracious to you.
God look on you with kindness and give you peace. **Amen.**

[Adapted from Numbers 6:24-26]

M The holy and blessed Trinity + bless us and keep us.
The face of God shine on us and be gracious to us.
God look on us with kindness and give us peace. **Amen.**

[Adapted from Numbers 6:24-26]

(A musical response may be sung; see Worship Resources 50, 105, 106, 148)

M Let us bless the Lord.
   Thanks be to God.
May the souls of the faithful departed,
through the mercy of God, rest in peace.
   Amen.

SERVICES OF THE ORDER OF SAINT LUKE

Profession of Vows[1]

Profession of Vows may follow a brief Service of the Word[2] and be succeeded by a Service of Eucharist, or it may be placed in the context of one of the hours of prayer in the Daily Office. The presider is usually the abbot or chapter prior.

Introduction and Charge

Dear friends in Jesus Christ:
Through our baptism, we are made into the one Body of Christ.

Through renewal of the baptismal covenant,
   we accept the call to service
   and affirm those vows made at the time of our entrance
   into this family we call the Church.

We come to affirm our commitment
   to living out our baptism
   through the Rule of Life and Service
   of the Order of Saint Luke.

Presentation and Baptismal Renewal

Brother/Sister N^3,
are the persons *(or "is the person")*
you present prepared by a commitment
to Christ as Lord,
to join with other members of the Order
in seeking to serve God and the Church
through the Order of Saint Luke
by study, service, gifts and practice
in order to live the sacramental life,
seeking to incarnate the life of hope,
promised and fulfilled in Jesus Christ?

The presenter responds (persons standing when presented)

---

[1] When used by the General Chapter in retreat or convocation, it should be noted that the service is the high point of our time together. Therefore, enough time should be allowed for it to unfold at its own pace. Persons who find it difficult to sit for an extended period of time are encouraged to stand or walk in the back of the chapel as need arises.

[2] At General Chapter, the service begins with a processional and a brief Service of the Word which may include an opening dialog, hymn, prayer of the day, scripture, and homily.

[3] At meetings of the General Chapter, the presentation is made by the provincial general. In local chapters, the prior designates another member of the Order to make the presentation.

They are *(or He/She is)* so committed.
I present to you *these persons (or, in the case of one person, NAME)*
seeking to make a first profession to the Order of Saint Luke.
> *Name, name, name . . .*

I present the professed members of the Order
making *[annual[4]]* renewal of their vows.

When appropriate[5], the following presentations are also made:

[I present those seeking to make lifelong profession to The Order.]
[I present those who have taken lifelong vows in The Order.]

I invite all other baptized persons present to stand with us.

The Presider asks the questions with all the baptized responding:

> God has consecrated you with water and the Holy Spirit.
> Acknowledging that our first calling is to be children of God
>   by adoption and grace, I now ask you:
>
> Do you reaffirm your renunciation of evil?
>   **I do.**
> Do you renew your commitment to Jesus Christ,
>   putting your whole trust in Him?
>   **I do.**

The Presider addresses the whole community which responds

> Will you do all in your power
>   to support one another in your life in Christ?
>   **By the strength and grace of God, we will.**

+PRAYER OVER THE WATER
> The Lord[6] be with you;
>   **and also with you.**
> Let us pray:
> Pour out your Holy Spirit,
>   and by this gift of water call to our remembrance
>   the grace declared to us in our baptism,
>   for You wash away our sins
>   and clothe us with righteousness throughout our lives,

---

[4] Annual renewal of vows ordinarily takes place in October, near to the Feast of Saint Luke on October 18. However, all members renew their vows in concert with new members at any profession service.

[5] Ordinarily these presentations are made only at a meeting of the General Chapter.

[6] Or "the Holy One" or "God."

that dying and rising with Christ
we may continue forever in the risen life of Jesus Christ our Savior,
who with You and the Holy Spirit lives and reigns forever.
Amen.

Water may be lifted up and allowed to fall back into the font, sprinkled over the congregation, or used in other symbolic ways, as the presider says:

Remember your baptism and be thankful.
Amen!

Profession of Vows

The presenter invites the candidates with these words:

If you are making your first profession, please come forward.

All members of the Order remain standing; others are seated..

The Presider receives the vows on behalf of the community:

I ask you who are now making your first profession,
in the presence of,
and in concert with, your brothers and sisters
both here present and throughout the Order:

Do you affirm the apostolic hope?
Candidates and members respond **I do.**

Do you live for the church of Jesus Christ?
I do.

Will you seek the sacramental life?
I will.

Will you promote the corporate worship of the Church?
I will.

Will you magnify the sacraments?
I will.

Do you accept the call to service
as put forth by the Rule of Life and Service
of The Order of Saint Luke?
I do.

Will you faithfully abide by the Rule of Life and Service of the Order
and indicate your commitment by study, service, gifts and practice?
I will.

Those making first profession remain standing; all others are seated.
Each candidate making their first profession then kneels or sits.

The presider places hands on the head of each candidate, being joined by other professed members, as all members raise their hands in blessing and the following prayer is offered.

Almighty God, send down your Holy Spirit upon *Name*
    who this day accepts your call to service
    as a member of this Order.
Uphold *him/her* by your power,
    inspire *him/her* with your Word,
    and sustain *him/her* with the means of grace
    that *he/she* may faithfully discharge your calling;
    through Jesus Christ our Lord. **Amen.**

[If annual renewal of vows takes place at this service, the presider addresses those who renewing their annual vows:]

[Will the members of the Order making annual renewal of their vows please come forward?

[Those making annual renewal of their vows come forward to kneel or sit as members of the Order raise their hands in blessing and the following prayer is offered:]

[Loving God, you abide with us in life and in death;
    in joy and in sorrow.
We give thanks for the grace given to *Name*
    who this day renews *his/her* vows to our Order.
Send down your Holy Spirit upon *him/her*.
Continue to uphold *him/her* by your power;
    renew him/her in your Word,
    and sustain *him/her* with the means of grace
    that *he/she* may seek always your will;
    through Jesus Christ our Lord. **Amen.**

[LIFELONG VOWS, ordinarily professed only at meetings of the General Chapter, are professed at this point; see page 91]

Collect for The Order of Saint Luke
    The Holy One be with you.
        And also with you.
    Let us pray:
        O Shepherd of us all,
            who inspired your servant Saint Luke the Physician
            to set forth in the gospel
            the love and healing power of Jesus:
        Grant, we ask you, your Spirit to the Order of Saint Luke,
            that we may proclaim the Apostolic hope,
            magnify the Sacraments,

**and embody Christ's healing grace for all creation;
through Jesus Christ our Lord. Amen.**

If the Eucharist is celebrated, it begins at this point with The Presentation of the Gifts (see p. 9, Worship Resources 34-36, 38), followed by the Great Thanksgiving. If no Eucharist is celebrated, it may conclude with a hymn, and a blessing and commission. In any case, the service concludes with the passing of the peace.

LIFELONG VOWS

(To be inserted in the service above before the Collect for The Order of Saint Luke. Note: At a earlier point in the life of the community, each candidate will have been invited to tell the story of his or her decision to make a life commitment to the Rule of Life and Service. This may include telling how they intend to live out their lifelong vows).

The Abbot continues[6]:

> My sisters and brothers in Christ,
>> we are gathered as a community
>> to witness the profession
>> of those who pray that the remainder of their lives
>> will be given to the living out of our Rule of Life and Service.

The Provincial General says:

> *Brother/Sister* Abbot,
>> these come *(or "this person comes")* to make a lifelong profession
>> of the Rule of Life and Service
>> and to declare their *(his/her)* devotion to the sacramental life.
>
> God has called them *(her/him)* to a life of continual worship
>> and to the constant use of the means of grace.
>> They seek *(She/He seeks)* to consecrate their lives *(his/her life)*
>> to presenting the Incarnate God to the world
>> and to being instruments of healing in the Church,
>> embodying Christ's healing grace for all creation.
>> Let those who desire the blessing of God and this community
>> in taking lifelong vows come forward, namely *Br./Sr. Chosen Name[7]*.
>
> *As each name is read, let the candidate respond:*
> **I am ready and willing.**

---

[6] Except in unusual circumstances, lifelong vows are made only at meetings of the General Chapter with the abbot presiding. The abbot may designate someone else to preside in his/her place.

[7] Inquiry should be made in advance as to what name the candidate chooses to use in the Order, whether a given name or a new name.

The Abbot says:
> You come before this community seeking our discernment
>> and affirmation of your call to the sacramental life.
> You have renewed your baptismal covenant
>> and confirmed the vows of our Rule of Life and Service.
> I ask you now,
>> in the presence of brothers and sisters here present
>> and in community with your sisters and brothers
>> throughout the Order:
>
> While you have life and breath,
>> will you seek to live according to the vows
>> you have confirmed this day
>> with your brothers and sisters in the Order of Saint Luke?
>>> **With God's help, I will.**
>
> Will you seek and serve Christ in all persons,
> loving your neighbor as yourself?
>>> **With God's help, I will.**
>
> Will you strive for justice and peace among all people,
>> respect the dignity of every human being,
>> and be a faithful steward of all that God has given you?
>>> **With God's help, I will.**

The Abbot addresses the community
> Brothers and sisters in Christ,
>> you have heard the testimony and call
>> of these who come seeking our discernment and affirmation.
> Is it your discernment that their call is truly of God?

The community responds: **That is our discernment.**

> Is it your will that we should affirm their call?
>> **That is our will. Thanks be to God!**

Each candidate then kneels or sits before the Abbot, placing a hand on a Bible, and making the following vow, as the life-vowed members of the Order raise their hands in blessing.

I, *Chosen Name*, by the grace of God
    consecrate myself to the service of God
    by commitment to the sacramental life.
Therefore, I promise to live the Christian life
    in The Order of Saint Luke
    by observing its Rule of Life and Service
    all the days of my life.
I trust in God alone for my strength.
May the grace of the Holy Spirit,
    the example of the apostles,
    and the bonds of this community always be my help.

The community responds

So may it be. Thanks be to God! Amen.

The abbot then blesses each new life-vowed member, being joined in the laying on of hands by other life-vowed members (including their companion in the discernment journey if present), as all members of the community raise a hand in blessing.

Loving God, you abide with us in life and in death,
    in joy and in sorrow.
We give thanks for the grace given to *Br./Sr.Chosen Name(s)*
    who this day have *(has)* made lifelong vows in our Order.
Send down your Holy Spirit upon them *(her/him)*.
Continue to uphold them *(him/her)* by your power,
  renew them *(her/him)* in your Word,
    and sustain them *(him/her)* with the means of grace
    that, throughout their lives *(her/his life)*,
    they *(he/she)* may keep these vows
    to the honor and glory of Your Name,
    through Jesus Christ our Lord. **Amen.**

As the new life-vowed member stands, an additional knot is tied in her or his cincture by the companion or another life-vowed member.

The service continues with the presider leading the community in The Collect for the Order of Saint Luke (p. 90 or Worship Resource 151). If the Eucharist is celebrated, it begins at this point with The Presentation of the Gifts (see p. 9, Worship Resources 34-36, 38), followed by the Great Thanksgiving.

Service of Investiture of Officers for The Order of Saint Luke

The presider is the previous abbot or prior if present, a prior abbot or prior, a canon of the Order, or a present or former general officer of the Order. If none of the above are present, another member of the Order may be designated to preside as the temporary vicar of the abbot.

The Service of Investiture may take place within one of the hours of the Daily Office, or in a Service of Word and Table where it takes place as a response to the Word and before the celebration of the Eucharist. In any case, the newly invested prior or abbot or their designate presides for the remainder of the service after being invested. When the Service of Investiture takes place apart from some other office or service, it may begin with the following:

>[Call to Praise and Prayer
>>O God, come to our assistance.
>
>>**O Lord, hasten to help us.**
>
>>Glory to you, O Trinity, most holy and blessed,
>
>>**one God, now and forever. Amen.**
>
>[Hymn and/or Psalter with Gloria
>[Prayer For Illumination
>[Reading From Holy Scripture
>>(a passage selected by the prior or abbot to be invested)
>
>[A Canticle such as the Te Deum Laudamus (see Worship
>>Resources 185)

+INVESTITURE SENTENCES
> Open for me the gates of righteousness;
>> **I will enter them and give thanks to the Lord.**
>
> The Lord has said:
> I will give you a shepherd after my own heart,
> who will feed you with knowledge and understanding.
>> [JEREMIAH 3:15]
>
>> **Glory to you, O Trinity, most holy and blessed,
>> one God, now and forever. Amen.**

+COLLECT
> The Holy One[1] be with you.
>> **And also with you.**
>
> Let us pray:

---

[1] Or "The Lord" or "God."

Mighty God, who called your servant Luke to be a physician of the soul: Pour out upon us, your children and servants today, a fresh measure of your Spirit that we may be faithful, devoting ourselves to the apostles' teaching, to *koinonia*[1], to the breaking of bread, and the prayers. May we receive your gifts with glad and generous hearts, praising you day by day. In the name of Jesus Christ our brother we pray. **Amen.**

[ADAPTED FROM ACTS 2:42-47 AND A COLLECT FROM THE 1549 BCP]

INVESTITURE

A representative of the chapter or general chapter presents the officers:

I present the following persons, duly elected by the members of the Order of Saint Luke, to be invested as our officers:

Brother/Sister N. to be our *[name of office]*
Brother/Sister N. to be our *[name of office]*
   Etc.
[each officer-elect stands when named]

The presider continues:

My brothers and sisters in the Order:
Do you recognize and receive these persons to be your officers?
We do.
Will you uphold them in their ministries with your prayers and your support?
We will.
My brother(s) and sister(s): It has pleased God to call you to be the pastors, shepherds, and officers *[of this chapter]* of the Order of Saint Luke. In order that we may know your commitment to fulfill this trust, I ask you to affirm these promises:

Will you exercise your ministry in obedience to Christ?
We (I) will obey Christ, and will serve in Christ's name.
Will you share with your fellow members in the governance of the Order; will you sustain them and take counsel with them, and will you guide and strengthen them as they minister in the Church of Jesus Christ?
We (I) will, by the grace given us (me).

---

[1] *Koinonia* refers to the beloved community in which we share our burdens, tears, cares, and apostolate.

Will you uphold the Rule of Life and Service of the Order of Saint Luke, and seek to enable your sisters and brothers in the Order to faithfully live their vows?

We (I) will, God being our (my) helper.

May the Lord who has given you the will to make these vows, give you the grace and power to perform them.

The officers-elect: Help us, Holy Spirit!

(Each officer kneels or sits to receive the laying on of hands by the chapter or, in the general chapter, by former abbots, as the presider prays:)

Gracious God, send down your Holy Spirit upon *Brother/Sister* _____, who this day accepts your call to service as _____ *(of this chapter)* of The Order of Saint Luke. Uphold *him/her* with your power, inspire *him/her* with your Word, and sustain *him/her* with your grace, that *he/she* may faithfully discharge your calling. **Amen.**

Each officer may then be anointed with oil and/or invested with a symbol of office, such as an OSL scapular, cross, or in the case of the abbot, the crozier. The "Veni Creator Spiritus" (Worship Resources 127) may then be sung. The newly invested abbot or prior concludes the service:

Collect for the Order of Saint Luke

The Holy One[1] be with you.

And also with you.

Let us pray:

O Shepherd of us all,
   who inspired your servant Saint Luke the Physician
   to set forth in the gospel
   the love and healing power of Jesus:
Grant, we ask you, your Spirit to the Order of Saint Luke,
   that we may proclaim the apostolic hope,
   magnify the Sacraments,
   and embody Christ's healing grace for all creation;
   through Jesus Christ our Lord. Amen.

If the Eucharist is celebrated, it takes place at this point beginning with the Invitation on p. 8. The newly invested abbot or prior or his or her designate presides at Table.

If the Eucharist is not celebrated, a hymn such as "Life and Service" (Worship Resources 143) is sung and the service concludes as follows:

---

1 Or "The Lord" or "God."

Abbot's Commendation and Blessing

[If the abbot of the Order is not present, the commendation may be given by the newly invested prior of the chapter, a prior abbot, one of the general officers, or the current prior of the chapter beginning with the words "And now, on behalf of Abbot x (first name of current abbot). I commend you to God . . . ."]

> And now I commend you to God
> > and to the word of God's grace
> > which is able to build you up
> > and to give you an inheritance with all the saints.
> >
> > > [Acts 20:32]

> The grace of our Lord Jesus Christ, and the love of God,
> > and the aid and comfort of the Holy Spirit be with you all. **Amen.**
> >
> > > [II Corinthians 13:14]

Passing the Peace

Intricate drawings of beasts were often used in Celtic sacred texts to invoke God's protection upon Creation.

WORSHIP RESOURCES

Invitation to Silence 1

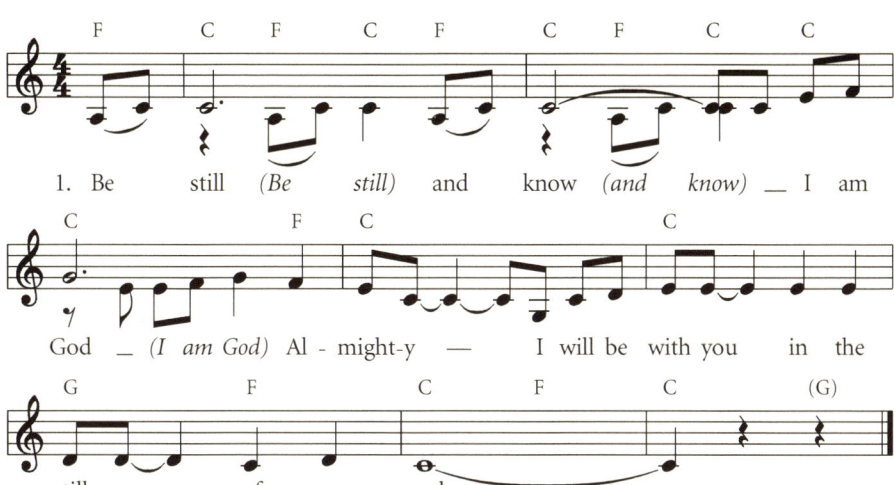

1. Be still *(Be still)* and know *(and know)* I am God *(I am God)* Almighty — I will be with you in the stillness of your soul.

2. Be still *(be still)* and know *(and know)* I break the bow *(I break the bow)* and chariot—I will be with you in the breaking of your soul.

3. Be still *(be still)* and know *(and know)* I am the One *(I am the One)* who suffers—I will be with you in the midnight of your soul.

4. Be still *(be still)* and know *(and know)* I am the joy *(I am the joy)* within you—I will be with you in the sunrise of your soul.

WORDS: Jim Manley
MUSIC: Jim Manley
© 1981, 1989 Hope Publishing Company, Carol Stream, IL 60188. All rights reserved. Used by permission.

Be Still and Know 2

WORDS: Psalm 46:10
MUSIC: Anonymous

Kyrie Eleison

May be used with Setting Two
WORDS: Ancient Greek
MUSIC: George R. Crisp, OSL
Music © 2010 George R. Crisp

Kyrie Eleison 4

May be used with Setting Three
WORDS: Ancient Greek
MUSIC: Russian Orthodox Liturgy

ORTHODOX KYRIE
Irr.

5 Kyrie Eleison

May be used with Setting One

WORDS: Ancient Greek
MUSIC: William J. Beasley, OSL, 2009
Music © 2009 Order of St. Luke

6 Kyrie Eleison

May be used with Setting Four

WORDS: Ancient Greek
MUSIC: African American Spiritual, arr. by Dwight W. Vogel, OSL
Arr. © 2011 Order of St. Luke

BURLEIGH
Irr.

KYRIE ELEISON

Have Mercy   7

First time: Unison melody
Second time: Add alto harmony
Third time: Add descant

WORDS: Robert S. Jarboe, OSL
MUSIC: Robert S. Jarboe, OSL
© 2006, 2011 Robert S. Jarboe. Used by permission.

THE LORD'S PRAYER

8 The Lord's Prayer

WORDS: Matthew 6:9-13
MUSIC: Lowell Mason, 1824
Words © 1988 English Language Liturgical Consultation (ELLC). Used by permission.

GREGORIAN
Irr.

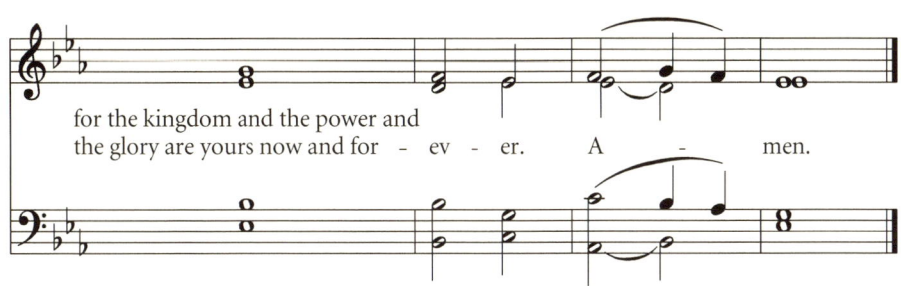

The Lord's Prayer 9

Our Father in heaven, hallowed be your name,

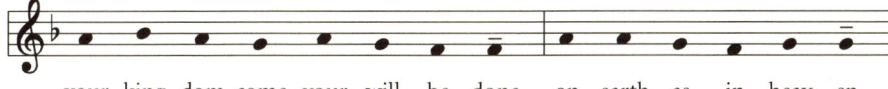

your kingdom come, your will be done, on earth as in heaven.

Give us today our daily bread. Forgive us our sins

as we forgive those who sin against us.

Save us from the time of trial, and deliver us from evil.

For the kingdom, the power, and the glory are yours,

now and forever. Amen.

WORDS: Matthew 6:9-13
MUSIC: Ambrosian chant, adapt. Mason Martens
Words © 1998 English Language Liturgical Consultation (ELLC). Used by permission.

AMBROSIAN
Irr.

THE LORD'S PRAYER
10 Our Father

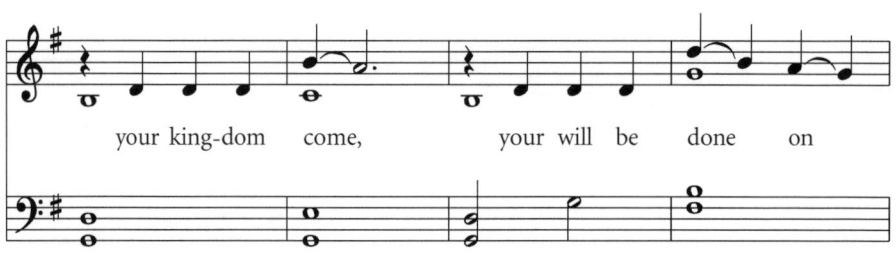

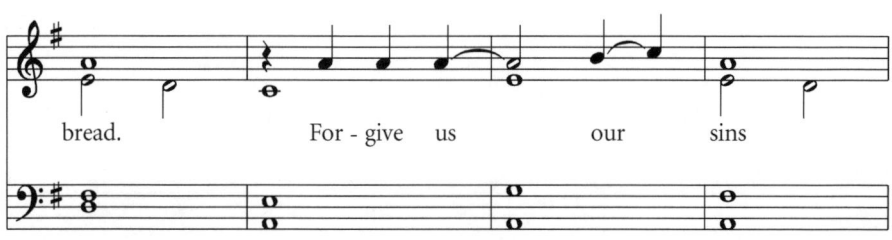

WORDS: Matthew 6:9-13 (ELLC)
MUSIC: John Erickson, 1977

LORD'S PRAYER
Irr.

Words © 1988 English Language Liturgical Consultation (ELLC). Used by permission.
Music © 1982 Hope Publishing Company, Carol Stream, IL 60188. Used by permission.

THE LORD'S PRAYER

THE LORD'S PRAYER

11 Our Father in Heaven

WORDS: Matthew 6:9-13
MUSIC: Jim Strathdee, 1982
Words © 1988 English Language Liturgical Consultation (ELLC). Used by permission.
Music © 1982 Desert Flower Music

THE LORD'S PRAYER

THE LORD'S PRAYER

12
The Prayer of Jesus

Ho-ly One, our on-ly home, hal-lowed be your

name. May your day dawn, your will be done,

here as in heav-en. Feed us to-day,

and for-give us as we for-give each oth-er.

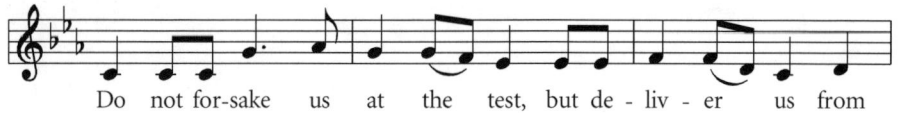
Do not for-sake us at the test, but de-liv-er us from

e-vil. For the glo-ry, the pow-er, and the mer-cy are

yours, now and for-ev-er. A-men;

A-men; A-men.

WORDS: Mother Thunder Mission (Matt. 6:9-13)
MUSIC: Native American melody, arr. Elise S. Eslinger
Arr. © 2005 The Upper Room

GOSPEL ACCLAMATION

Zimbabwe Alleluia   13

May be used with Eucharistic Setting Four

WORDS: Traditional
MUSIC: Adapt. from Zimbabwe

Alleluia   14

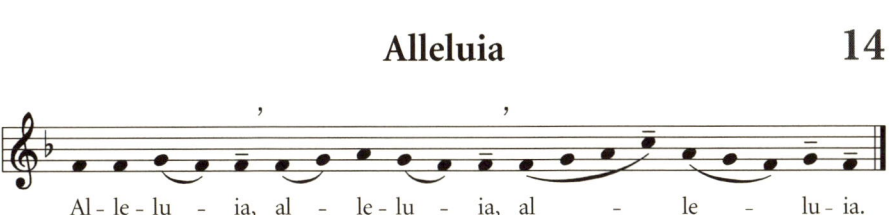

May be used with Eucharistic Setting Three

WORDS: Traditional
MUSIC: Traditional chant

GOSPEL ACCLAMATION

15 Alleluia

May be used with Eucharistic Setting One
WORDS: Traditional
MUSIC: William J. Beasley, OSL
Music © 2009 Order of Saint Luke

16 Alleluia

May be used with Eucharistic Setting Two
WORDS: Traditional
MUSIC: George R. Crisp, OSL
Music © 2010 George R. Crisp

GOSPEL ACCLAMATION

GOSPEL ACCLAMATION

17   Gospel Acclamation for Lent

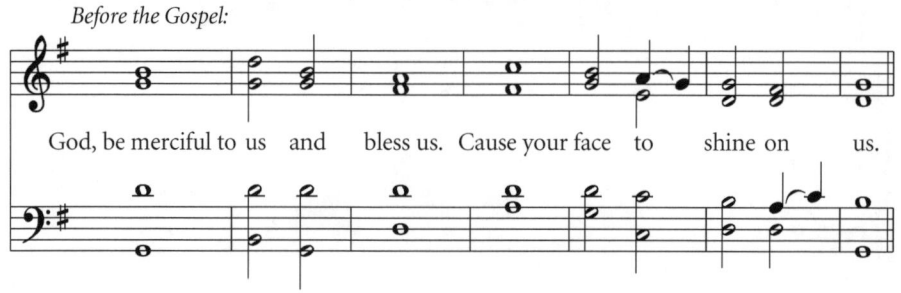

Before the Gospel: God, be merciful to us and bless us. Cause your face to shine on us.

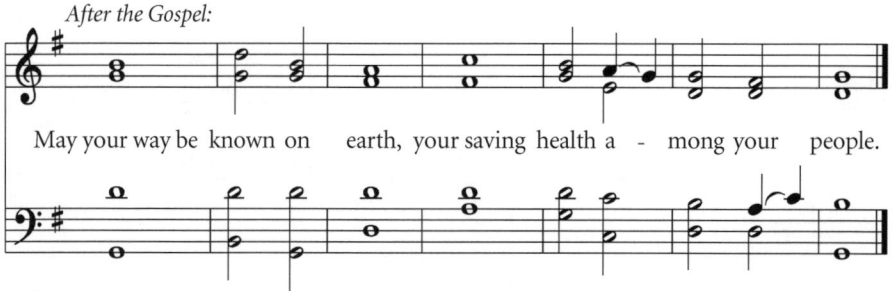

After the Gospel: May your way be known on earth, your saving health among your people.

WORDS: Traditional
MUSIC: *The Methodist Hymnal,* 1935

18   Gloria Christi, Gratia Tibi

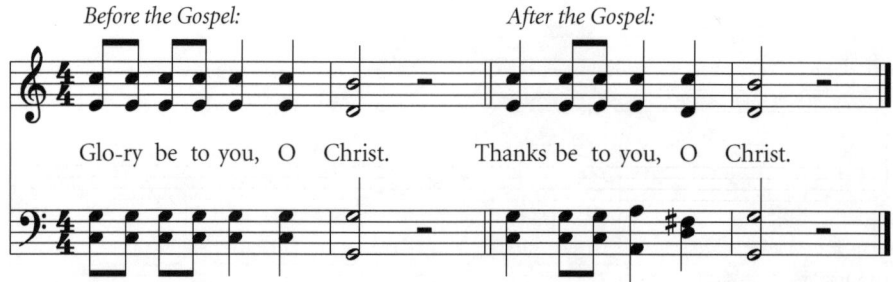

Before the Gospel: Glory be to you, O Christ. *After the Gospel:* Thanks be to you, O Christ.

WORDS: Traditional
MUSIC: John L. Playford 1674-1730

Jesus, Lamb of God
(*Agnus Dei*)

May be used with Setting One

WORDS: English Language Liturgical Consultation (ELLC).
MUSIC: William J. Beasley, OSL
Words © 1988 English Language Liturgical Consultation. Used by permission. Music © 2009 Order of St. Luke.

AGNUS DEI
20   Jesus, Lamb of God
(Agnus Dei)

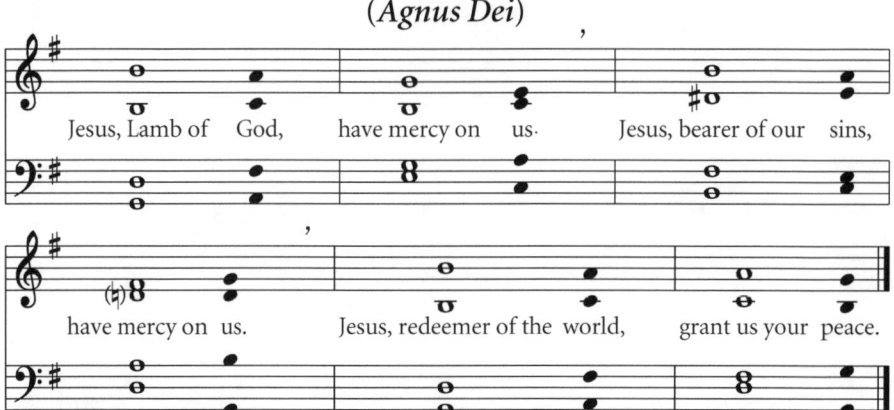

May be used with Setting Three
WORDS: English Language Liturgical Consultation (ELLC)
MUSIC: Adapted from chants by Stephen Elvey (1805-1860) and James Turle (1802-1882)
Words © 1988 English Language Liturgical Consultation. Used by permission.

21   Jesus, Lamb of God
(Agnus Dei)

May be used with Setting Two
WORDS: Traditional
MUSIC: George R. Crisp, OSL
Music © 2010 George R. Crisp

AGNUS DEI
22
Jesus, Lamb of God
(*Agnus Dei*)

May be used with Setting Four

WORDS: ELLC, alt.
MUSIC: John E. Gould, 1871
Words © 1988 English Language Liturgical Consultation. Used by permission.

PILOT
7.7.7.7.7.7

GATHERING HYMNS

Come, Sinners, to the Gospel Feast
23

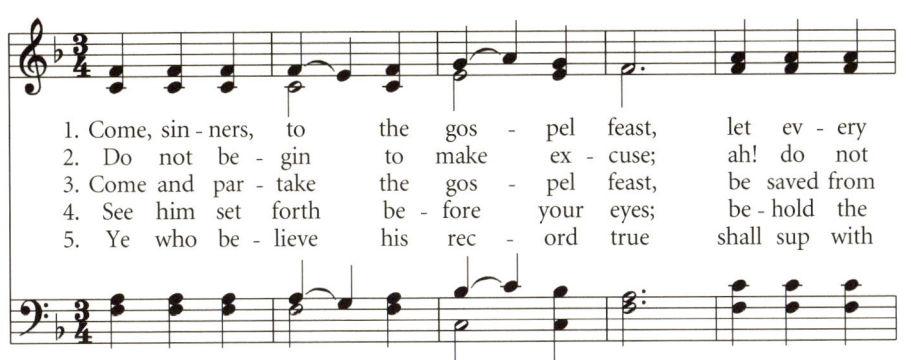

1. Come, sin-ners, to the gos-pel feast, let ev-ery
2. Do not be-gin to make ex-cuse; ah! do not
3. Come and par-take the gos-pel feast, be saved from
4. See him set forth be-fore your eyes; be-hold the
5. Ye who be-lieve his rec-ord true shall sup with

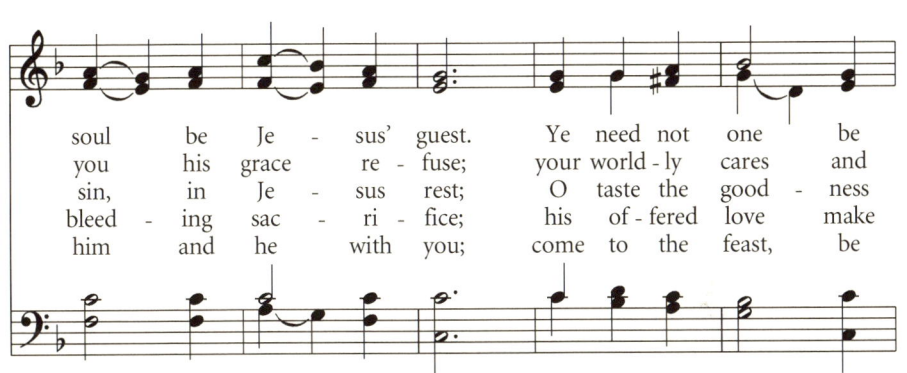

soul be Je - sus' guest. Ye need not one be
you his grace re - fuse; your world-ly cares and
sin, in Je - sus rest; O taste the good - ness
bleed - ing sac - ri - fice; his of-fered love make
him and he with you; come to the feast, be

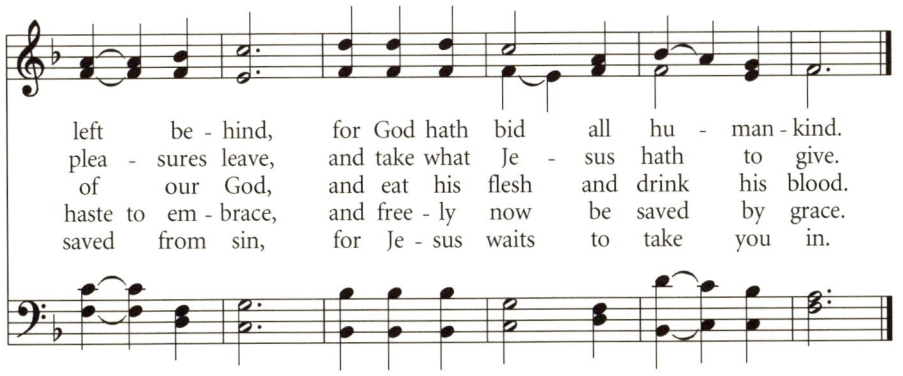

left be - hind, for God hath bid all hu - man-kind.
plea - sures leave, and take what Je - sus hath to give.
of our God, and eat his flesh and drink his blood.
haste to em - brace, and free - ly now be saved by grace.
saved from sin, for Je - sus waits to take you in.

WORDS: Charles Wesley, 1747 (Lk. 14:16-24) Alternate
MUSIC: *Katholisches Gesangbuch*, ca. 1774; adapt. from *Metrical Psalter*, 1855

HURSLEY
LM

GATHERING HYMNS

24   God, Whose Love Is Reigning o'er Us

1. God, whose love is reign-ing o'er us, source of
2. Word of God from na-ture bring-ing spring-time
3. Ho-ly God of an-cient glo-ry, choos-ing
4. Cove-nant, new a-gain in Je-sus, Star-child
5. Lift we then our hu-man voic-es in the

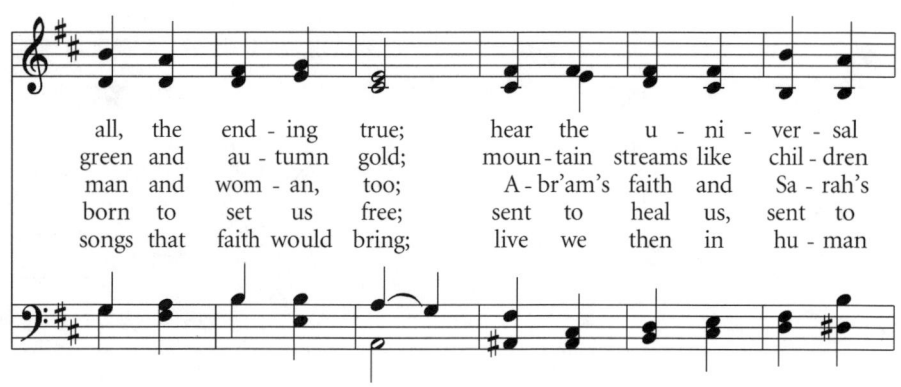

all, the end-ing true; hear the u-ni-ver-sal
green and au-tumn gold; moun-tain streams like chil-dren
man and wom-an, too; A-br'am's faith and Sa-rah's
born to set us free; sent to heal us, sent to
songs that faith would bring; live we then in hu-man

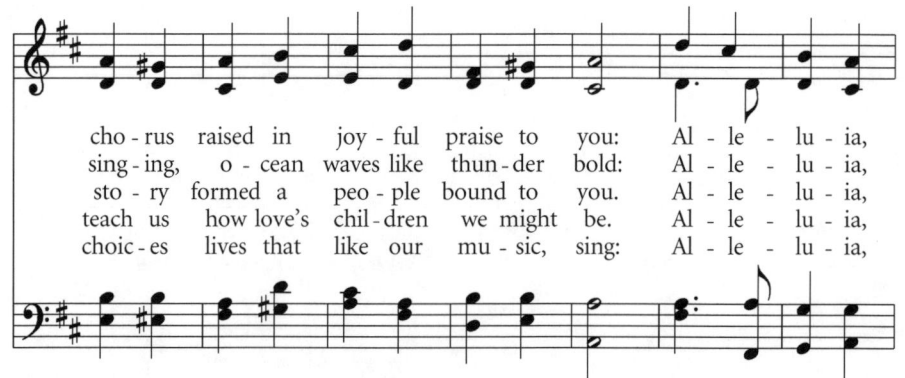

cho-rus raised in joy-ful praise to you: Al-le-lu-ia,
sing-ing, o-cean waves like thun-der bold: Al-le-lu-ia,
sto-ry formed a peo-ple bound to you. Al-le-lu-ia,
teach us how love's chil-dren we might be. Al-le-lu-ia,
choic-es lives that like our mu-sic, sing: Al-le-lu-ia,

WORDS: William Boyd Grove, OSL, 1980   LAUDA ANIMA
MUSIC: John Goss, 1869   87.87.87
Words © 1980 William Boyd Grove. Used by permission.

GATHERING HYMNS

Al - le - lu - ia, wor - ship an - cient, wor - ship new.
Al - le - lu - ia, as cre - a - tion's tale is told.
Al - le - lu - ia, to your cove - nant keep us true.
Al - le - lu - ia, ris - en Christ, our Sav - ior he!
Al - le - lu - ia, joined in love our prais - es ring!

Let All Mortal Flesh   25

1. Let all mor - tal flesh keep si - lence and with fear and trem - bling stand;
2. King of kings, yet born of Ma - ry, as of old on earth he stood,
3. Rank on rank the host of heav - en spreads its van - guard on the way,
4. At his feet the six-winged ser - aph, cher - u - bim with sleep - less eye,

pon - der noth - ing earth - ly - mind - ed, for with bless - ing in his hand,
Lord of lords in hu - man ves - ture, in the bod - y and the blood
as the Light of Light de - scend - eth from the realms of end - less day,
veil their fa - ces to the Pres - ence, as with cease - less voice they cry:

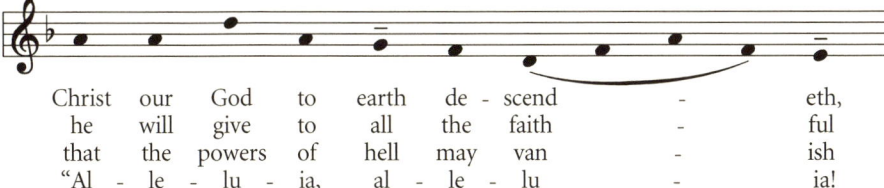

Christ our God to earth de - scend - eth,
he will give to all the faith - ful
that the powers of hell may van - ish
"Al - le - lu - ia, al - le - lu - ia!

our full hom - age to de - mand.
his own self for heaven - ly food.
as the dark - ness clears a - way.
Al - le - lu - ia, Lord Most High!"

WORDS: Liturgy of St. James; para. Gerard Moultrie (1829-1885)
MUSIC: PICARDY, 87.87.87, French carol, 17th cent.; melody from *Chansons populaires de France, 1860*

GATHERING HYMNS

26 Deck Yourself, My Soul, with Gladness

1. Deck your-self, my soul, with glad-ness, leave be-hind all gloom and sad-ness; come in-to the day-light's splen-dor, there with joy your prais-es ren-der un-to God, whose grace un-bound-ed has this won-drous ban-quet found-ed; come, for now the Lord most ho-ly stoops to you in like-ness low-ly.
2. Sun, who all my life does bright-en; Light, who does my soul en-light-en; Joy, your won-drous gift be-stow-ing; Fount, from which all good is flow-ing; at your feet I cry, my Mak-er, let me be a fit par-tak-er of this bless-ed food from heav-en, for our good, your glo-ry giv-en.
3. Je-sus, source of life and plea-sure, tru-est friend and dear-est trea-sure, by your love I am in-vit-ed, be your love with love re-quit-ed. From this ban-quet let me mea-sure, Lord, how vast and deep its trea-sure; through the gifts that here you give me, as your guest in heaven re-ceive me.

WORDS: Johann Franck (1618-1677), trans. Catherine Winkworth, 1863, and John Casper Mattes, 1913, alt.
MUSIC: Johann Crüger, 1649

SCHMÜCCKE DICH
LMD

GATHERING HYMNS

As Grain on Scattered Hillsides
27

1. As grain on scattered hillsides, when gathered, makes one bread,
   God, gather all your people as one in Christ our head.
   We come from many places and we are not the same,
   yet your strong love has called us to meet in Jesus' name.

2. A grain of wheat is fruitless until in earth it lies;
   then, dying to its old life, it bears and multiplies.
   So may we die to hatred, to all our hurtful ways,
   reborn to common living, to love, to work, to praise.

3. Like yeast that brings new ferment so lifeless dough may rise,
   your Spirit is the leaven of life that satisfies.
   As salt enhances flavor, enriches, and preserves,
   may earth rejoice to savor a church that heals and serves.

4. O Christ, our risen Savior; O Spirit, holy dove,
   come now and move among us; make us a sign of love.
   Come knead and blend each texture with strong and gentle hands,
   that we may be one body, one loaf in many lands.

WORDS: Ruth Duck, 1986, 1990
MUSIC: *Gesangbuch*, Meiningen, 1693; harm. Felix Mendelssohn, 1847
Words © 1992 GIA Publications, Inc. All rights reserved. Used by permission.

MUNICH
76.76 D

GATHERING HYMNS

Give Thanks to the Source
29

1. Give thanks to the Source who brings forth earth's goodness: the bread on our table, the fruit of the vine. Give thanks to the Love who welcomes the wandering, invents new beginnings, and calls us to dine.
2. Remember the Word, incarnate among us, whose table is open to all who draw near. Recall Jesus Christ in living and dying, in rising to new life, set free from our fear.
3. We pray for the gift of life-giving Spirit that we may know Jesus in sharing this meal. So may we depart refreshed for the journey, to live by the Gospel, to love and to heal.

Reflecting Br. Dwight Vogel's summary of the Great Thanksgiving: "Praise God; remember Jesus; pray for the Spirit."

WORDS: Ruth Duck, 2005
MUSIC: Jane Marshall, 1982
ANNIVERSARY SONG
11.11.11.11
Words © 2005 GIA Publications, Inc. Music © 1982 Hope Publishing Company, Carol Stream, IL 60188.
All rights reserved. Used by permission.

GATHERING HYMNS

30 Planets Humming As They Wander

1. Plan-ets hum-ming as they wan-der, stars a-flame with si-lent song, gal-ax-ies are spin-ing end-less mel-o-dies, a-far but strong. God's cre-a-tion tunes a time-less hymn as far as we can gaze. Heaven-ly bod-ies help us hear the u-ni-ver-sal song of praise.
2. At-oms quiv-er-ing in-side us, cells a-buzz with en-er-gy, par-ti-cles are chant-ing ti-ny psalms in ho-ly syn-er-gy. All these mol-e-cules pro-vide us pat-terns of the craft of God, of-fering up me-lod-ic first fruit, grate-ful hymns which leave us awed.
3. Hu-man voic-es praise our Mak-er, part of the cre-at-ed choir: rum-bling tones of space be-low us, neu-tron's des-cant ev-er higher. Hymns a-rise from all a-round us, thank-ful praise our whole life long, to the One who made us, knows us, Au-thor of the end-less song!

Commissioned by the School of Theology of Boston University, Boston, Massachusetts, U.S.A., in honor of Carl P. Daw, Jr.

WORDS: Heather Josselyn-Cranson, OSL, 2010
MUSIC: Heather Josselyn-Cranson, OSL, 2010
© 2010 Heather Josselyn-Cranson

MUSICA MUNDANA
8.7.8.7 D

Maker of the Earth and Ocean

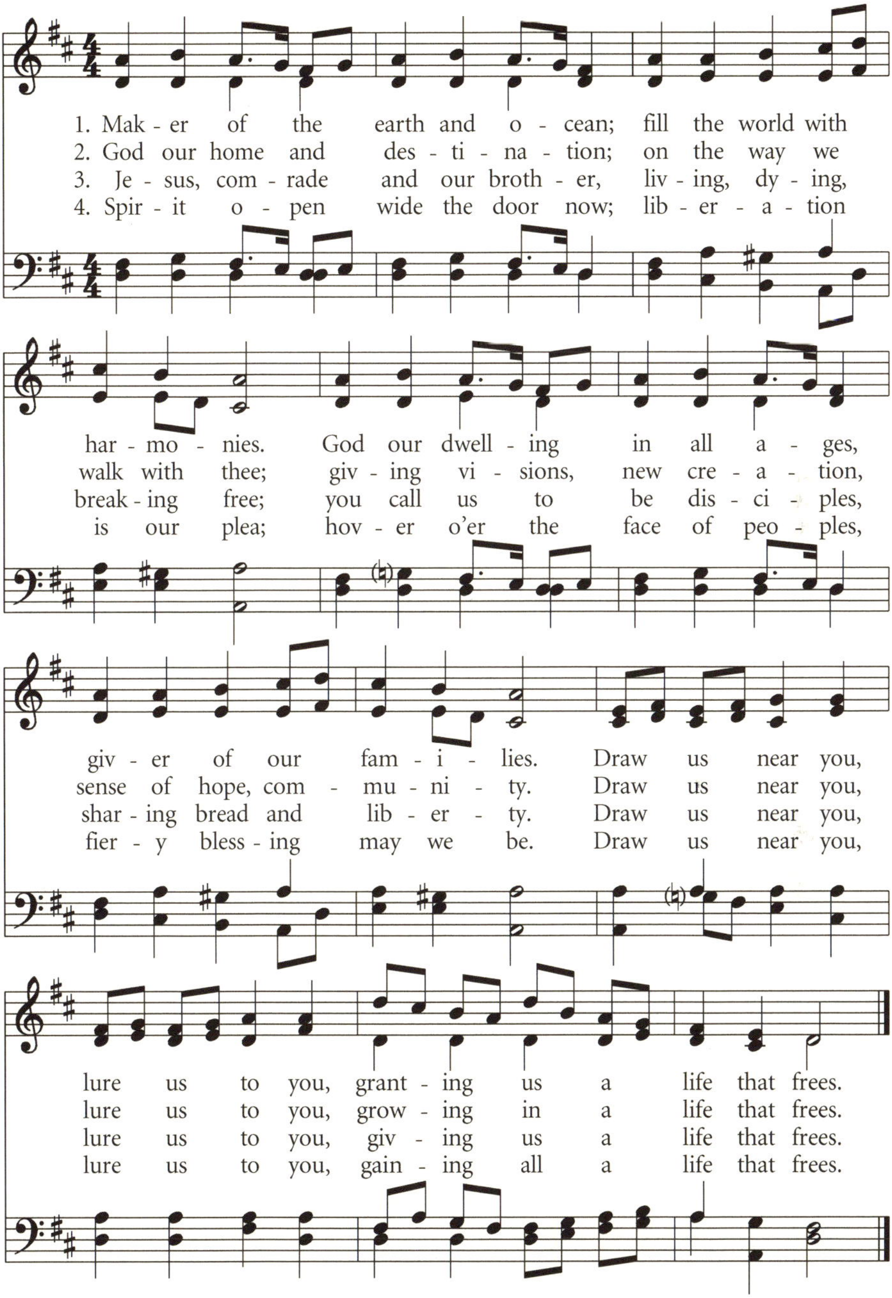

WORDS: Patricia Patterson, 2007
MUSIC: *The European Magazine and Review,* 1792; harm. *The Methodist Hymn and Tune Book,* 1889, alt.

SICILIAN MARINERS
87.87.87

GATHERING HYMNS

32 We Meet at His Table

1. We meet at his table, Jesus the Savior, as by the Spirit we are called and led; and while at his table we find a blessing: grace undeserving, as we receive the cup and bread.
2. The grain which was scattered now has been gathered for us to break and then in faith receive; and wine of the vineyard: gift of creation, poured for salvation, new life in Christ, as we believe.
*3. We come to this table filled with thanksgiving as with this feast we will be blessed and fed; for God's loving mercy brings us forgiveness: wonderful wholeness, found in the gifts of cup and bread.

*For a Sending Forth, sing the original words for the third stanza: "We rise from this table" and "as with this feast we have been blessed."

WORDS: George R. Crisp, OSL, 2000, alt.
MUSIC: George R. Crisp, OSL, 2000
© 2000 George R. Crisp/Giraffe Music

MEETING
Irr.

PRESENTATION OF THE GIFTS

Invitation 33

Come from the east and the west, from the north and the south,
 and gather at Christ's table.
Whoever you are, and wherever you are on your journey of faith,
 you are welcome to receive the bread and wine made holy.
But be forewarned: this is dangerous food;
 it can transform your life.

TAR, Trad.

The Gifts of God for the People of God 34

WORDS: Richard Bruxvoort Colligan, 2004
MUSIC: Richard Bruxvoort Colligan, 2004
© 2004 This Here Music. Used by permission.

GIFTS
10.7.10.7

PRESENTATION OF THE GIFTS

35 As the Grains of Wheat

WORDS: Marty Haugen (1950-)
MUSIC: Marty Haugen (1950-)
© 1990 GIA Publications, Inc. All rights reserved. Used by permission.

AS THE GRAINS
Irr.

PRESENTATION OF THE GIFTS

PRESENTATION OF THE GIFTS

36 At This Table

1. At this ta-ble, bread is bro-ken, and the wine is free-ly poured.
2. At this ta-ble, we are bro-ken, and our lives are formed a-new.
3. At this ta-ble, Love is giv-en—God shows us a bet-ter way.

Je-sus o-pens arms wide to us, giv-ing us his bod-y, blood.
Je-sus o-pens hearts to oth-ers—care no more for just a few.
We are nour-ished by the Spir-it with the bread blessed here to-day.

We are gath-ered here to-geth-er at the ta-ble Christ has set;
We are called to serve the hun-gry, heal the sick, and clothe the poor.
As we gath-er at the ta-ble, blesed by what we will re-ceive:

men and wom-en, man-y col-ors — all are wel-come, all are fed.
Look-ing 'round we see our sis-ters, find our broth-ers ev-ery-where.
bod-y giv-en to feed oth-ers. Through us Christ is known in-deed.

WORDS: W. Vincent Eller, OSL, 2006
MUSIC: John Wyeth's *Repository of Sacred Music*, 1813
Words © 2006 Order of Saint Luke

NETTLETON
87.87 D

Here, O My Lord, I See Thee

COMMUNION
37

1. Here, O my Lord, I see thee face to face;
   here would I touch and handle things unseen;
   here grasp with firmer hand eternal grace,
   and all my weariness upon thee lean.

2. This is the hour of banquet and of song;
   this is the heavenly table spread for me;
   here let me feast, and feasting still prolong
   the hallowed hour of fellowship with thee.

3. Here would I feed upon the bread of God,
   here drink with thee the royal wine of heaven;
   here would I lay aside each earthly load,
   here taste afresh the calm of sin forgiven.

4. Feast after feast thus comes and passes by;
   yet, passing, points to the glad feast above,
   giving sweet foretaste of the festal joy,
   the Lamb's great bridal feast of bliss and love.

MUSIC: Edward Dearle, 1874

PENITENTIA
10 10.10 10

COMMUNION

38 Jesus Took the Bread

1. Je-sus took the bread, dai-ly gift of God,
2. Je-sus blessed the bread, thanked the God of grace,
3. Je-sus broke the bread; then he poured the wine.
4. Je-sus gives the bread at our ta-ble still,

formed of wheat and sweat and toil, sun, rain, and sod.
thanked the One who made all worlds, all time, all space.
Bro-ken bod-y, life poured out, God gives as sign.
gives the cup to those who seek God's lov-ing will.

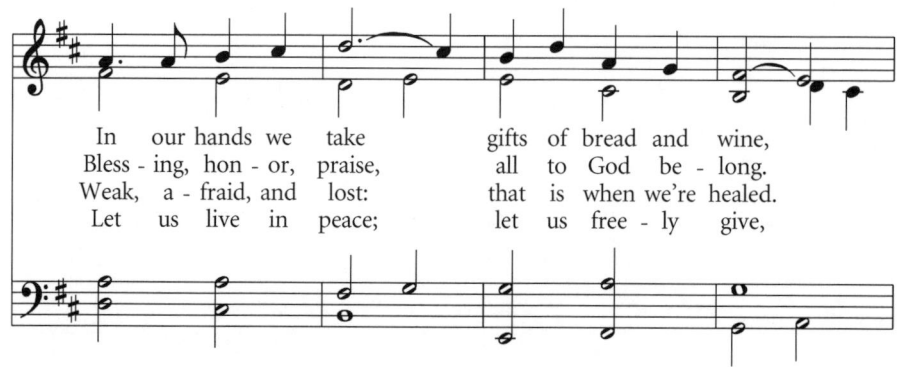

In our hands we take gifts of bread and wine,
Bless-ing, hon-or, praise, all to God be-long.
Weak, a-fraid, and lost: that is when we're healed.
Let us live in peace; let us free-ly give,

WORDS: Ruth Duck, 1982, alt.
MUSIC: Ruth Duck, arr. Randall Sensmeier
© 1992 GIA Publications, Inc. Used by permission. All rights reserved.

NEW HOPE
10.11.10.12

COMMUNION

gath - ered from the fields of earth, signs of love di - vine.
Let us lift our hearts to God in a thank - ful song.
In our hu - man bro - ken - ness, there God is re - vealed.
shar - ing love with all the world dai - ly as we live.

Thee We Adore, O Savior 39

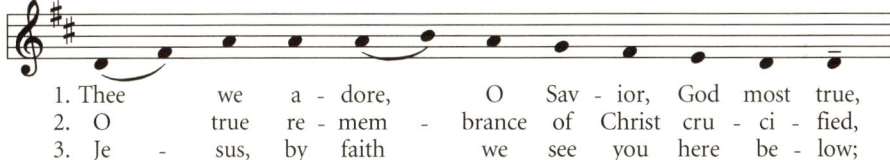

1. Thee we a - dore, O Sav - ior, God most true,
2. O true re - mem - brance of Christ cru - ci - fied,
3. Je - sus, by faith we see you here be - low;

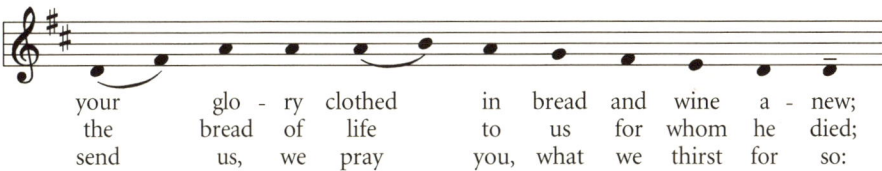

your glo - ry clothed in bread and wine a - new;
the bread of life to us for whom he died;
send us, we pray you, what we thirst for so:

our heart to you in true de - vo - tion bow,
lend us this life then; feed and feast our mind,
in - crease our faith and love, that we may know

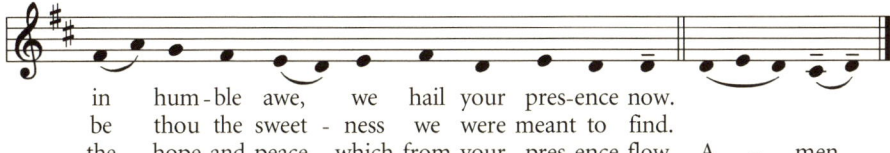

in hum - ble awe, we hail your pres - ence now.
be thou the sweet - ness we were meant to find.
the hope and peace which from your pres - ence flow. A - men.

WORDS: Thomas Aquinas, 1227-1274; tr. Gerard Manley Hopkins, 1844-1889,   ADORO TE DEVOTE
      James R. Woodford, 1820-1885, alt.   10 10 10 10
MUSIC: Plainsong mode V; *Processionale*, Paris, 1697

COMMUNION

40   O the Depth of Love Divine

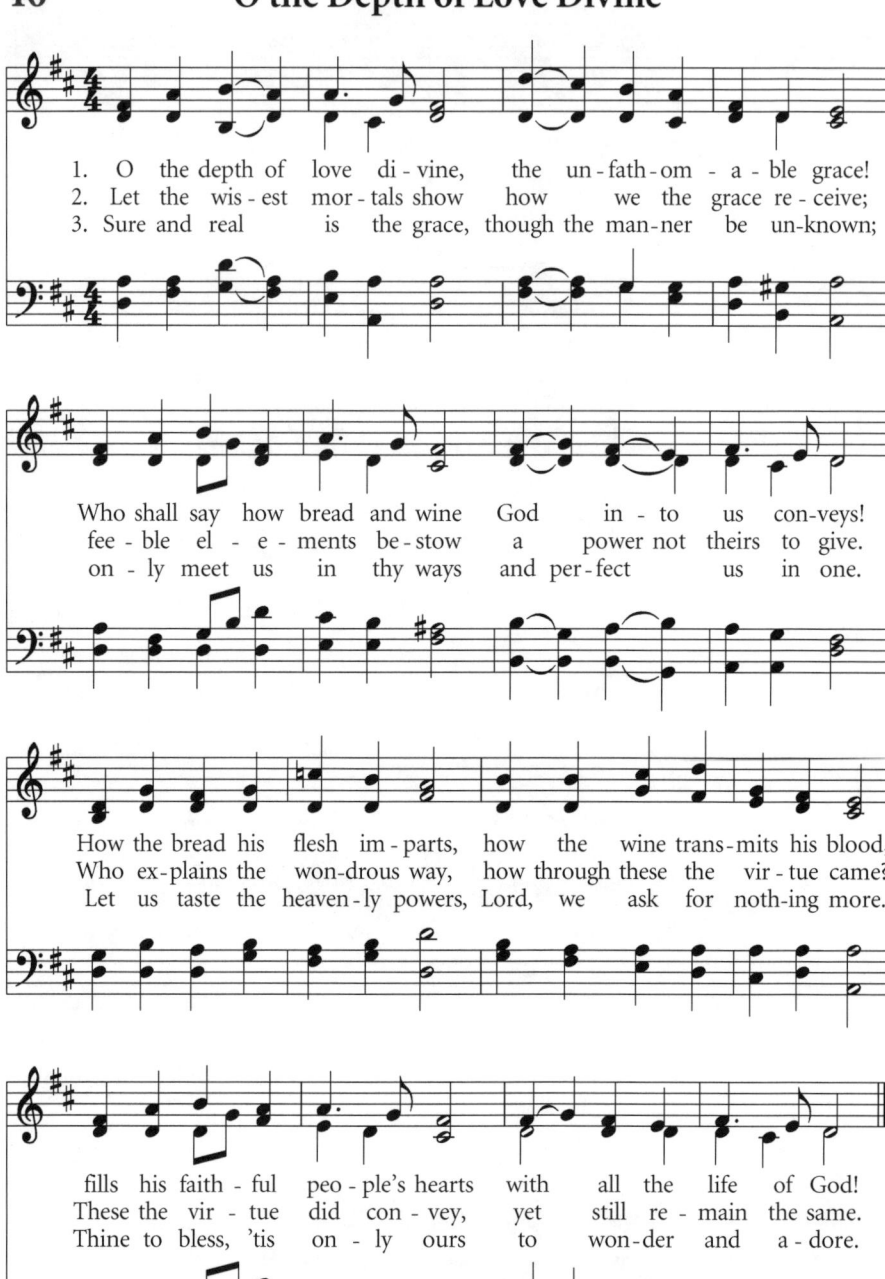

1. O the depth of love divine, the unfathomable grace!
   Who shall say how bread and wine God into us conveys!
   How the bread his flesh imparts, how the wine transmits his blood,
   fills his faithful people's hearts with all the life of God!

2. Let the wisest mortals show how we the grace receive;
   feeble elements bestow a power not theirs to give.
   Who explains the wondrous way, how through these the virtue came?
   These the virtue did convey, yet still remain the same.

3. Sure and real is the grace, though the manner be unknown;
   only meet us in thy ways and perfect us in one.
   Let us taste the heavenly powers, Lord, we ask for nothing more.
   Thine to bless, 'tis only ours to wonder and adore.

WORDS: Charles Wesley, 1745 (Jn. 6:35-38)   HOLLINGSIDE
MUSIC: J. B. Dykes, 1823-1876   7.7.7.7 D

COMMUNION
Bread of the World
41

1. Bread of the world in mercy broken,
2. Look on the heart in sorrow broken,

wine of the soul in mercy shed,
look on the tears by sinners shed;

by whom the words of life were spoken
and be your feast to us the token

and in whose death our sins are dead.
that by your grace our souls are fed.

WORDS: Reginald Heber, 1827 (Jn. 6:35-38)
MUSIC: John S. B. Hodges, 1868

EUCHARISTIC HYMN
98.98

COMMUNION

42 Shepherd of Souls

1. Shep-herd of souls, re-fresh and bless
2. We would not live by bread a-lone,
3. Be known to us in break-ing bread,
4. Lord, sup with us in love di-vine;

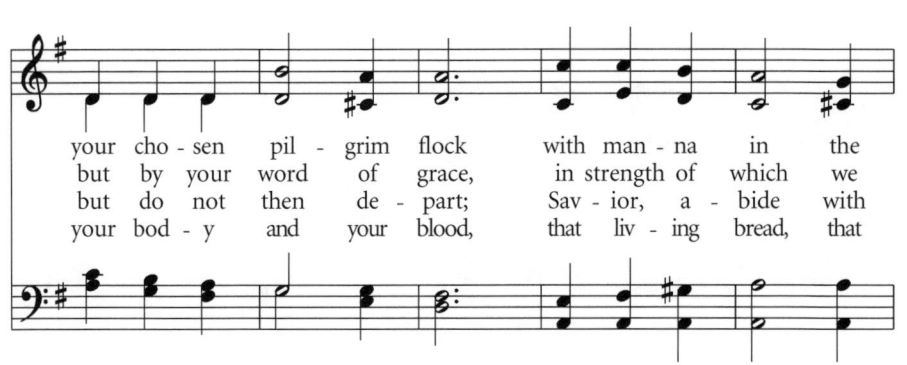

your cho-sen pil-grim flock with man-na in the
but by your word of grace, in strength of which we
but do not then de-part; Sav-ior, a-bide with
your bod-y and your blood, that liv-ing bread, that

wil-der-ness, with wa-ter from the rock.
trav-el on to our a-bid-ing place.
us, and spread your ta-ble in our heart.
heaven-ly wine, be our im-mor-tal food.

WORDS: Sts. 1 and 2, James Montgomery, 1825, alt.; sts. 3 and 4, Anonymous,
in *A Collection of Hymns*, United Bretheren, Philadelphia, 1832, alt.
MUSIC: J. B. Dykes, 1866

ST. AGNES
CM

COMMUNION
Only Bread
43

1. This is on-ly bread, you know, from seed that died in the
2. He was on-ly bread, you know, bro-ken like the
3. We are on-ly bread, you know, a farm-er once went
4. This is on-ly bread, you know, a sim-ple mir-a-

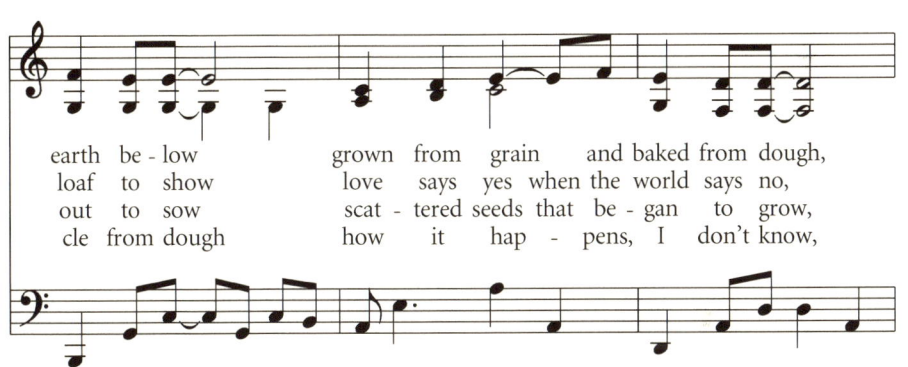

earth be-low grown from grain and baked from dough,
loaf to show love says yes when the world says no,
out to sow scat-tered seeds that be-gan to grow,
cle from dough how it hap-pens, I don't know,

Last time

this is on-ly bread.
this is on-ly bread.
this is on-ly bread.
this is on-ly bread.

WORDS: Jim Manley, 1990
MUSIC: Jim Manley, 1990; arr. Kristin Burns; adapt. Jim Strathdee
© 1990 Jim Manley. All rights reserved.

ONLY BREAD
Irr.

COMMUNION

44 Breaking of the Bread

1. Flee-ing from the ci-ty with the smell of death so strong, a stran-ger on the road in-vites him-self to walk a-long, and com-ing to the house we tell him stay and rest your head, and Christ is known to us in the break-ing of the bread.

2. Meet-ing in the ci-ty with the load of life so strong, we gath-er in the church to share our strug-gles and a song. We break the loaf and pour the wine and the old worn words are said, and Christ is known to us in the break-ing of the bread.

WORDS: Luke 24; Jim Manley, 1988
MUSIC: Jim Manley; arr. William McGee
© 1988 Jim Manley. All rights reserved.

COMMUNION

3. Weary over dinner with the day that went so long,
   we gather 'round the table too worn out to sing a song,
   but someone says a simple prayer, we pause to bow our head,
   and Christ is known to us in the breaking of the bread.
   Refrain

4. Fleeing from the city with a bedroll on our back,
   we rest beside the mountain stream and lean against our pack.
   The canteen and the loaf go 'round and simple words are said,
   and Christ is known to us in the breaking of the bread.
   Refrain

5. Fleeing from the graveside we have gathered at the home,
   friends drop by and bring in food and caring as they come.
   We sit around and talk about the living and the dead,
   and Christ is known to us in the breaking of the bread.
   Refrain

6. Lying in the hospital as night drifts into day,
   friends come by to see us and they help us with the tray.
   It's only toast and broth but over them the words are said,
   and Christ is known to us in the breaking of the bread.
   Refrain

7. Returning to the city where the homeless people wait
   it's our day to pass out food at the shelter by the gate.
   It's only tins and vegetables, but gentle words are said,
   and Christ is known to us in the breaking of the bread.
   Refrain

COMMUNION

45 Remember

The broken bread the out-poured wine reveal God's love for you. So come to feast and come to dine; remember as you do.

1. Remember Cana's wedding day? The Lord told them to pour the water which became the wine much better than before.
2. Remember at the marriage feast? The king sent out the call "It does not matter who you are, my table is for all."
3. Remember how the multitude was gathered and was fed? For Jesus blessed and multiplied the fish and loaves of bread.
4. Remember at the sinners' feast, when Jesus gave the call? "I came to seek and save the lost; to serve the least of all."

WORDS: Robert S. Jarboe, OSL, 2006
MUSIC: Robert S. Jarboe, OSL, 2006
© 2006 Robert S. Jarboe. Used by permission.

REMEMBER
8.6.8.6

SENDING FORTH
God Be with You
46

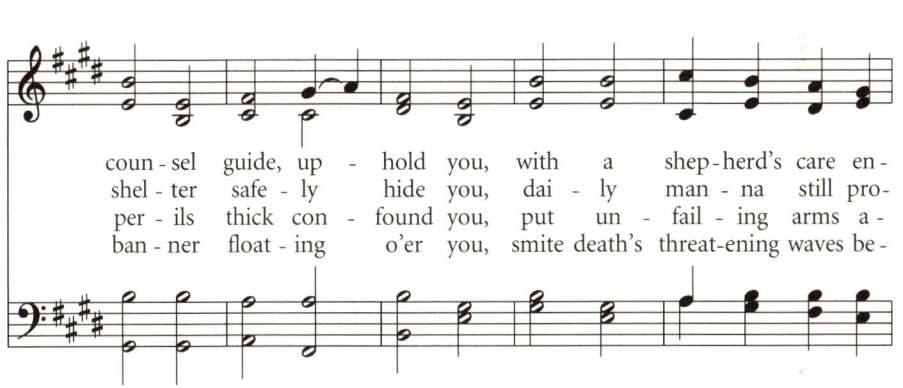

1. God be with you will we meet again; by good coun-sel guide, up-hold you, with a shep-herd's care en-fold you: God be with you till we meet a-gain.
2. God be with you till we meet again; wings of shel-ter safe-ly hide you, dai-ly man-na still pro-vide you: God be with you till we meet a-gain.
3. God be with you till we meet again; when life's per-ils thick con-found you, put un-fail-ing arms a-round you: God be with you till we meet a-gain.
4. God be with you till we meet again; keep love's ban-ner float-ing o'er you, smite death's threat-ening waves be-fore you: God be with you till we meet a-gain.

WORDS: Jeremiah E. Rankin, 1880, alt.
MUSIC: Anna J. Morse, 1941

KEMPER
98.89

SENDING FORTH

47 Peace Before Us

WORDS: David Haas, 1987 (based on a Navajo prayer) PEACE
MUSIC: David Haas, 1987 Irr.
© 1987 GIA Publications. All rights reserved. Used by permission.

SENDING FORTH

49 Go in Christ's Name

Go in Christ's name; em-bod-y God's love. Bring heal-ing
grace and peace from a-bove. Be sac-ra-ments of Christ's liv-ing
way. Blessed by the Spir-it to work and to pray.

WORDS: Dwight W. Vogel, OSL, 2007
MUSIC: Melody by Dwight W. Vogel, OSL, 2007; harm. Robert B. Davis, OSL, 2007
© 2007 Order of Saint Luke

PILGRIM
9.9.9.11

50 Christ Beside Us

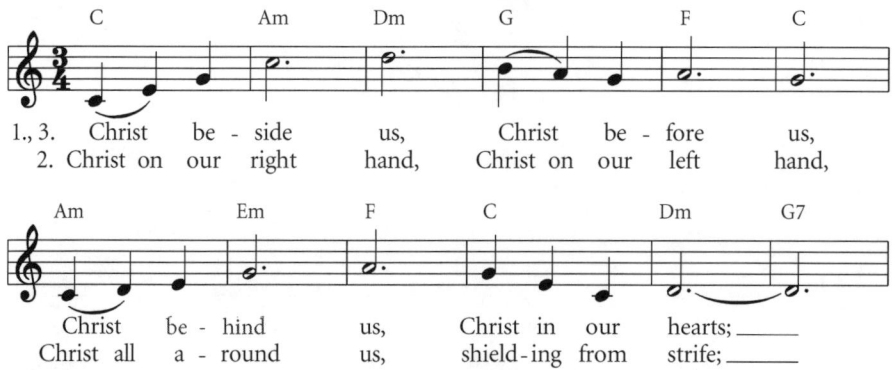

1., 3. Christ be-side us, Christ be-fore us,
2. Christ on our right hand, Christ on our left hand,
Christ be-hind us, Christ in our hearts;
Christ all a-round us, shield-ing from strife;

WORDS: St. Patrick's Breastplate, alt. Dwight W. Vogel, OSL, 2011
MUSIC: Traditional Gaelic melody

BUNESSAN
55.54 D

For You Shall Go Out with Joy 51

(Go in Joy)

May be performed by four groups, each singing and repeating a single line.

WORDS: Don E. Saliers, OSL, 1977 (Isa. 55:12)
MUSIC: Don E. Saliers, OSL, 1977

BUCKHANNON
Irr.

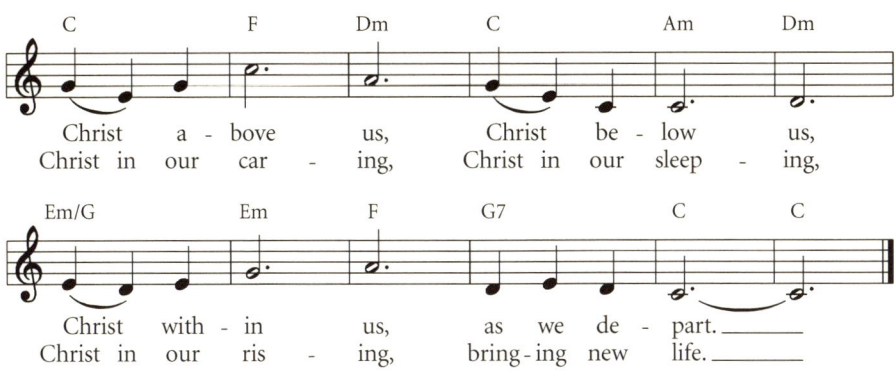

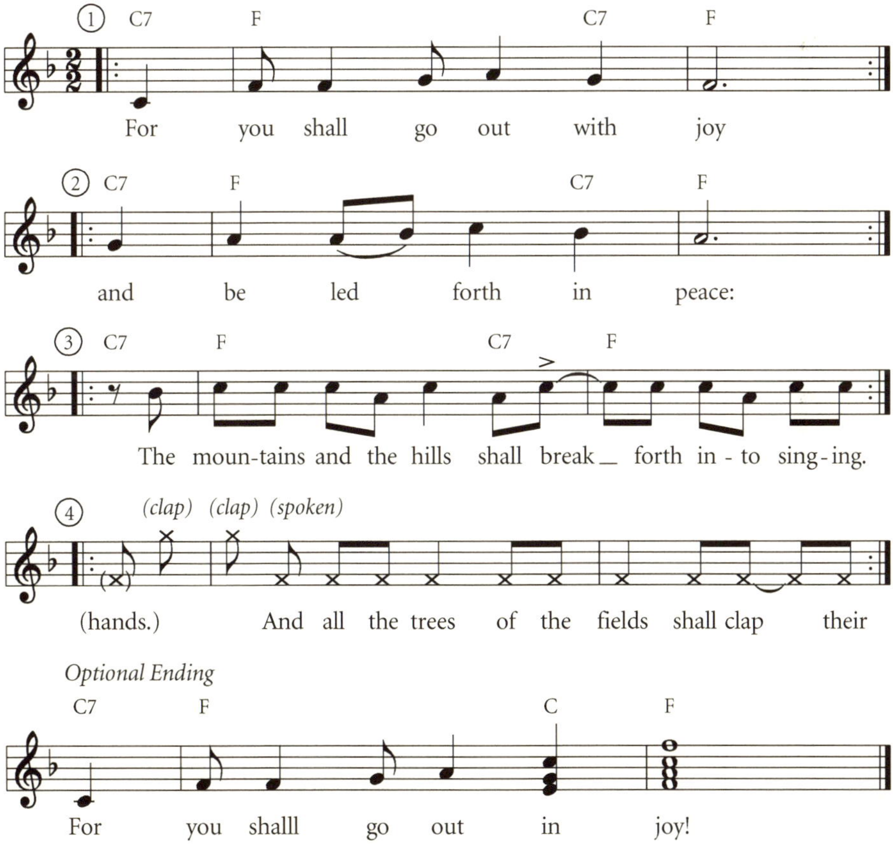

SENDING FORTH

52

Song of Shalom
(*Pues Si Vivimos*)

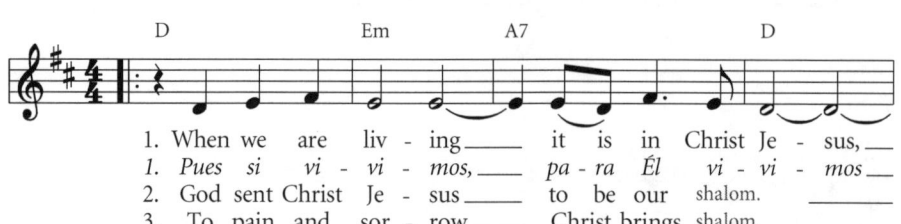
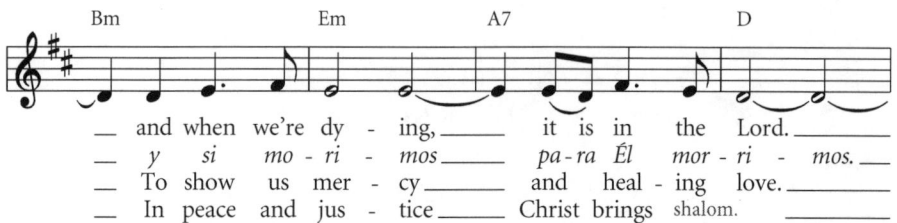
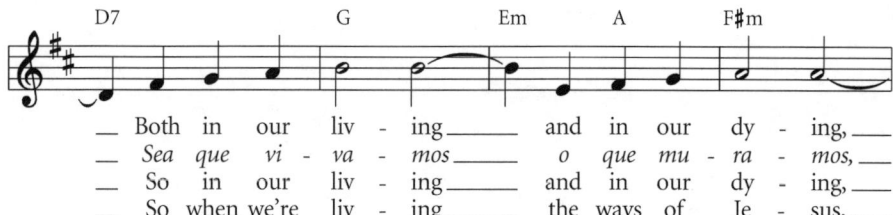
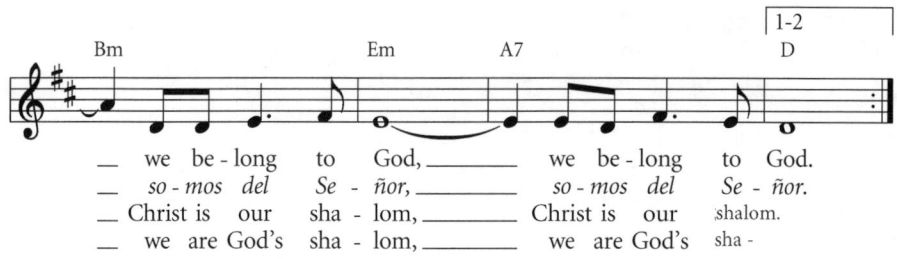
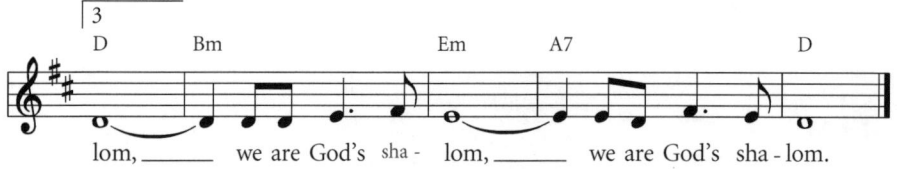

WORDS: St. 1, Anonymous (Rom. 14:8-9), trans. Elise S. Eslinger;
        sts. 2-3, Elise S. Eslinger
MUSIC: Mexican melody
Sts. 2-3 © 1983 Elise S. Eslinger

SOMOS DEL SEÑOR
Irr.

Morning Prayer   53
Opening Sentence

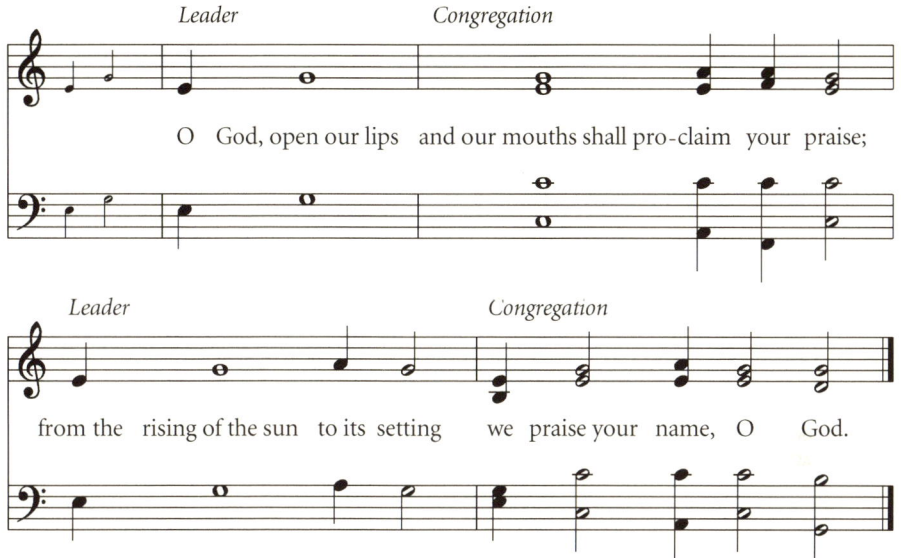

Leader: O God, open our lips *Congregation:* and our mouths shall proclaim your praise;

Leader: from the rising of the sun to its setting *Congregation:* we praise your name, O God.

WORDS: Adapted from Psalm 51:15; 113:3
MUSIC: Thomas Tallis, ca. 1564

Morning Prayer   54

ADONAI,
passionate presence,
mystery here and holy,
known in relationship
and revealed in a thousand stories:
awaken us each morning to your indwelling,
and at day's end,
  hide us under the shadow of your wings. **Amen.**

[DTB]

CANTICLE OF ZECHARIAH

55 Now Bless the God of Israel
(*Benedictus*)

1. Now bless the God of Is-ra-el, who comes in love and power, who rais-es from the roy-al house de-liv-erance in this hour. Through ho-ly proph-ets God has sworn to free us from a-larm, to save us from the heav-y hand of all who wish us harm.

2. Re-mem-ber-ing the cov-e-nant, God res-cues us from fear, that we might serve in ho-li-ness and peace from year to year; and you, my child, shall go be-fore to preach, to proph-e-sy, that all may know the ten-der love, the grace of God most high.

3. In ten-der mer-cy, God will send the day-spring from on high, our ris-ing sun, the light of life for those who sit and sigh. God comes to guide our way to peace, that death shall reign no more. Sing prais-es to the Ho-ly One! O wor-ship and a-dore!

WORDS: Luke 1:68-79, Ruth Duck, 1985
MUSIC: English melody, arr. Heather Josselyn-Cranson, 2011, alt.
Words © 1992 GIA Publications. Arr. © 2011 Order of Saint Luke.

KINGSFOLD
CMD

MORNING HYMNS

57 Christ, Whose Glory Fills the Skies

1. Christ, whose glory fills the skies, Christ, the true the only light, Son of Righteousness, arise, triumph o'er the shades of night; Day-spring from on high be near; Day-star, in my heart appear.

2. Dark and cheerless is the morn unaccompanied by thee; joyless is the day's return, till thy mercy's beams I see; till they inward light impart, cheer my eyes and warm my heart.

3. Visit then this soul of mine; pierce the gloom of sin and grief; fill me, Radiancy divine, scatter all my unbelief; more and more thyself display, shining to the perfect day.

WORDS: Charles Wesley, 1740
MUSIC: J. G. Werner's *Choralbuch*, 1815; harm. by William H. Havergal, 1861

RATISBON
77.77.77

MORNING HYMNS

O Splendor of God's Glory Bright   58

1. O splendor of God's glory bright, eternal source of light from light, O Light of light light's living spring, O Day all days illumining.
2. O true Sun, on us let your glance now fall with brilliant radiance; the Spirit's sanctifying beam upon our earthly senses stream.
3. O holy Source of all, we pray, let your light shine on us this day. O blest Source of all grace and might, now banish sin from our delight.
4. To guide whate'er we seek to do, with love all envy to subdue; to make ill fortune turn to fair, and give us grace your love to share.

WORDS: Ambrose of Milan, 4th cent., trans. Robert Bridges, 1899, alt.   SPLENDOR PATERNAE
MUSIC: Sarum plainsong, mode 1   LM

A Commissioning Commendation   59

May the word of Christ dwell in us richly.
Whatever we do in word or deed,
let us do everything in the name of the Lord Jesus,
giving thanks to God.

[ADAPTED FROM COLOSSIANS 3:16a, 17 OSL]

MORNING HYMNS

New Every Morning
61

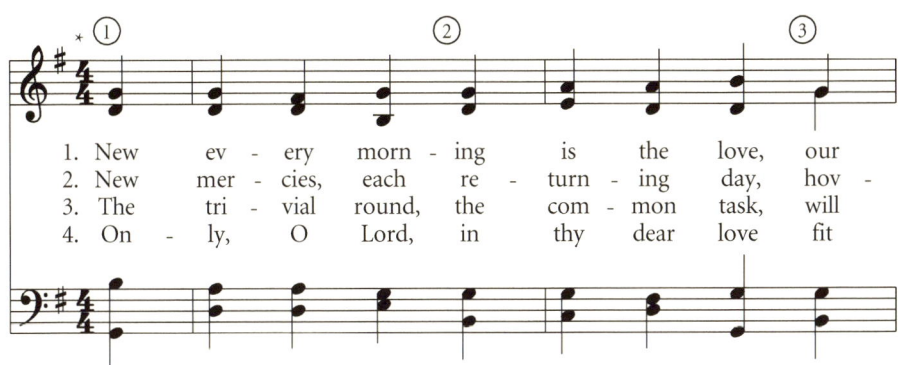

1. New ev - ery morn - ing is the love, our
2. New mer - cies, each re - turn - ing day, hov -
3. The tri - vial round, the com - mon task, will
4. On - ly, O Lord, in thy dear love fit

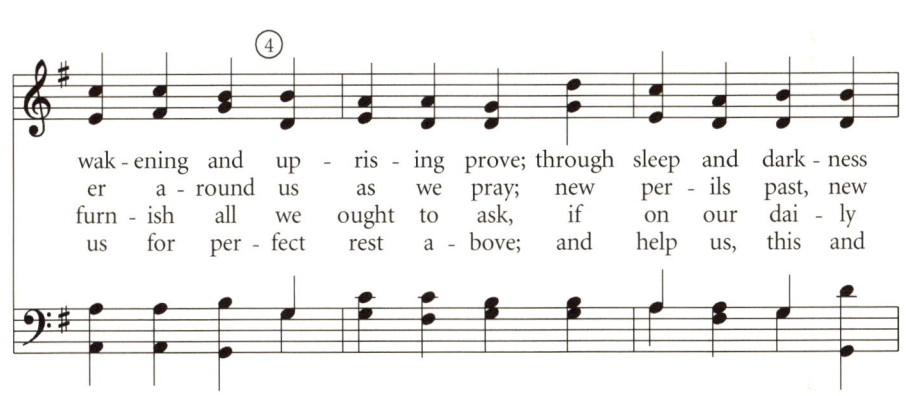

wak - ening and up - ris - ing prove; through sleep and dark - ness
er a - round us as we pray; new per - ils past, new
furn - ish all we ought to ask, if on our dai - ly
us for per - fect rest a - bove; and help us, this and

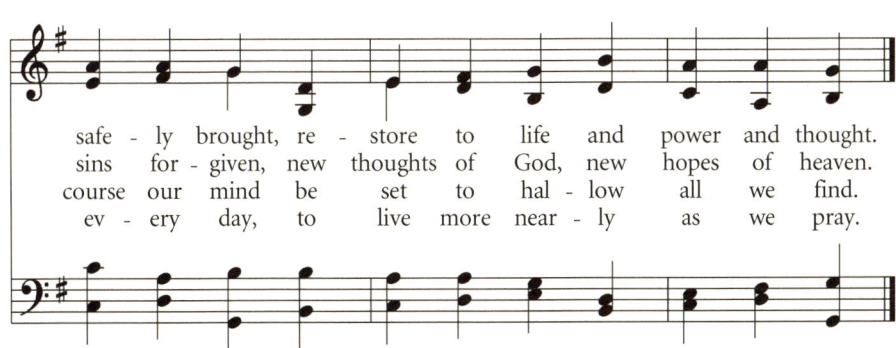

safe - ly brought, re - store to life and power and thought.
sins for - given, new thoughts of God, new hopes of heaven.
course our mind be set to hal - low all we find.
ev - ery day, to live more near - ly as we pray.

*May be sung as a canon. Omit accompaniment, singing unison.

WORDS: John Keble, 1822
MUSIC: Thomas Tallis, ca. 1550

TALLIS' CANON
LM

MORNING HYMNS

62 In the Morning I Will Sing

WORDS: Psalm 63:1-8, adapt. from *Good News Bible*
MUSIC: David Goodrich
Words © 1976 American Bible Society. Used by permission. Music © 1983 David Goodrich.

MORNING HYMNS

OPENING OF EVENING PRAYER

Entrance of the Light   63

Leader: Jesus Christ, you are the light of the world,
All: the light no darkness can over-come.

Leader: Stay with us, for it is evening,
All: and the day is nearly over.

Leader: For with you is the fountain of life,
All: and in your light do we see light.

WORDS: Adapted from John 8:12, Luke 24:29, and Psalm 35:9
MUSIC: Adapted from chants by Stephen Elvey (1805-186) and James Turle (1802-1882)

Thanksgiving for the Light   64

Thanks be to you, O God, author of eternal light.
Continually shine forth upon us who watch for you,
that our lips may praise you, our lives bless you,
and our meditation glorify you;
though Jesus Christ, the Light of the world we pray. **Amen.**

[SARUM BREVIARY, A.D. 1085, ALT.]

PHOS HILARON

65 Joyous Light
(Phos Hilaron)

1. Joy-ous light of heaven-ly glo-ry, lov-ing glow of God's own face; you who sing cre-a-tion's sto-ry, shine of ev-ery land and race. Now as eve-ning falls a-round us, we shall raise our songs to you, God of day-break, God of shad-ows, come and raise our songs to you,

2. In the stars that grace the dark-ness, in the blaz-ing sun of dawn, in the light of peace and wis-dom, we can hear your qui-et song. Love that fills the night with won-der, love that warms the wea-ry soul, love that bursts all chains a-sun-der, set us

3. You who made the heav-en's splen-dor, ev-ery danc-ing star of night, make us shine with gen-tle jus-tice, let us each re-flect your light. Might-y God of all cre-a-tion, gen-tle Christ who lights our way, lov-ing Spir-it of sal-va-tion, lead us

WORDS: Marty Haughen, 1986
MUSIC: Marty Haugen, 1986
© 1990 GIA Publications

67 Evening Prayer Canticle

I call to you, O God, come to me *quickly;**
hear my voice when I cry to *you.*
Keep guard over my mouth, *O Lord,**
watch the door of my *lips.*
Keep my heart from slipping in-to *evil;**
let me not be busy with e-vil-*doers.*
My eyes are turned toward you, O Lord my *God.**
In you I take refuge, do not deprive me of *life.*
ANTIPHON

Commonly chanted to psalm tone two or spoken in unison. May be accompanied by the lighting of incense.
WORDS: Selected from Psalm 141, trans. Arlo D. Duba, 1986
MUSIC: Arlo D. Duba, 1986
© 1986 Arlo D. Duba. Used by permission.

68 Evening Prayer Canticle

WORDS: Selected from Psalm 141, trans. Arlo D. Duba
MUSIC: Heather Josselyn-Cranson, OSL, 2010
Words © 1986 Arlo D. Duba. Used by permission. Music © 2010 Order of Saint Luke.

EVENING PRAYER CANTICLE

EVENING PRAYER CANTICLE

69 Evening Prayer Canticle
(Metrical)

1. Come quickly, Lord, I call on you, and hear my voice, my cry for help. Control my lips and tongue, O Lord, and save my heart from evil's grasp. Let my prayer rise like incense, Lord, my hands an evening sacrifice.
2. Help me accept rebuke as grace, and guard me from all bitterness. All wicked ways may I resist and never share in sensuous feasts. Let my praise rise like incense, Lord, my hands an evening sacrifice.
3. Protect me from the Evil One, and rule my life through Christ your Son. With Holy Fire my sins consume, and flood my soul with love divine. My heart shall rise like incense, Lord, my life, your living sacrifice.

WORDS: Sarah Flynn, OSL, 1997
MUSIC: Attr. to Dimitri S. Bortniansky, 1825
Words © 1997 Order of Saint Luke

ST. PETERSBURG
88.88.88

CANTICLE OF MARY

My Soul Gives Glory to My God
(*Magnificat*)

70

1. My soul gives glo-ry to my God. My
2. My God has done great things for me: yes,
3. From age to age to all who fear, such
4. Love casts the might-y from their thrones, pro-
5. Praise God, whose lov-ing cov-e-nant sup-

heart pours out its praise. God lift-ed up my
ho-ly is God's name. All peo-ple will de-
mer-cy love im-parts, dis-pens-ing jus-tice
motes the in-se-cure, leaves hun-gry spir-its
ports those in dis-tress, re-mem-ber-ing past

low-li-ness in man-y mar-vel-ous ways.
clare me blessed, and bless-ings they shall claim.
far and near, dis-miss-ing self-ish hearts.
sat-is-fied the rich seem sud-den-ly poor.
prom-is-es with pres-ent faith-ful-ness.

WORDS: Miriam Therese Winter, based Luke 1:46b-55; 1 Sam. 2:1-10, 1987
MUSIC: Melody from *Kentucky Harmony,* 1816; harm. C. Winfred Douglas, 1940
Words © 1987 Miriam Therese Winter. Used by permission.

MORNING SONG
CM

CANTICLE OF MARY

71 Canticle of the Turning
(Magnificat)

1. My soul cries out with a joy-ful shout that the
2. Though I am small my God, my all, you
3. From the halls of power to the for-tress tower, not a
4. Though the na-tions rage from age to age, we re-

God of my heart is great, and my spir-it sings of the
work great things in me, and your mer-cy will last from the
stone will be left on stone. Let the king be-ware for your
mem-ber who holds us fast: God's mer-cy must de-

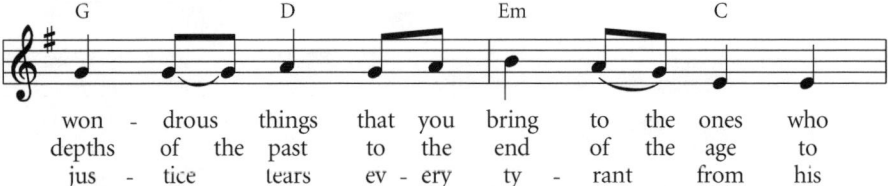

won - drous things that you bring to the ones who
depths of the past to the end of the age to
jus - tice tears ev - ery ty - rant from his
liv - er us from the con - quer-or's crush - ing

wait. You fixed your sign on your ser - vant's plight, and my
be. Your ver - y name puts the proud to shame, and to
throne. The hun - gry poor shall weep no more, for the
grasp. This sav - ing word that our fore-bears heard is the

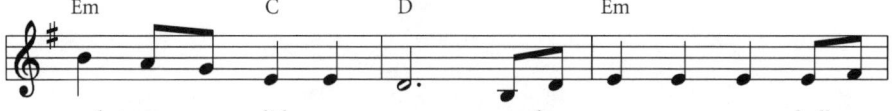

weak-ness you did not spurn, so from east to west shall my
those who would for you yearn, you will show your might, put the
food they can nev - er earn; there are ta - bles spread, ev - ery
prom - ise which holds us bound till the spear and rod can be

WORDS: Rory Cooney (Luke 1:46-55)   STAR OF COUNTY DOWN
MUSIC: Trad. Irish; adapt. Rory Cooney   Irr.
Words and adpt. © 1990 GIA Publications, Inc. Used by permission. All rights reserved.

CANTICLE OF MARY

A Prayer for Transformation 72

Arise, O Spirit of Life,
that through you we may begin to live.
Descend upon us;
transform us into such human beings
  as your heart longs to see
    – renewed into the image of Christ,
  and going on from glory to glory.
O God, Supreme Good,
make yourself known to us,
and glorify yourself in our inner being. **Amen.**

[GERHARD TERSTEEGEN, 1731]

Stay with Us 74

1. Stay with us, till night has come: our praise to you this day be sung. Bless our bread, o-pen our eyes: Je-sus, be our great sur-prise.
2. Walk with us, our spir-its sigh: hear when our wea-ry spir-its cry, feel a-gain our loss, our pain: Je-sus, take us to your side.
3. Walk with us, the road will bend: make all our weep-ing, wail-ing end. Wipe our tears, for-give our fears: Je-sus, lift the heav-y cross.
4. Talk with us, till we be-hold a joy-ful life you will un-fold: heal our eyes to see the prize: Je-sus, take us to the light.
5. Stay with us, till day is done: no tears nor dark shall dim the sun. Cheer the heart, your grace im-part: Je-sus, bring e-ter-nal life.

WORDS: Herbert Brokering (Luke 24:13-35)
MUSIC: Walter L. Pelz
© 1980 Concordia Publishing House. Used by permission.

STAY WITH US
78.77

An Evening Commendation 75

Good Shepherd*, bless your flock this night. Give your peace, your help, your love to the sheep of your fold so that we may be united in peace and love as one body, one spirit, in one hope of our calling, through your boundless love. Amen.

[LITURGY OF SAINT MARK, 4TH C., ALT.]

* Or "God" or "Holy One"

EVENING HYMNS

76 As the Shadows Deepen

WORDS: George R. Crisp, OSL, 2000
MUSIC: George R. Crisp, OSL, 2000
© 2000 George R. Crisp/Giraffe Music. All rights reserved.

ST. LUKE
55.76 D

EVENING HYMNS

The Day You Gave, O Lord, Is Ended 77

1. The day you gave, O Lord, is end-ed; the dark-ness
2. We thank you that your church, un-sleep-ing while earth rolls
3. As o'er each con-ti-nent and is-land the dawn leads
4. So be it, Lord; your throne shall nev-er, like earth's proud

falls at your be-hest; to you our morn-ing hymns as-
on-ward in-to light, through all the world her watch is
on an-oth-er day, the voice of prayer is nev-er
em-pires, pass a-way. Your king-dom stands, and grows for-

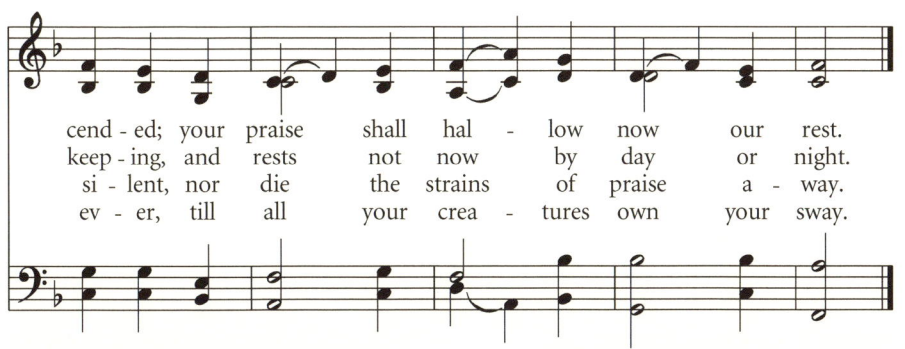

cend-ed; your praise shall hal-low now our rest.
keep-ing, and rests not now by day or night.
si-lent, nor die the strains of praise a-way.
ev-er, till all your crea-tures own your sway.

WORDS: John Ellerton, 1870 (Ps. 113:2-3), alt. ST. CLEMENT
MUSIC: Clement Cottevill Scholefield, 1874 98.98

EVENING HYMNS
78 O Strength and Stay

1. O Strength and Stay upholding all creation, who with us day and night ever abides; yet day by day as light in due gradation from hour to hour changes, you still guide.
2. Grant to life's day a peaceful, faithful ending, an eve untouched by shadows of decay, the brightness of your grace at death be blending with dawning glories of eternal day.
3. Hear us, O God, most gracious and forgiving, through Jesus Christ your co-eternal Word, who, with the Holy Spirit, by our living now and to endless ages be adored.

WORDS: St. Ambrose, 340-97; trans. John Ellerton, 1826-1893, and F. J. A. Hort, 1818-1892, alt.
MUSIC: John Bacchus Dykes, 1823-1876

STRENGTH AND STAY
11.10.11.10

NIGHT HYMNS

Creator of the Stars of Night   79

1. Cre - a - tor of the stars of night,
   your peo - ple's ev - er - last - ing light,
   O Christ, Re - deem - er of us all,
   we pray you hear us when we call.

2. When this old world drew on toward night,
   your came but not in splen - dor bright,
   not as a mon - arch, but the child
   of Ma - ry, blame - less moth - er mild.

3. Come in your ho - ly might, we pray,
   re - deem us for e - ter - nal day;
   now come, O Sav - ior, to set free
   your own in glo - rious lib - er - ty.

4. At your great name, O Je - sus, now
   all knees must bend, all hearts must bow:
   all things on earth with one ac - cord,
   like those in heaven, shall call you Lord.

WORDS: Latin, 9th cent.; ver. *Hymnal 1940*, alt. CONDITOR ALME SIDERUM
MUSIC: Plainsong, Mode IV LM

Night Prayer   80

God of the day and of the night:
as the evening deepens,
bring our work to a close
and prepare us for rest and peace at the last. **Amen.**

DTB ALT.

NIGHT HYMNS

81 All Praise to Thee, My God, This Night

1. All praise to thee, my God, this night, for
2. For-give me, Lord, for your dear Son, the
3. Teach me to live, that I may dread the
4. O may my soul on you re-pose, and
5. Praise God, from whom all bless-ings flow; praise

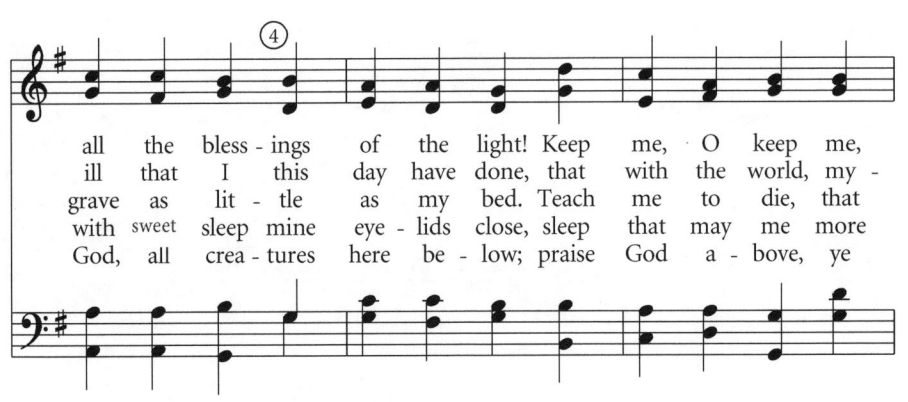

all the bless-ings of the light! Keep me, O keep me,
ill that I this day have done, that with the world, my-
grave as lit-tle as my bed. Teach me to die, that
with sweet sleep mine eye-lids close, sleep that may me more
God, all crea-tures here be-low; praise God a-bove, ye

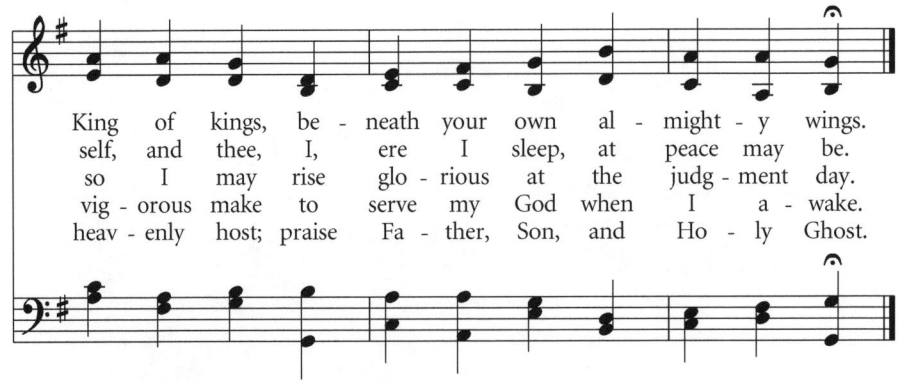

King of kings, be-neath your own al-might-y wings.
self, and thee, I, ere I sleep, at peace may be.
so I may rise glo-rious at the judg-ment day.
vig-orous make to serve my God when I a-wake.
heav-enly host; praise Fa-ther, Son, and Ho-ly Ghost.

May be sung without accompaniment as a unison canon.

WORDS: Thomas Ken, ca. 1674
MUSIC: Thomas Tallis, 1567

TALLIS' CANON
LM

NIGHT HYMNS

Fast Falls the Night 82

1. Fast falls the night: stay with us, Lord, and banish every care and fear. When all we trusted fades or fails, help of the helpless you are near.
2. Our lives run swiftly on toward death; our strength shall ebb our glory pass. Let sleep rehearse us night by night to rest in you, O God, at last.
3. Come shed the radiance of your cross upon our closing eyes this night; then when your endless day has dawned, death's sleep will yield to boundless light.

WORDS: Aelred Seton Shanley, 1999, from *Hymns for Morning and Evening Prayer* WHEN JESUS WEPT
MUSIC: William Billings, 1770, *New England Psalm Singer* LM
Words © 1999 Aelred Seton Shanley. Used by permission.

Commendation 83

O God, the light of the minds who know you,
the life of the souls who love you,
and the strength of thoughts that seek you;
help us so to know you that we might truly love you,
and so to love you that we might truly serve you,
whose service is perfect freedom;
through Jesus Christ our Lord. **Amen**.

GELASIAN SACRAMENTARY, A.D. 492, ALT

NIGHT HYMNS

84 Come Down, O Love Divine

WORDS: Bianco of Siena, 1434; trans. Richard F. Littledale, 1867, alt.
MUSIC: Ralph Vaughan Williams, 1906

DOWN AMPNEY
6 6 11 D

NIGHT HYMNS
86 Now, God, Be with Us

1. Now, God, be with us for the night is closing;
both light and darkness are of your disposing,
and, 'neath your shadow, here to rest we yield us for you will shield us.

2. Let peaceful thoughts be ours when sleep o'ertakes us,
our earliest thoughts be yours when morning wakes us,
all day to serve you through all we are doing, your praise pursuing.

3. O God, your name be praised, your kingdom given.
Your will be done on earth as 'tis in heaven;
keep us in life, forgive our sins, deliver now and forever.

WORDS: Petrus Herbert, 1566; trans. Catherine Winkworth, 1863, alt.
MUSIC: *Paris Antiphoner*, 1681; harm. Heather Josselyn-Cranson, OSL, 2011
Harm. © 2011 Order of Saint Luke

CHRISTE SANCTORUM
11.11.11.5

NIGHT HYMNS

God, Who Made the Earth and Heaven 87

1. God, who made the earth and heav-en, dark-ness and light,
2. When the con-stant sun re-turn-ing un-seals our eyes,

who the day for toil has giv-en, for rest the night:
may we, born a-new like morn-ing, to la-bor rise.

may your an-gel guards de-fend us, slum-ber sweet your mer-cy send us;
Gird us for this task that calls us, let not ease and self en-thrall us,

ho-ly dreams and hopes at-tend us, this live-long night.
strong through you what-e'er be-fall us, O God most wise!

WORDS: St. 1, Reginald Heber, 1827; st. 2, Frederick Lucian Hosmer, 1912 (Gen. 1:1-15) AR HYD Y NOS
MUSIC: Trad. Welsh melody; harm. Luther Orlando Emerson, 1906 84.84.888.4

CANTICLE OF SIMEON

88   Br. Timothy's Last Commendation

"Life is short and we have never too much time for gladdening the hearts of those who are traveling the journey with us. Oh, be swift to love, make haste to be kind!"* For the joyous light of our Lord Jesus Christ and the love of God and the sustaining community of the Holy Spirit is with us, now and unto ages of ages. **Amen.**

* These words of Henri-Frederic Amiel (1821-1881) were used by Chaplain General Timothy J. Crouch, OSL, in his valedictory benediction to the Order shortly before his death in 2005.

89   Canticle of Simeon
(*Nunc Dimittis*)

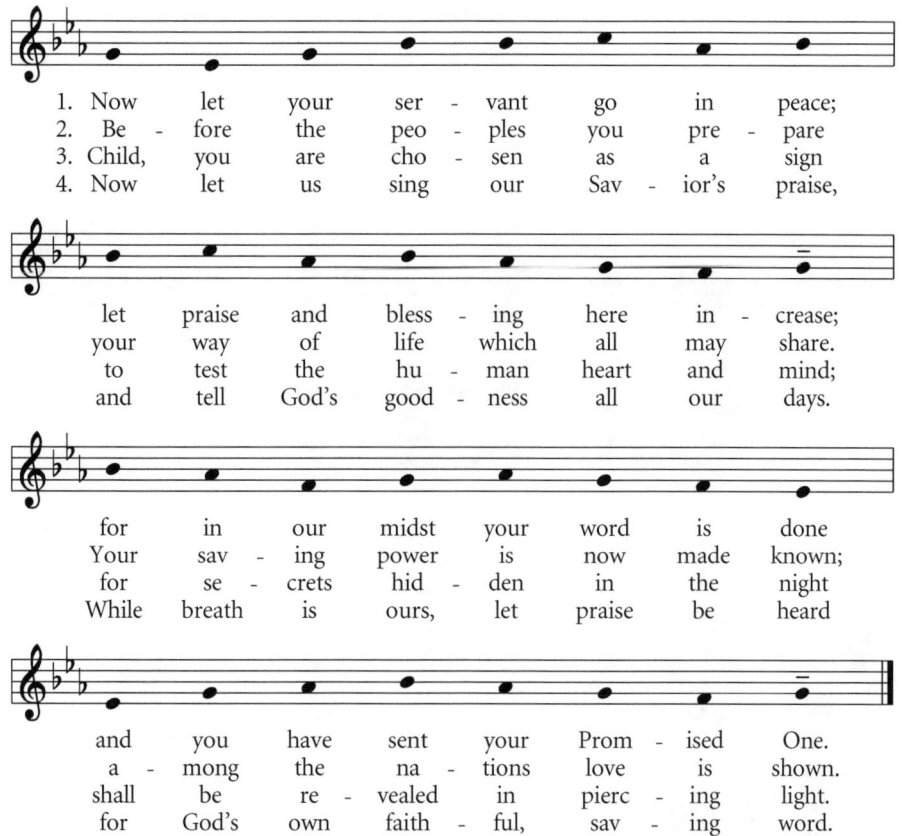

1. Now let your ser- vant go in peace; let praise and bless- ing here in- crease; for in our midst your word is done and you have sent your Prom- ised One.
2. Be- fore the peo- ples you pre- pare your way of life which all may share. Your sav- ing power is now made known; a- mong the na- tions love is shown.
3. Child, you are cho- sen as a sign to test the hu- man heart and mind; for se- crets hid- den in the night shall be re- vealed in pierc- ing light.
4. Now let us sing our Sav- ior's praise, and tell God's good- ness all our days. While breath is ours, let praise be heard for God's own faith- ful, sav- ing word.

WORDS: Ruth Duck, based on Luke 2:29-35, 1978   CONDITOR ALME SIDERUM
MUSIC: Plainsong Mode IV   LM
Words © 1992 GIA Publications, Inc.

Canticle of Simeon
(*Nunc Dimittis*)

1. Ho-ly One, now let your ser-vants go in peace. Your word has been ful-filled.
2. We our-selves, we know the heal-ing you've pre-pared, and all the world can see.
3. We pro-claim the light to show you to the world, for glo-ry, Is-ra-el.
4. Ho-ly One, now let your ser-vants go in peace. Your word has been ful-filled.

WORDS: Richard Bruxvoort-Colligan
MUSIC: Richard Bruxvoort-Colligan
© 2004 This Here Music. Used by permission.

A Prayer at the End of Day

God who sees us,*
sun sets but there is no sunset on your mercy:
In this evening hour take us to yourself,
join us with heaven's praise,
and embrace your world in our prayers. **Amen.**

[DTB]

*El Roi—Hagar's name for God when God saw her affliction (Genesis 16:13)

HEALING

94 Give Thanks to God Who Hears Our Cries

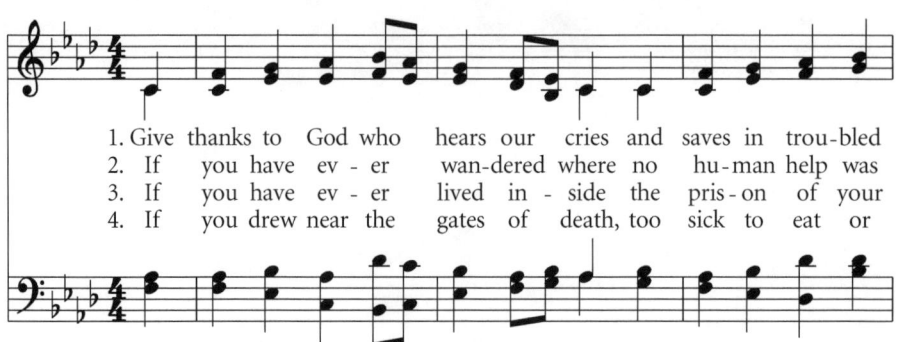

1. Give thanks to God who hears our cries and saves in trou-bled
2. If you have ev - er wan-dered where no hu-man help was
3. If you have ev - er lived in - side the pris - on of your
4. If you drew near the gates of death, too sick to eat or

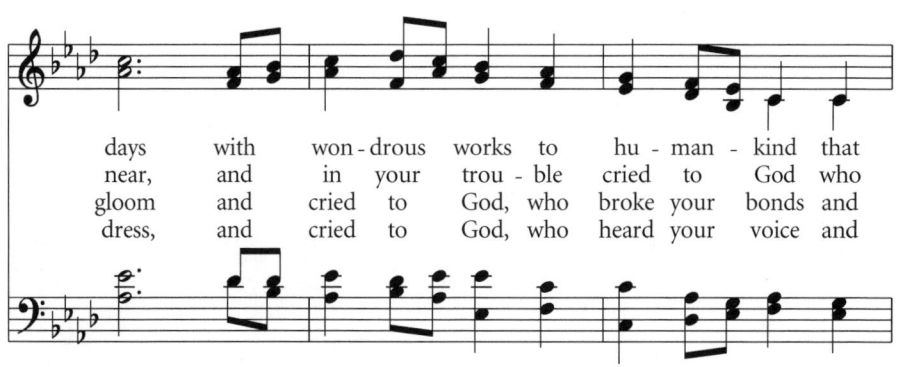

days with won-drous works to hu - man - kind that
near, and in your trou - ble cried to God who
gloom and cried to God, who broke your bonds and
dress, and cried to God, who heard your voice and

call for high - est praise. Let all who know God's
res - cued you from fear, then thank the God of
raised you from your tomb, then praise the One who
healed all your dis - tress, then sing with sounds of

WORDS: Ruth Duck, 2007
MUSIC: Wyeth's *Repository of Sacred Music,* 1813; harm. Richard Proulx
Words © 2007 Ruth Duck. Harm. © 1975 GIA Publications. Used by permission.

MORNING SONG
86.86.86

HEALING

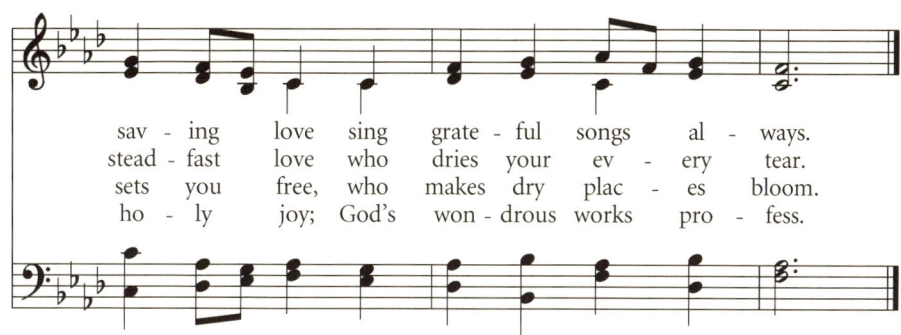

saving love sing grateful songs always.
steadfast love who dries your every tear.
sets you free, who makes dry places bloom.
holy joy; God's wondrous works profess.

5. If you have felt your courage fail
before a violent sea
and cried to God, who stilled the storm,
and made the wild wind flee,
then in the congregation praise
the God who heard your plea.

6. So praise the One whose love is great,
whose kindness is well-known.
Consider well the healing hand
and help you have been shown,
and tell the world what God has done.
Praise God and God alone!

Take, Oh, Take Me As I Am   95

Take, oh, take me as I am; summon out what I shall be; set your seal upon my heart and live in me.

WORDS: John L. Bell, b. 1949
MUSIC: John L. Bell
© 1995 Iona Community, admin. by GIA Publications, Inc.

TAKE ME AS I AM
77.74

HEALING

When We Must Bear Persistent Pain 97

1. When we must bear persistent pain and suffer with no cure in sight, come, Holy Presence, breathe your peace with gifts of warmth and healing light.
2. Support us as we learn new ways to care for bodies newly frail. Help us endure, and live and love. Help our complaint when patience fails.
3. We thank you for the better days when we may smile to greet the sun to do your work with clearing mind and bless your name when day is done.
4. In ease or pain, in life or death, to you our fragile lives belong, and so we trust you in all things. You are our hope, our health, our song.

WORDS: Ruth Duck, b. 1947　　　　　　　　　CONDITOR ALME SIDERUM
MUSIC: Plainsong, Mode IV　　　　　　　　　　　　　　　　　　　LM
Words © 2005 GIA Publications, Inc.

A 9th Century Prayer for Healing 98

ADONAI, give strength to the weary,
aid to the sufferers, comfort to the sad,
relief to those in pain and help to those in tribulation. **Amen.**

[AMBROSIAN SACRAMENTARY, 9TH C. ALT.]

RECONCILIATION
99 The Beatitudes

WORDS: Matthew 5:3-12, Russian Orthodox liturgy
MUSIC: *Beatitudes*, Russian Orthodox hymn

RECONCILIATION

RECONCILIATION

RECONCILIATION
Heal Me, Hands of Jesus
100

1. Heal me hands of Jesus, and search out all my pain; restore my hope, remove my fear, and bring me peace again.
2. Cleanse me blood of Jesus, take bitterness away; let me forgive as one forgiven and bring me peace today.
3. Know me, mind of Jesus, and show me all my sin; dispel the memories of guilt and bring me peace within.
4. Fill me, joy of Jesus; anxiety shall cease, and heaven's serenity be mine, for Jesus brings me peace!

WORDS: Michael Perry, 1982
MUSIC: Norman L. Warren, 1982
SUTTON COMMON
SM
Words and Music © 1973 The Jubilate Group (Admin. Hope Publishing Company, Carol Stream, IL 60188). All rights reserved. Used by permission.

God Calls Us to Forgive
101

1. God calls us to forgive just as we are forgiven, that we may fully live as the children of God.
2. Wherever we may go, may we love as God loves us, so that the Word may grow and the world fill with peace.

WORDS: Robert S. Jarboe, OSL
MUSIC: Robert S. Jarboe, OSL
© 2001 Robert S. Jarboe

RECONCILIATION
102 I Heard the Voice of Jesus Say

1. I heard the voice of Jesus say, "Come unto me and rest; lay down, O weary one, lay down your head upon my breast." I came to Jesus, as I was, weary and worn and sad; I
2. I heard the voice of Jesus say, "Behold, I freely give the living water; thirsty one, stoop down, and drink, and live." I came to Jesus, and I drank of that life-giving stream; my
3. I heard the voice of Jesus say, "I am this dark world's light; look unto me, thy morn shall rise, and all thy day be bright." I looked to Jesus, and I found in him my star, my sun; and

WORDS: Horatius Bonar, 1808-1889
MUSIC: John B. Dykes, 1823-1876

VOX DILECTI
CMD

RECONCILIATION

found in him a rest-ing place, and he has made me glad.
thirst was quenched, my soul re-vived, and now I live in him.
in that light of life I'll walk, till trav-el-ing days are done.

Come, God, and Hear My Cry   103

1. Come, God, and hear my cry; my spir-it thirsts for you.
2. The proph-et's ech-oes filled a parched and with-ered place
3. Far from that des-ert land, we search for life made new.
4. Lead us where wa-ters flow, that we may find re-birth.

My bod-y with-ers, wea-ry, dry. Come, Spir-it God, re-new!
where pil-grims wea-ry with the world came long-ing for your grace.
Where dry leaves toss in win-ter's wind, we wait, O God, for you.
O Hope of ev-ery thirst-y soul, come rain up-on the earth.

WORDS: Ruth Duck, b. 1947
MUSIC: William Damon's *Psalmes*, 1579
Words © 2005 GIA Publications, Inc.

SOUTHWELL
55.65

RECONCILIATION

104   For the Healing of the Nations

1. For the heal-ing of the na-tions, Lord, we pray with one ac-cord; for a just and e-qual shar-ing of the things that earth af-fords; to a life of love in ac-tion help us rise and pledge our word.

2. Lead us for-ward in-to free-dom; from de-spair your world re-lease, that, re-deemed from war and ha-tred, all may come and go in peace. Show us how through care and good-ness fear will die and hope in-crease.

3. All that kills a-bun-dant liv-ing, let it from the earth be banned; pride of sta-tus, race, or school-ing, dog-mas that ob-scure your plan. In our com-mon quest for jus-tice may we hal-low life's brief span.

4. You, Cre-a-tor God, have writ-ten your great name on hu-man-kind; for our grow-ing in your like-ness bring the life of Christ to mind, that by our re-sponse and ser-vice earth its des-ti-ny may find.

WORDS: Fred Kaan, 1965 (Rev. 21:1-22:5)   RHUDDLAN
MUSIC: Trad. Welsh melody from E. Jones' *Musical Relics of the Welsh Bards*, 1800   87.87.87
Words © 1968 Hope Publishing Company

TRANSITUS
All Shall Be Well
105

May be sung as a canon.

WORDS: Julian of Norwich, ca. 1400
MUSIC: Dwight W. Vogel, OSL, 2011
Music © 2011 Order of Saint Luke

Dona Nobis Pacem
106

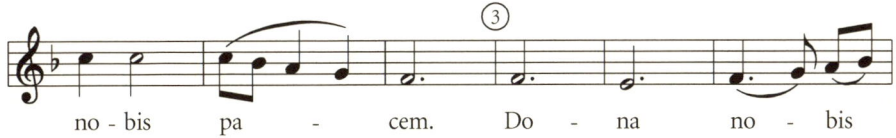

May be sung as a canon.

WORDS: Trad. Latin
MUSIC: Trad.

DONA NOBIS PACEM
Irr.

ADVENT
O Come, O Come, Emmanuel
108

1. O come, O come, Emmanuel.
   The darkness of this earth dispel.
   Bring light and justice here below
   that we in paths of righteousness may go.

2. O come, thou Wisdom from on high,
   and order all things far and nigh;
   to us the path of knowledge show,
   and cause us in her ways to go.

3. O come, O come thou Lord of might,
   who to thy tribes on Sinai's height
   in ancient times did give the law,
   in cloud, and majesty, and awe.

4. O come, thou Branch of Jesse's tree,
   an ensign of thy people be.
   Before thee rulers silent fall;
   all peoples on thy mercy call.

Rejoice! Rejoice! Emanuel shall come to earth; let love dispel all fear.

5. O come, thou Key of David, come,
   and open wide your heavenly home.
   Make safe the path to endless day;
   to hell's destruction, close the way.

6. O come, thou Day-spring, come and cheer
   our spirits by thine advent here.
   Disperse the gloomy clouds of night,
   and death's dark shadows put to flight.

7. O come, Desire of nations, bind
   all peoples in one heart and mind;
   bid envy, strife, and quarrels cease;
   fill the whole world with heaven's peace.

WORDS: Latin, ca. 9th cent., tr. st. 1, Eva Fleischner, 2008; sts. 2 and 7, Heny Sloane Coffin, 1916; sts. 3 and 6, adapt. from JohnMason Neale, 1851
MUSIC: Plainsong, Mode I, *Processionale,* 15th cent.; adapt. Thomas Helmore (1811-1890)

VENI, VENI, EMMANUEL
LM with Refrain

ADVENT
109 O Come, Divine Messiah

WORDS: Abbé Pellegrin, 1708; tr. Sister Mary of St. Phillip, 1887, alt.
MUSIC: 16th cent. noël, ca. 1544; acc. by Arthur Hutchings, 1980

VENEZ DIVIN MESSIE
Irr. with Refrain

ADVENT

ADVENT
110 God With Us: Emmanuel

WORDS: George R. Crisp, OSL, 2000
MUSIC: George R. Crisp, OSL, 2000
© 2000 George R. Crisp/Giraffe Music. All rights reserved.

NEWPORT
87.87 D

CHRISTMAS
112 Of the Parent's Heart Begotten

1. Of the Parent's heart begotten,* ere the worlds began to be,
2. By his word was all created; he commanded and 'twas done,
3. This is he whom seer and wise ones sang in ages long gone by;
4. Sing ye heights of heaven, adore him; angels and archangels, sing!
5. Christ to thee with God the Parent, and Holy Spirit to thee,

Christ is Alpha and Omega, he the source the ending be,
earth and sky and boundless ocean, universe of three-in-one,
this is he of old revealed in the page of prophecy
where-so-e'er you be, O faithful, let your joyous anthems ring,
hymn and praise and high thanksgiving and unwearied praises be,

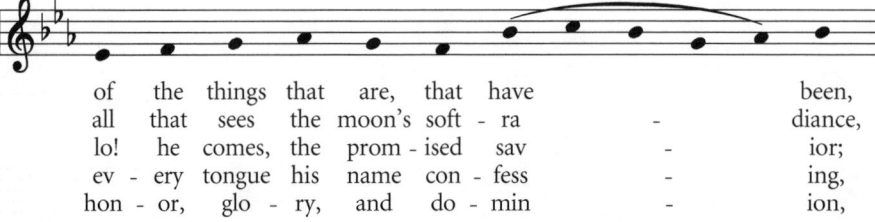

of the things that are, that have been,
all that sees the moon's soft radiance,
lo! he comes, the promised savior;
every tongue his name confessing,
honor, glory, and dominion,

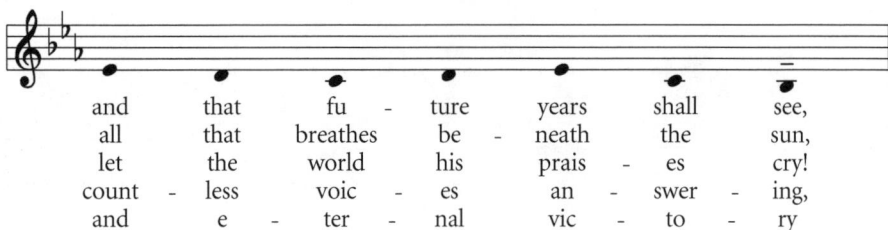

and that future years shall see,
all that breathes beneath the sun,
let the world his praises cry!
countless voices answering,
and eternal victory

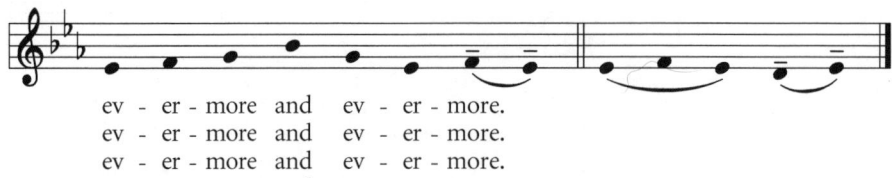

evermore and evermore.
evermore and evermore.
evermore and evermore.
evermore and evermore.
evermore and evermore. A - men.

*Latin: *"Corde natus ex parentis"* (literally: "Of the Parent's heart begotten")

WORDS: Aurelius Clemens Prudentius, 348-413; tr. John Mason Neale, 1854,
    Henry W. Baker, 1851-1861, and Roby Furly Davis, 1908, alt.
MUSIC: 13th cent. plainsong melody, adapt. Theodoricus Petrus of Nyland, 1582

EPIPHANY

Brightest and Best of the Stars of the Morning   115

1. Brightest and best of the stars of the morning,
dawn on our darkness and lend us your aid;
Star of the East, the horizon adorning,
guide where our infant Redeemer is laid.

2. Cold on his cradle the dewdrops are shining;
low lies his head with the beasts of the stall;
angels adore him in slumber reclining,
Maker, and Monarch, and Savior of all.

3. Say, shall we yield him, in costly devotion,
odors of Edom and offerings divine,
gems of the mountain, and pearls of the ocean,
myrrh from the forest, and gold from the mine?

4. Vainly we offer each ample oblation;
vainly with gifts would His favor secure:
richer by far is the heart's adoration;
dearer to God are the prayers of the poor.

WORDS: Reginald Heber (1783-1826)
MUSIC: J.P. Harding (1861-1892)

MORNING STAR
11.10.11.10

EPIPHANY
116   I Am the Light of the World

In response to a Christmas poem by Howard Thurman
WORDS: Jim Strathdee, 1969
MUSIC: Jim Strathdee, 1969
© 1969 Desert Flower Music. Used by permission.

EPIPHANY

LENT
Lord Jesus, Who Through Forty Days   118

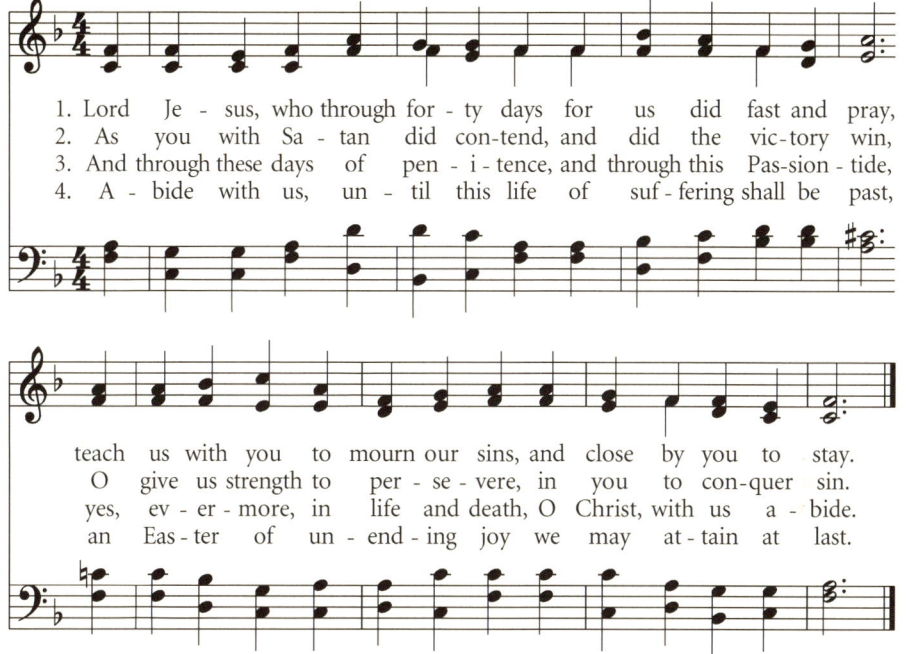

1. Lord Jesus, who through forty days for us did fast and pray, teach us with you to mourn our sins, and close by you to stay.
2. As you with Satan did contend, and did the victory win, O give us strength to persevere, in you to conquer sin.
3. And through these days of penitence, and through this Passiontide, yes, evermore, in life and death, O Christ, with us abide.
4. Abide with us, until this life of suffering shall be past, an Easter of unending joy we may attain at last.

WORDS: Claudia F.I. Hernaman, 1873, alt. (Mark 1:12-13: Luke 4:1-13)   ST. FLAVIAN
MUSIC: Day's *The Whole Booke of Psalms*, 1562

A Lenten Prayer   119
Anticipating the Easter Vigil

Immersed in baptismal waters of God's grace,
we journey toward the shadows and
the cross and
the grave and
the fire and
the book and
the font and
the table and
the Life of all that lives.
Merciful God, bring us back to the place
that grace and penitence brought us
when we first believed. **Amen.**

[DTB]

LENT

120   Dark Road to Jerusalem

1. On the dark road to Jerusalem, Jesus, you set your face, though knowing in your heart of hearts it could be your dying place. You could not turn from cross's pain, nor run from evil's power. No other witness to God's reign, but this courageous hour.

2. Our faith flows from your faithfulness, our lives from your life-blood. Against oppressive forces now we walk the self-same road. Your goodness is transforming strength, your kingdom earthly call. We see beyond the terror tree, life healing for us all.

WORDS: Patricia J. Patterson, 2008
MUSIC: English folk tune; arr. Heather Josselyn-Cranson, 2011, alt.
Words © 2008 Patricia Patterson. Used by permssion. Arr. © 2011 Order of Saint Luke.

KINGSFOLD
CMD

When I Survey the Wondrous Cross

LENT 121

1. When I sur-vey the won-drous cross on which the
2. For-bid it, Lord, that I should boast save in the
3. See, from his head, his hands, his feet, sor-row and
4. Were the whole realm of na-ture mine, that were a

Prince of glo-ry died, my rich-est gain I
death of Christ, my God; all the vain things that
love flow min-gled down; did e'er such love and
pres-ent far too small: love so a-maz-ing,

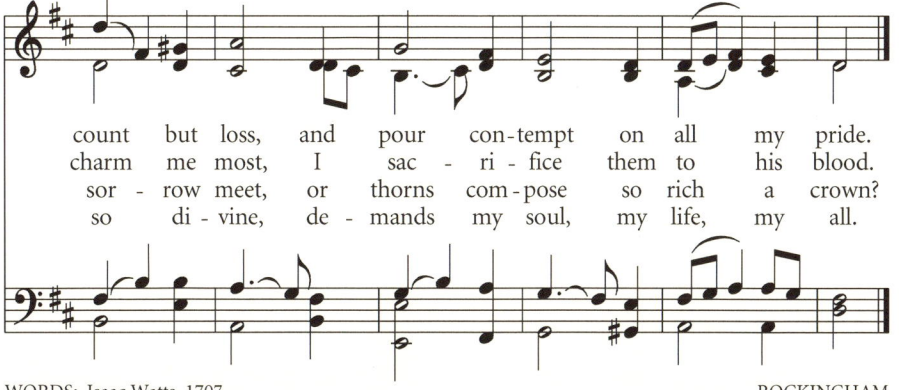

count but loss, and pour con-tempt on all my pride.
charm me most, I sac-ri-fice them to his blood.
sor-row meet, or thorns com-pose so rich a crown?
so di-vine, de-mands my soul, my life, my all.

WORDS: Isaac Watts, 1707
MUSIC: From the *Second Supplement to Psalmody in Minature*; adapt. Edward Miller, 1790; harm. Samuel Webbe, 1740-1816

ROCKINGHAM
LM

THE GREAT FIFTY DAYS

122   Come, You Faithful, Raise the Strain

WORDS: Exodus 15; John of Damascus, 8th cent.; tr. John Mason Neale, 1859, alt.   ST. KEVIN
MUSIC: Johann Leisentritt's *Catholicum Hymnologicum Germanicum*, Bautzen, 3rd ed., 1854   76.76 D

THE GREAT FIFTY DAYS

124   A Thousand Resurrections

1. A thou-sand res-ur-rec-tions are hap-pening ev-ery day,
in cour-age and with pa-tience where peo-ple walk the way.
They rec-og-nize the Sav-ior in break-ing of the bread,
and cry out: Christ is ris-en, al-though we thought him dead.

2. Death can-not break our spir-it, nor pain de-stroy like knife.
With God be-hind, be-fore us, we live a trans-formed life.
The gar-den tomb is emp-ty, the hill-top cross is gone;
life's man-y cru-ci-fix-ions will end in ear-ly morn.

3. What-ev-er fate or trag-edy. God will not let us go.
With love's in-sis-tent urg-ing, we change, we rise, we grow.
There is an Eas-ter morn-ing re-served for each and all;
be-yond the cross-'s shad-ow, a sun-rise wake-up call.

WORDS: Patricia J. Patterson, 2005   RISING
MUSIC: Constance E. Cimos, 2005   Irr.
Words © 2005 Patricia J. Patterson. Music © 2005 Constance E. Kimos.

Awareness and Assurance in Eastertide   125

Your light has filled our lives,
but we have not shared it with others.
   Lord, have mercy.
You have marked us as your own in baptism,
but we have not lived as your faithful people.
   Christ, have mercy.
You have called us to be a light to the nations,
but we have hidden our light under a bushel.
   Lord, have mercy.
Transform us by the power of your Holy Spirit
so that we may live our baptism as your new creation,
forgiven and made whole
by your matchless love in Jesus Christ.
   Thanks be to God! Amen.

[DWV, 1998, OSL]

THE GREAT FIFTY DAYS

126   O Christ, Our Hope
(Jesu, Nosta Redemptio)

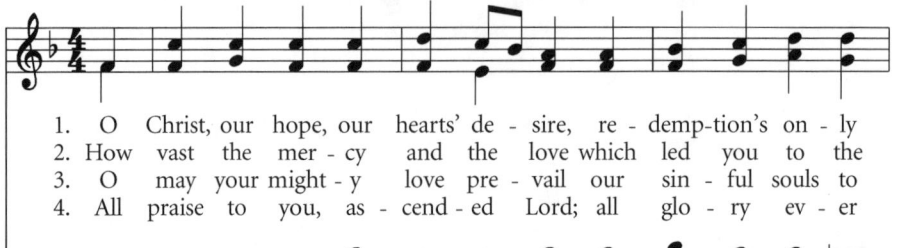

1. O Christ, our hope, our hearts' de-sire, re-demp-tion's on-ly
2. How vast the mer-cy and the love which led you to the
3. O may your might-y love pre-vail our sin-ful souls to
4. All praise to you, as-cend-ed Lord; all glo-ry ev-er

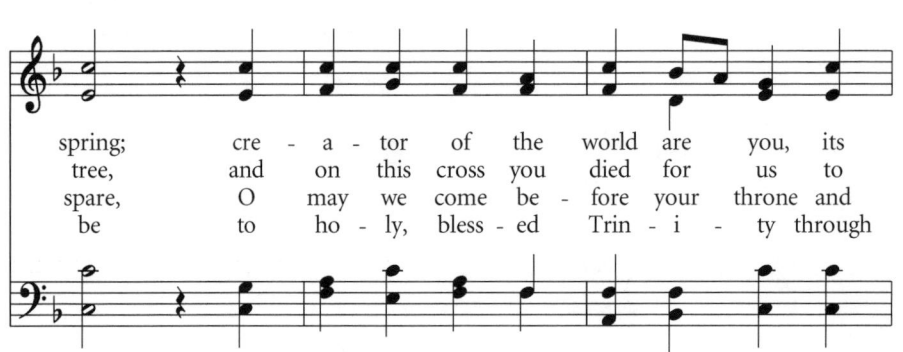

spring; cre-a-tor of the world are you, its
tree, and on this cross you died for us to
spare, O may we come be-fore your throne and
be to ho-ly, bless-ed Trin-i-ty through

Sav-ior and its King, its Sav-ior and its King.
set your peo-ple free, to set your peo-ple free.
find ac-cept-ance there, and find ac-cept-ance there!
all e-ter-ni-ty, through all e-ter-ni-ty.

WORDS: Latin hymn, ca. 8th cent.; tr. John Chandler, 1837, alt.   LOBT GOTT, IHR CHRISTEN (Hermann)
MUSIC: Nicholas Hermann, 1554, alt.   8.6.8.66

PENTECOST

O Creator Spirit, By Whose Breath 127
(*Veni, Creator Spiritus*)

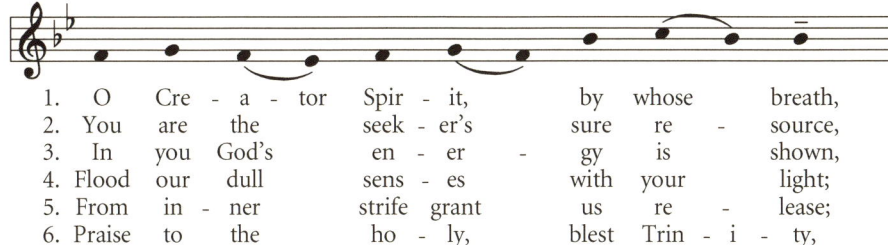

1. O Cre - a - tor Spir - it, by whose breath,
2. You are the seek - er's sure re - source,
3. In you God's en - er - gy is shown,
4. Flood our dull sens - es with your light;
5. From in - ner strife grant us re - lease;
6. Praise to the ho - ly, blest Trin - i - ty,

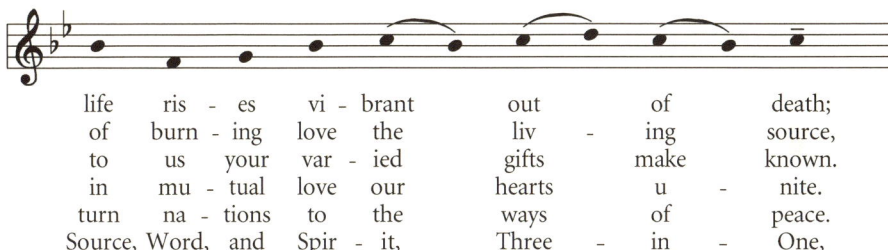

life ris - es vi - brant out of death;
of burn - ing love the liv - ing source,
to us your var - ied gifts make known.
in mu - tual love our hearts u - nite.
turn na - tions to the ways of peace.
Source, Word, and Spir - it, Three - in - One,

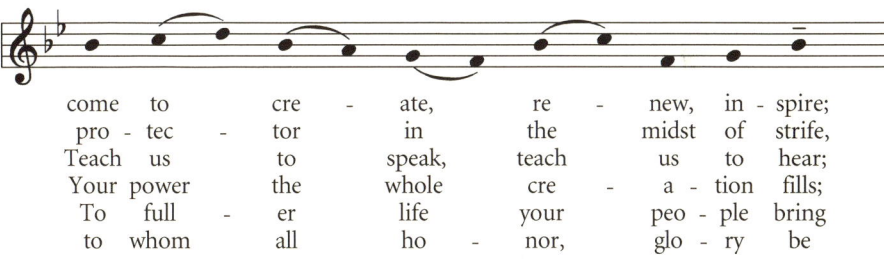

come to cre - ate, re - new, in - spire;
pro - tec - tor in the midst of strife,
Teach us to speak, teach us to hear;
Your power the whole cre - a - tion fills;
To full - er life your peo - ple bring
to whom all ho - nor, glo - ry be

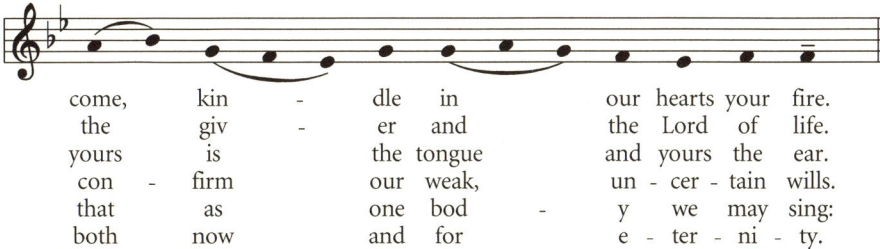

come, kin - dle in our hearts your fire.
the giv - er and the Lord of life.
yours is the tongue and yours the ear.
con - firm our weak, un - cer - tain wills.
that as one bod - y we may sing:
both now and for e - ter - ni - ty.

WORDS: Attr. Rabanus Maurus, 776-856; tr. John Webster Grant, b. 1919, alt. VENI, CREATOR SPIRITUS
MUSIC: Plainsong, Mode 8 LM

PENTECOST

128 Spirit, Spirit of Gentleness

WORDS: Jim Manley, 1978
MUSIC: Jim Manley, 1978
© 1978 Jim Manley. Used by permssion. All rights reserved.

SPIRIT
Irr.

PENTECOST

129   A Pentecost Prayer

Great Spirit, hear and help us as we pray.
You were there at Creation, Dove of God,
  bright wings over chaos.
Your word came to Abram and Sarai,
  calling them to journey far in faith.
You blew from heaven and the sea opened,
  delivering your ancient people from the destroyer.
To Mary, You whispered the eternal Word,
  the Christ she bore in Bethlehem.
You birthed the church in wind and fire at Pentecost,
  and still you blow, out of the desert places,
  through city's canyons.
Shelter us beneath your wings, call us, deliver us,
  inspire us, fill us with hope and power
  and set us alight in these dark times.
Through you we pray to God for Jesus' sake. **Amen.**

DONALD F. CHATFIELD

130   Holy Spirit, Truth Divine

1. Holy Spirit, Truth divine, dawn upon this soul of mine;
   Word of God and inward light, wake my spirit, clear my sight.
2. Holy Spirit, Love divine, glow within this heart of mine;
   kindle every high desire; perish self in thy pure fire.
3. Holy Spirit, Power divine, fill and nerve this will of mine;
   grant that I may strongly live, bravely bear, and nobly strive.
4. Holy Spirit, Right divine, King within my conscience reign;
   be my Lord, and I shall be firmly bound, forever free.

WORDS: Samuel Longfellow, 1864   CANTERBURY
MUSIC: Adapt. from Orlando Gibbons, 1623   77.77

ORDINARY TIME

132   Come, Thou Fount of Every Blessing

1. Come, thou Fount of ev-ery bless-ing, tune my heart to sing thy grace; streams of mer-cy, nev-er ceas-ing, call for songs of loud-est praise. Teach me some me-lo-dious son-net, sung by flam-ing tongues a-bove. Praise the mount! I'm fixed up-on it, mount of thy re-deem-ing love.
2. Here I raise my Eb-e-ne-zer; hith-er by thy help I'm come; and I hope, by thy good plea-sure, safe-ly to ar-rive at home. Je-sus sought me when a stran-ger, wan-dering from the fold of God; he, to res-cue me from dan-ger, in-ter-spersed his pre-cious blood.
3. O to grace how great a debt-or dai-ly I'm con-strained to be! Let thy good-ness, like a fet-ter, bind my wan-dering heart to thee. Prone to wan-der, Lord, I feel it, prone to leave the God I love; here's my heart, O take and seal it, seal it for thy courts a-bove.

WORDS: Robert Robinson, 1758 (1 Sam. 7:12)   NETTLETON
MUSIC: Wyeth's *Repository of Sacred Music, Part Second*, 1813   87.87 D

Love Divine, All Loves Excelling

ORDINARY TIME 133

1. Love divine, all loves excelling, joy of heaven, to earth come down;
fix in us thy humble dwelling; all thy faithful mercies crown!
Jesus, thou art all compassion, pure, unbounded love thou art;
visit us with thy salvation; enter every trembling heart.

2. Breathe, O breathe thy loving Spirit into every troubled breast!
Let us all in thee inherit; let us find that second rest.
Take away our bent to sinning; Alpha and Omega be;
end of faith, as its beginning, set our hearts at liberty.

3. Come, Almighty to deliver, let us all thy life receive;
suddenly return and never, nevermore thy temples leave.
Thee we would be always blessing, serve thee as thy hosts above,
pray and praise thee without ceasing, glory in thy perfect love.

4. Finish, then, thy new creation; pure and spotless let us be.
Let us see thy great salvation perfectly restored in thee;
changed from glory into glory, till in heaven we take our place,
till we cast our crowns before thee, lost in wonder, love, and praise.

WORDS: Charles Wesley, 1747
MUSIC: John Zundel, 1870

BEECHER
87.87 D

SAINTS
134 Ye Watchers and Ye Holy Ones

WORDS: John Athelstan Laurie Riley, 1906
MUSIC: *Geistliche Kirchengesänge*, 1623; harm. Ralph Vaughan Williams, 1906

LASST UNS ERFREUEN
88.44.88 with Refrain

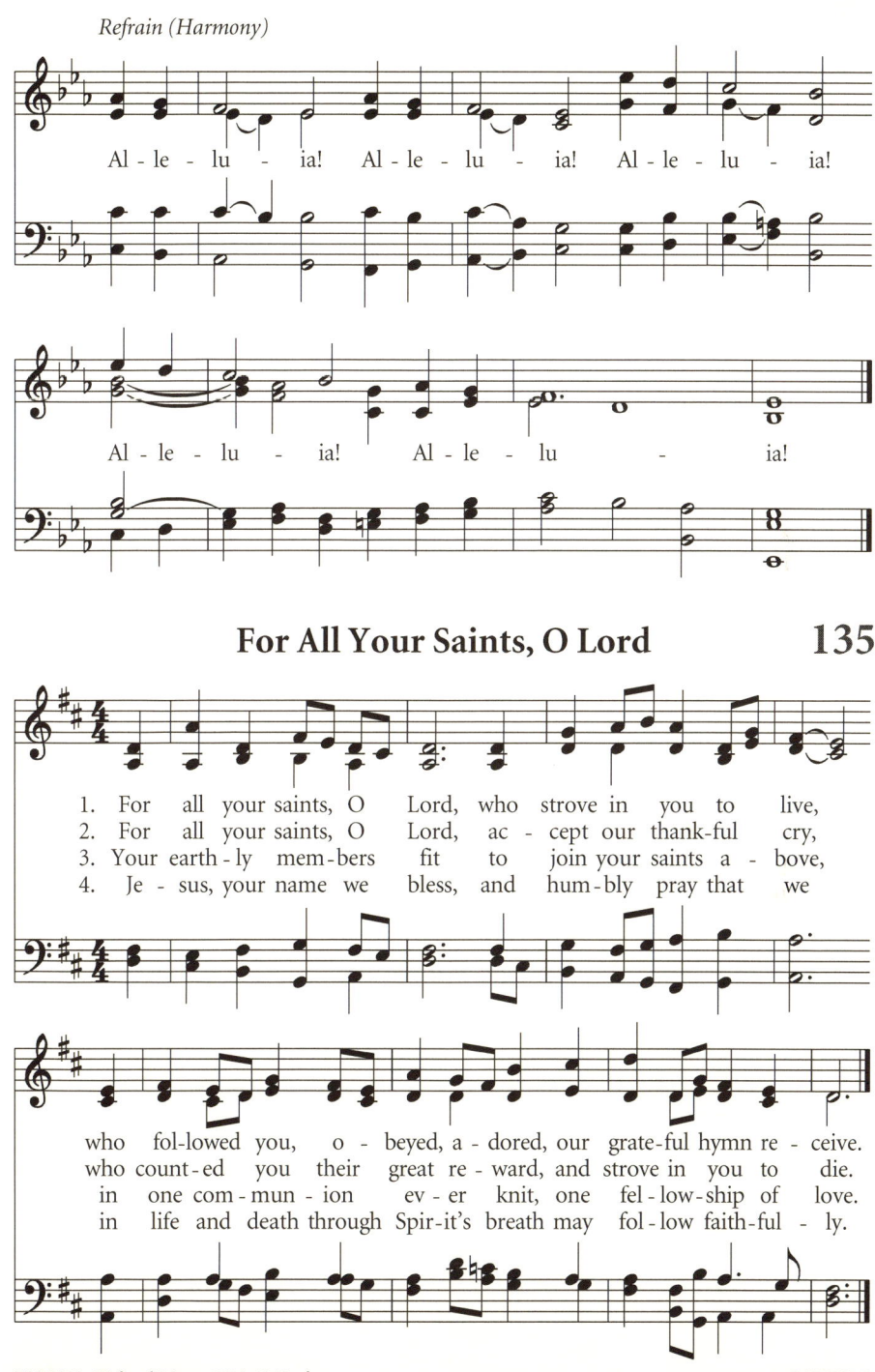

For All Your Saints, O Lord 135

1. For all your saints, O Lord, who strove in you to live,
who followed you, obeyed, adored, our grateful hymn receive.
2. For all your saints, O Lord, accept our thankful cry,
who counted you their great reward, and strove in you to die.
3. Your earthly members fit to join your saints above,
in one communion ever knit, one fellowship of love.
4. Jesus, your name we bless, and humbly pray that we
in life and death through Spirit's breath may follow faithfully.

WORDS: Richard Mant, 1776-1848, alt.
MUSIC: Charles Lockhart, 1745-1815

CARLISLE
66.86 (SM)

A Thanksgiving for the Light on Marian Feasts   137

Blessed are you, God of all grace,
for in Jesus Christ you are our light and our life;
to you be glory and praise forever.
You gave your living Word to Mary, Birth Giver,
that through the Holy Spirit
she might bear the Word made flesh,
who brings light out of darkness,
and with your Spirit renews the face of the earth.
All praise and thanks to you,
most holy and blessed Trinity,
one God, now and for ages of ages. **Amen.**

[DWV, OSL]

MARY, MOTHER OF JESUS

138   The Word Whom Earth and Sea and Sky

WORDS: Latin, 7th-8th cent.; sts. 1 and 3, tr. *Hymns Ancient and Modern*, 1861,
        after John Mason Neale, 1818-1866; st. 2, tr. Anne K. LeCroy, b. 1930
MUSIC: Melody and bass Orlando Gibbons, 1583-1625; adapt. and harm. from *The English Hymnal*, 1906

SONG 34
LM

MARY, MOTHER OF JESUS

Mary, Woman of the Promise

139

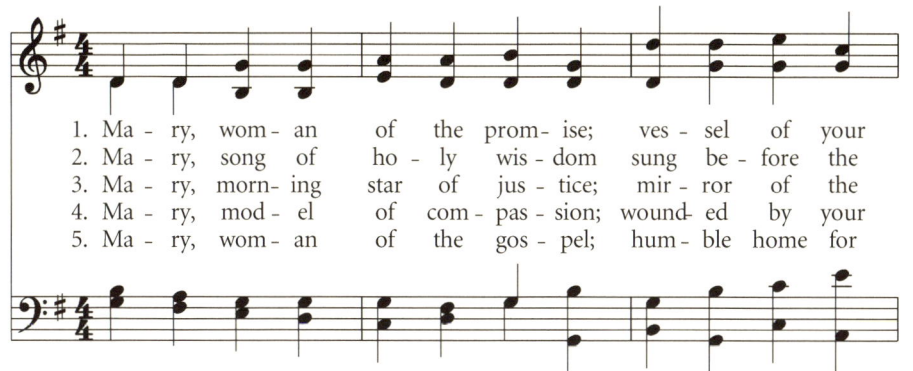

1. Ma - ry, wom - an of the prom - ise; ves - sel of your
2. Ma - ry, song of ho - ly wis - dom sung be - fore the
3. Ma - ry, morn - ing star of jus - tice; mir - ror of the
4. Ma - ry, mod - el of com - pas - sion; wound - ed by your
5. Ma - ry, wom - an of the gos - pel; hum - ble home for

peo - ple's dreams: through your o - pen
world be - gan: faith - ful to the
Ra - diant Light: in the shad - ows
off - spring's pain: when our hearts are
trea - sured seed: help us to be

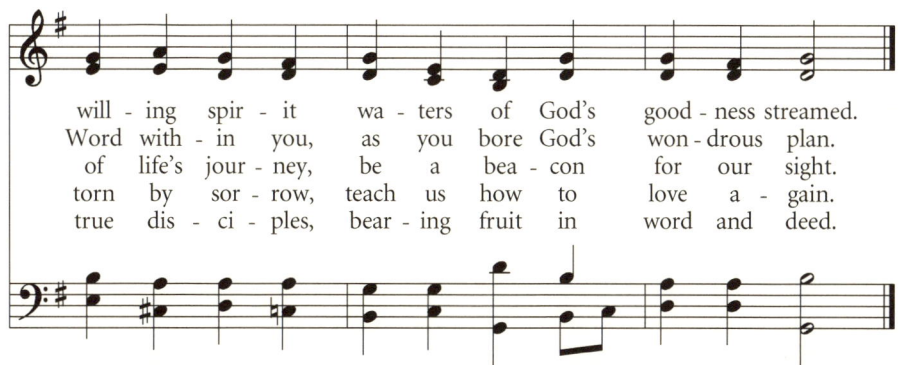

will - ing spir - it waters of God's good - ness streamed.
Word with - in you, as you bore God's won - drous plan.
of life's jour - ney, be a bea - con for our sight.
torn by sor - row, teach us how to love a - gain.
true dis - ci - ples, bear - ing fruit in word and deed.

WORDS: Mary Frances Fleischaker, 1988
MUSIC: Attr. to C. F. Witt, 1715; adapt. Henry J. Gauntlett, 1861
Words © 1988 Mary Francis Fleischaker, O.P.

STUTTGART
87.87

SAINT LUKE THE EVANGELIST

140 Hymn for the Feast of Saint Luke

1. O sisters, brothers, let us sing of Luke, evangelist and saint, healer of hearts and bodies faint.
2. Saint Luke the gospel did proclaim. "Glory on high," the angels sang, God's peace on earth for all Christ brings.
3. Luke's Gospel for the Gentiles wrote, in storied songs glad tidings brought, and women, children, sinners sought.
4. At close of day with Simeon say, "My eyes have seen your glory, Lord. Let now your servant go in peace."

Refrain
Alleluia, alleluia, alleluia.

WORDS: Sarah Flynn, OSL, 2008
MUSIC: *Schönes Geistlichen Gesangbuch*, 1609; harm. from *The Pilgrim Hymnal*, 1958
Words © 2008 Sarah Flynn, 2011 Order of Saint Luke

GELOBT SIE GOTT
888 with Alleluias

SAINT LUKE THE EVANGELIST

O Blessed Luke
141

1. O blessed Luke! whose sacred page, so rich in words of truth and love, pours on the Church from age to age the healing unction from above.
2. How many a soul with guilt oppressed has learned to hear the joyful sound, in that account of sin confessed, of parent's love for lost and found?
3. How many a child of sin and shame has refuge found from guilty fears through her, who to the Savior came with costly ointments and with tears!
4. What countless worshippers have sung, in lowly church or lofty choir, the song that loosed the silent tongue of him who was the Baptist's sire!
5. So grant us, Lord, like him to live, in loving service, faithful, free, 'til you at last the summons give, and we, with him, your face shall see.

WORDS: William Dalrymple Maclagan, 1826-1910, alt.; Heather Josselyn-Cranson, OSL, 2011
MUSIC: Melody by J. H. Schein, 1586-1630, in his revised *Cantional*, 1645; harm. J. S. Bach, 1865-1750

EISENACH
88.88 (LM)

LUKAN EUCHARISTIC MUSIC

144 Setting One

SANCTUS

Ho-ly, ho-ly, ho-ly, God of love and jus-tice, heav-en and earth are full of your glo-ry. Glo-ry be to you, O God. Blest is the one who comes in the name of God. Ho-san-na, ho-san-na, ho-san-na in the high-est!

WORDS: Adapted from traditional sources
MUSIC: William J. Beasley, OSL, 2009
Music © 2009 Order of Saint Luke

LUKAN EUCHARISTIC MUSIC

AMEN

WORDS: Trad.
MUSIC: William J. Beasley, OSL, 2009
Music © 2009 Order of Saint Luke

145   Setting Two

SANCTUS

Ho-ly, ho-ly, ho-ly Lord, God of power and might, heav-en and earth are full of your glo-ry. Ho-

WORDS: English Language Liturgical Consultation (ELLC)
MUSIC: George R. Crisp, OSL, 2010
Words © 1988 English Language Liturgical Consulation (ELLC). Music © 2010 George R. Crisp.

LUKAN EUCHARISTIC MUSIC

LUKAN EUCHARISTIC MUSIC

MEMORIAL ACCLAMATION

Christ has died. Christ has ris-en. Christ will come a-gain!

WORDS: English Language Liturgical Consultation (ELLC)
MUSIC: George R. Crisp, OSL, 2010
Words © 1988 English Language Liturgical Consulation (ELLC). Music © 2010 George R. Crisp.

GREAT AMEN

A-men, a-men, a-men.

WORDS: Trad.
MUSIC: George R. Crisp, OSL, 2010
Music © 2010 George R. Crisp

LUKAN EUCHARISTIC MUSIC

Setting Three

146

SANCTUS

Ho - ly, Ho - ly, Ho - ly God of jus - tice and love!
Heav - en and earth are full, full of your glo - ry.
Save us; ho - san - na. Bless-ed is the One who comes
in the name of our God. Ho - san - na; save us.

WORDS: Adapt. from traditional responses
MUSIC: Adapt. from 11th cent. *Sanctus* trope, DIVINUM MYSTERIUM;
arr. Dwight W. Vogel, OSL, 2011
Arr. © 2011 Order of Saint Luke

MYSTERY OF FAITH

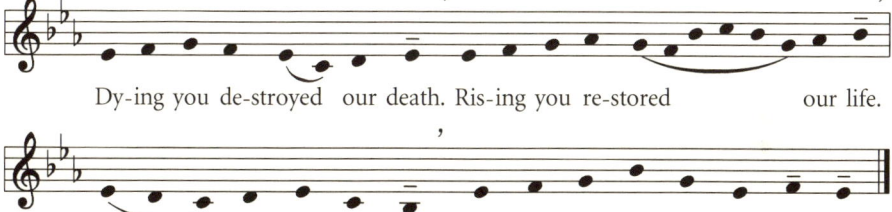

Dy-ing you de-stroyed our death. Ris-ing you re-stored our life.
Come Lord Je - sus Christ, come in res - ur - rec - tion glo - ry!

WORDS: Adapt. from traditional responses
MUSIC: Adapt. from 11th cent. *Sanctus* trope, DIVINUM MYSTERIUM;
arr. Dwight W. Vogel, OSL, 2011
Arr. © 2011 Order of Saint Luke

AMEN

A - men. A - men. A - men.

WORDS: Trad.
MUSIC: Adapt. from 11th cent. *Sanctus* trope, DIVINUM MYSTERIUM;
arr. Dwight W. Vogel, OSL, 2011
Arr. © 2011 Order of Saint Luke

LUKAN EUCHARISTIC MUSIC

Setting Four
147 Salvation, Glory, and Power to God

WORDS: Heather Murray Elkins, OSL
MUSIC: Trad. Scottish melody, from *The Hesperian Harp*, 1847
Words © 2011 Heather Murray Elkins. Used by permission.

CANDLER
LMD

LUKAN EUCHARISTIC MUSIC

What Wondrous Love Is This 148

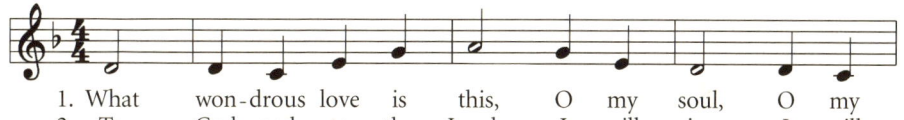
1. What wondrous love is this, O my soul, O my
2. To God and to the Lamb I will sing, I will

soul, what wondrous love is this, O my soul! What
sing, to God and to the Lamb, I will sing; to

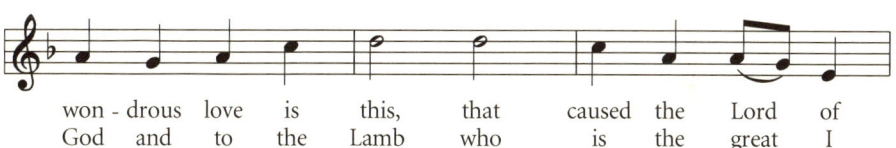
wondrous love is this, that caused the Lord of
God and to the Lamb who is the great I

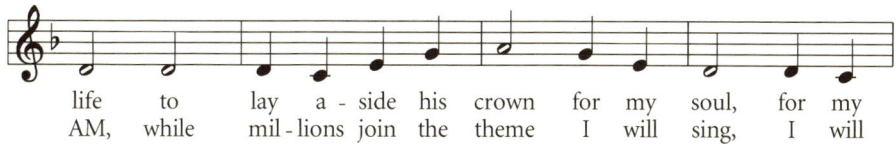
life to lay aside his crown for my soul, for my
AM, while millions join the theme I will sing, I will

soul, to lay aside his crown for my soul.
sing; while millions join the theme I will sing.

WORDS: USA folk hymn
MUSIC: USA folk hymn

WONDROUS LOVE
12 9.12 9

149 Praise God, from Whom All Blessings Flow

Praise God, from whom all bless-ings flow; praise God, all crea-tures here be-low; praise God, blest ho-ly Trin-i-ty; both now and for e-ter-ni-ty. A-men.

WORDS: Thomas Ken, 1674, alt.
MUSIC: Attr. to Louis Bourgeois, 1551

OLD 100th
LM

OSL Resources

Litany for The Order Of Saint Luke   150

Sisters and brothers,
in peace let us pray to the Lord saying,
> **Merciful God, hear our prayer.**

For the life and work of the Order of Saint Luke
that we may be ever guided by your Spirit,
> Merciful God, **hear our prayer.**

For our affirmation of the apostolic hope
that we may always abide in Christ our hope,
and bring good news to all who hunger and thirst
for the coming of your kin-dom,
> Merciful God, **hear our prayer.**

For the magnifying of the sacraments
as signs of your Presence
and as means of grace for your Church,
> Merciful God, **hear our prayer.**

For the Church as the Body of Christ,
that we may affirm our diverse gifts,
and mend our divisions
so that our common life may be a source of healing grace for all,
> Merciful God, **hear our prayer.**

For faithfulness to our baptismal covenant
that we may live the sacramental life
in communion with you
through daily prayer and eucharistic living,
> Merciful God, **hear our prayer.**

For integrity and fidelity in the corporate worship of our churches,
that we may celebrate the Gospel in Spirit and in Truth,
> Merciful God, **hear our prayer.**

That we may respond to your call to service
in the Order, the Church and the world,
being midwives of justice, peace and compassion
for the sake of your kin-dom,
> Merciful God, **hear our prayer.**

For those who have died
whom we commend to your eternal love and goodness,
   (especially . . . .)
   Merciful God, **hear our prayer.**

SF/DWV

(to be followed by collectively praying the Collect for The Order)

151   Collect for The Order Of Saint Luke

O Shepherd of us all,
who inspired your servant Saint Luke the Physician
to set forth in the gospel
the love and healing power of Jesus:
Grant, we ask you, your Spirit to the Order of Saint Luke,
that we may proclaim the Apostolic hope,
magnify the Sacraments,
and embody Christ's healing grace for all creation;
through Jesus Christ our Lord. Amen.

OSL

152   Intercessions for The Order of Saint Luke

Hear our prayer and let our cry come to you
   for Brother/Sister (first name) our abbot,
     for the officers of the General Chapter,
      [Brother/Sister (first names),
   for our priors,
     [*or* for Brother/Sister (first name) our prior,
   for our brothers and sisters in the Order (especially . . .),
   for a sense of community with others in the Order,
   for grace to live for you and with each other
   as we live our Rule of Life and Service.
Merciful God,
   hear our prayer.

OSL

Affirmation of Vows — 153

Sisters and brothers in the Order of Saint Luke.
let us affirm the vows of life and service we share:

We affirm the apostolic hope.
We live for the Church of Jesus Christ.
We seek the sacramental life.
We promote the corporate worship of
  the Church.
We magnify the sacraments.
We accept the call to service.

May the Holy Spirit work within us
that we may be faithful in living into these vows.

OSL

CONFESSION / AWARENESS AND ASSURANCE

Prayer of General Confession — 154

Mighty and most merciful God,
we have erred and strayed from your ways like lost sheep.
We have followed too much the devices and desires
  of our own hearts.
We have left undone those things which we ought to have done,
and done those things which we ought not to have done;
and we are diminished in soul and body.
Have mercy on us.

Spare those, O God, who confess their faults.
Restore those who are penitent,
according to your promises declared to us
  in Christ Jesus our Lord.
And grant, O most merciful God, for Jesus' sake,
that we may hereafter live a godly, righteous, and sober life
to the glory of your holy name. Amen.

BCP ALT.

PRAYERS OF AWARENESS

155   A Prayer of Confession

Merciful God,
we have not loved you with our whole heart
nor our neighbors as ourselves.
For the sake of your Son Jesus Christ,
forgive what we have been,
accept us as we are,
and guide what we shall be,
through Jesus Christ our Lord. Amen.

SUPPLEMENT TO THE BCP, ALT.

156   A Prayer of Awareness

God of all mercy,
we confess that we have sinned against you,
opposing your will in our lives.
We have denied your goodness in each other,
in ourselves, and in the world you have created.
We repent of the sins we have done.
We commit ourselves to resist evil, injustice and oppression
in whatever forms they present themselves,
especially when they are done in your name.
We seek your power to deliver us from sins that still beset us.
Forgive, restore, and strengthen us
through our Savior Jesus Christ,
that we may abide in your love
and always discern and do your will. Amen.

© 1998, THE CHURCH PENSION FUND, ALT TWBE

157   A Prayer for Restoration

Blessed be the holy and blessed Trinity, one God —
Hope-bringing,
  Light-sharing,
    Water-quenching,
      Bread-breaking,
        Wine-pouring,
Grace-bearing,
  Peace-making,

Justice-seeking,
    Earth-restoring
God of ALL that was and is and ever will be.
Blessed be God forever!   **Amen.**

Let us seek God's forgiving grace
in the presence of God and of one another.

silence for reflection

Gracious, life-giving God,
  **Give us eyes to see when we are blinded by assumptions
    that keep us from seeing your Light.**
  Give us courage to act when we are afraid to risk.
  Give us wisdom to set straight our cultural biases.
  **Give us humility to recognize the earth and all its inhabitants
    as your good work which we are called to tend.**
  **Give us hope to share
    when discouragement threatens to immobilize us.**
  Give us whatever it takes to embrace the least and the last.

**With deep gratitude and open hearts we come to you,
  seeking to be faithful followers of Your Way.**
Heal us and use us,
for we pray in the name of Jesus.
Amen.   LJV

A Personal Prayer of Confession   158

(especially appropriate for Evening Prayer or Compline when prayed alone)

Holy and gracious God,
I have sinned against you this day.
Some of my sin I know–
for there are thoughts and words and deeds
which trouble me;
some is known only to you.
I come to you in the name of Jesus,
asking for forgiveness.
Heal, renew, restore me,
and let me rest in your peace. Amen.

ADAPTED FROM TRADITIONAL PRAYERS, OSL

PRAYERS OF AWARENESS

159   An Assurance of Forgiveness

The message we have heard from Jesus
we proclaim to you:
God is light
and in God there is no darkness at all!
If we walk in the light as Jesus is in the light,
we have *koinonia** with one another,
and the grace of our Lord Jesus Christ
cleanses us from all sin.
Brothers and sisters in Christ, we are a forgiven people!
   Thanks be to God!

ADAPTED FROM I JOHN 1:5,7, OSL

160   Words of Assurance

May the God whose mercy is from everlasting to everlasting
forgive us all our sins,
strengthen us in all goodness,
and by the power of the Holy Spirit
keep us in eternal life.
Brothers and sisters in Christ, we are a forgiven people!
   Thanks be to God!

ADAPTED FROM I TIMOTHY 1:15; I PETER 2:24, OSL

161   An Affirmation of Reconciliation

We have this assurance from God:
through Christ our sins are not counted against us,
but we are reconciled to God
and given the message of reconciliation.
Brothers and sisters in Christ,
anyone who is in Christ is a new creation;
the old has passed away, the new has come.
   Thanks be to God!

ADAPTED FROM II CORINTHIANS 5:17-19, OSL

---

* Or: "sustaining community"

AFFIRMATIONS OF FAITH

The Apostles' Creed 162

I believe in God, the Father almighty,
creator of heaven and earth.

I believe in Jesus Christ, God's only Son, our Lord,
who was conceived by the Holy Spirit,
born of the Virgin Mary,
suffered under Pontius Pilate,
was crucified, died, and was buried;
he descended to the dead.
On the third day he rose again;
he ascended into heaven,
he is seated at the right hand of the Father,
and he will come to judge the living and the dead.

I believe in the Holy Spirit,
the holy catholic Church,
the communion of saints,
the forgiveness of sins,
the resurrection of the body,
and the life everlasting. Amen.

<small>ENGLISH LANGUAGE LITURGICAL CONSULTATION, 1988; USED BY PERMISSION</small>

The Nicene Creed 163

We believe in one God,
the Father, the Almighty,
maker of heaven and earth,
of all that is, seen and unseen.

We believe in one Lord, Jesus Christ,
the only Son of God,
eternally begotten of the Father,
God from God, Light from Light,
true God from true God,
begotten, not made,
of one Being with the Father;
through him all things were made.
For us and for our salvation
he came down from heaven,
was incarnate of the Holy Spirit and the Virgin Mary
and became truly human.

AFFIRMATIONS OF FAITH

For our sake he was crucified under Pontius Pilate;
he suffered death and was buried.
On the third day he rose again
in accordance with the Scriptures;
he ascended into heaven
and is seated at the right hand of the Father.
He will come again in glory to judge the living and the dead,
and his kingdom will have no end.

We believe in the Holy Spirit, the Lord, the giver of life,
who proceeds from the Father and the Son,
who with the Father and the Son is worshiped and glorified,
who has spoken through the prophets.
We believe in one holy catholic and apostolic Church.
We acknowledge one baptism for the forgiveness of sins.
We look for the resurrection of the dead,
and the life of the world to come. Amen.

ENGLISH LANGUAGE LITURGICAL CONSULTATION, 1988; USED BY PERMISSION

164   A New Creed

Leader:
We are not alone, we live in God's world.

People:
We believe in God:
   who has created and is creating,
   who has come in Jesus, the Word made flesh,
     to reconcile and make new,
   who works in us and others by the Spirit.
We trust in God.
We are called to be the church:
   to celebrate God's presence,
   to live with respect in Creation,
   to love and serve others,
   to seek justice and resist evil,
   to proclaim Jesus, crucified and risen,
     our judge and our hope.
In life, in death, in life beyond death,
   God is with us.
We are not alone.
Thanks be to God. Amen.

THE UNITED CHURCH OF CANADA, 1968, 1980, 1994

A Creed for This Community

We believe in God,
eternal yet ever moving One,
who creates and is creating,
who keeps covenant,
who sets before us
   the ways of life and death.

We believe in Jesus,
the Servant-Advocate
who lived the way of dying/rising,
who embodied justice and reconciliation,
who, with authority,
calls us to share this way and this embodying.

We believe in the Holy Spirit,
sustaining Presence and transforming Power,
who dwells among us in clarity and mystery,
who inspires us individually and corporately,
who challenges, prods, emboldens.

We believe that the Church,
community of faith and caring,
covenant and promise,
which nurtures our pilgrimage,
calls us to be witnesses
to God's truth, love and justice.

We believe that our believing affects
our daily walking and talking,
our doubting and struggling,
our decisions and choice making,
and our responses to persons and systems.

As brothers and sisters in this community,
we intend to raise questions hopefully,
to work for justice lovingly,
and, by God's grace,
to share our ministry
faithfully and passionately.

ADAPTED FROM A CREEDAL STATEMENT FOR THE GENERAL COMMISSION ON THE STATUS AND ROLE OF WOMEN OF THE UNITED METHODIST CHURCH BY BARBARA B. TROXELL, OSL. USED BY PERMISSION.

A Celtic-style icon of Saint Luke.

PRAYERS OF THE PEOPLE
Sung Intercessions   166

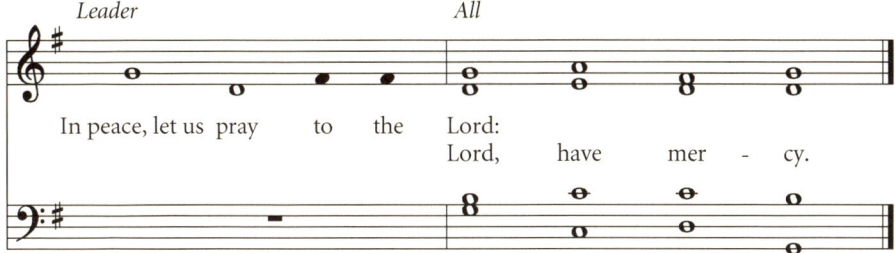

In peace, let us pray to the Lord:
Lord, have mercy.

MUSIC: Byzantine Chant

For those who hunger and thirst for righteousness, let us pray . . .
For those who are weak in body, mind or spirit, let us pray . . .
For those captive to wealth and violence, let us pray . . .
For the lonely, despondent, down-trodden or oppressed, let us pray . . .
For justice, freedom and peace throughout the world, let us pray . . .
For refugees and exiles, and for all in danger, let us pray . . .
In thanksgiving for prophets, poets and salty disciples, let us pray . . .
In thanksgiving for God's love and grace, let us pray . . .

[DTB, TAR, TJC]

(May be followed by an appropriate collect)

A Litany of Intercession   167

Gracious God,
who loves all and forgets none,
we bring to you our prayers for all your children.

For all whom we love, watch over, and for whom we care;
    Merciful God, **hear our prayer.**

For all prisoners and captives,
and those who suffer from oppression,
that you will manifest your mercy toward them,
and make all hearts as merciful as your own;
    Merciful God, **hear our prayer.**

For all who bear the cross of suffering,
the sick in body or mind;
    Merciful God, **hear our prayer.**

For all those who are troubled by the sin or suffering
of those they love;
   Merciful God, **hear our prayer.**

For all who are absorbed in their own grief,
that they may be raised to share the sorrow of others,
and know the saving grace of the cross;
   Merciful God, **hear our prayer.**

For all perplexed by the deeper questions of life
and overshadowed with doubt,
that your light may guide them;
   Merciful God, **hear our prayer.**

For all who are tried by temptations or weakness,
that your mercy may be their strength;
   Merciful God, **hear our prayer.**

For all who are lonely and sad in the midst of others' joy,
that they may know you as their friend and comforter;
   Merciful God, **hear our prayer.**

For the infirm and aged and for all who are dying,
that they may find their strength in you
and live in your light at evening time;
   Merciful God, **hear our prayer.**

For all forgotten by us, but dear to you;
   Merciful God, **hear our prayer.**

Compassionate God, hear our prayers,
answer them according to your will,
and make us channels of your infinite grace,
through Jesus Christ we pray.
        Amen.   WCC Publications ©1989

168   A Prayer of Thanksgiving and Supplication

(In the silence following each petition, specific names or situations may be lifted up, quietly aloud, or in silence.)

   Great God of power and love,
   we thank you for abiding with us in Jesus
   through Word and Sacrament.
   In the intimacy of the Spirit we plead:

dance in your Church . . .
embrace the suffering . . .
defend the oppressed . . .
forgive the guilty . . .
release the prisoner . . .
guide the powerful . . .
center the distracted . . .
strengthen the tempted . . .
hear the needy . . .
welcome the dying . . .
complete what is lacking in us . . .
and all for your love's sake. **Amen.**

[DTB in OSL DO, III]

Suffrages (A) 169

Show us your mercy, O Lord;
   and grant us your salvation.
Clothe your ministers with righteousness;
   let your people sing with joy.
Give peace, O Lord, in all the world;
   for only in you can we live in safety.
Lord, keep this nation under your care;
   and guide us in the way of justice and truth.
Let your way be known upon earth;
   your saving health among all nations.
Let not the needy, O Lord, be forgotten;
   nor the hope of the poor be taken away.
Create in us clean hearts, O God;
   and sustain us by your Holy Spirit.

[BCP]

Suffrages (B) 170

O God, save your people and bless your heritage;
   direct and sustain us with your Holy Spirit.
Day by day we praise you;
   and we worship you forever, world without end.
O God, keep us this day without sin;
   have mercy on us, Lord, have mercy.

O God, let your steadfast love be upon us;
> **for our trust is in you.**

O God, in you have we trusted;
> **let evil never overwhelm us.**

[Adapted from a Byzantine Evening Liturgy]

171   Prayer of Affirmation

O God:
Because you are the source of all life and love and being,
> **we call you Creator.**

Because we know the story of your presence among your Covenant People,
and we honor their tradition,
> **we call you Lord.**

Because Jesus Christ, your obedient child,
knew you intimately and spoke of you so,
> **we call you Father.**

Because you are present in the act of birth,
and because you shelter, nurture, and care for us,
> **we call you Mother.**

Because you hold us up
and give us strength and courage when we are weak and in need,
> **we call you Sustainer.**

Because we have known you in our pain and suffering,
> **we call you Comforter.**

Because beyond pain lies your promise of all things made new,
> **we call you Hope.**

Because you are the means of liberation and the way to freedom,
> **we call you Deliverer.**

Because you have chosen to come among us
 and share our common lot, — suffering and dying —
> **we call you Companion.**

Because you rose victorious, bringing new life,
> **we call you Redeemer.**

Confident that you will hear,
we call upon you with all the Names that make you real to us –
names that create images in our minds and hearts —
images which our souls can understand and touch.
And yet we know that you are more than all of these.
> **Blessing and power, glory and honor be unto you, our God. Amen.**

[Timothy J. Crouch, alt. OFB ©2012 OSL]

PRAYERS OF THE PEOPLE
The Spirit Prayer 172

As we remember the prayer Jesus taught us, we pray together:

Eternal Spirit,
Life Giver, Pain Bearer, Love Maker,
Source of all that is and that shall be,
Father and Mother of us all,
Loving God, in whom is heaven:
The hallowing of your name echo through the universe!
The way of your justice
be followed by the peoples of the world!
Your heavenly will be done by all created beings!
Your commonwealth of peace and freedom
sustain our hope and come on earth.
With the bread we need for today, feed us.
In the hurts we absorb from one another, forgive us.
In times of temptation and test, strengthen us.
From trials too great to endure, spare us.
From the grip of all that is evil, free us.
For you reign in the glory of the power that is love,
now and for ever. Amen.

[JIM COTTER, *PRAYER AT NIGHT*;
CAIRNS PUBLICATIONS, 1991. USED BY PERMISSION.]

Veni Sancte Spiritus 173

(Community left may pray the lines to the left, with community right responding with the indented lines, or a liturgist may read the lines to the left with the community as a whole responding with the indented lines.)

Come, Holy Spirit, come;
radiate your light divine.
> **Source of all gifts, come;**
> **shine within our hearts.**

Great Comforter,
the soul's most welcome guest:
> **in labor you are rest,**
> **in heat, coolness,**
> **in woe, reassurance and relief.**

O blessed Light,
shine within our hearts and fill our inmost being.

> Without you, nothing is free from taint of ill;
> nothing is good in thought or deed.
> Heal what is wounded;
> **strengthen what is weak;**
> cleanse what is filthy;
> **water what is parched;**
> bend what is stubborn;
> **melt what is frozen;**
> warm what is chill,
> **guide what is devious.**
>
> On the faithful who trust in you,
> pour out your sevenfold gifts;
> **give us boundless mercy—**
> **your salvation—**
> **joy unending.**
> **Amen.**

[ADAPTED BY DWV FROM THE THIRTEENTH CENTURY PRAYER OF ARCHBISHOP STEPHEN LANGTON AS TRANSLATED BY E. CASWALL (1814-1878); ADAPTED FROM *THE DAILY OFFICE: A BOOK OF HOURS FOR DAILY PRAYER AFTER THE USAGE OF THE ORDER OF SAINT LUKE*, © 1994 BY THE ORDER OF SAINT LUKE.]

SENDING FORTH: BLESSINGS AND COMMISSIONINGS

174 The Apostolic Blessing

(May be used alone or in conjunction with any sending forth.)

The grace of our Lord Jesus Christ and the love of God and the *koinonia*[1] of the Holy Spirit be with all of you.

[II CORINTHIANS 13:14, OSL]

175 The Aaronic Blessing

May God bless us and keep us. May God's face shine upon us and be gracious to us. May God lift up the divine countenance upon us, and give us peace.

[ADAPTED FROM NUMBERS 6:24-26, OSL]

---

[1] Or "sustaining community;" NRSV = "communion."

SENDING FORTH

A Resurrection Blessing from Hebrews   176

May the God of peace, who brought back from the dead our Lord Jesus, the great shepherd of the sheep, by the blood of the eternal covenant, make us complete in everything good so that we may do God's will, working among us that which is pleasing to God, through Jesus Christ to whom be glory forever and ever.

[HEBREWS 13:20-21, NRSV]

A Commissioning Commendation   177

May the High God of Heaven refresh you,
the Galilean freedom of the Son lift you,
and the Hush of Holy Breath overtake you.
The Holy Three welcome you away and at home,
here and now and in every time and place.   [DTB]

A Sending Forth   178

We have seen strange things today.
Let us ponder them in our hearts
  as we go from here,
    filled with the power of the Holy Spirit,
    to love and to serve God and our neighbor in all that we do.

[MJO'D, LUKE 5:26 AND LUKE 2:19]

A Closing Prayer   179

God be in my head;
   and in my understanding.
God be in my eyes,
   and in my looking;
God be in my mouth,
   and in my speaking;
God be in my heart,
   and in my thinking;
God be at my end,
   and at my departing. Amen.

A SARUM PRIMER, 1588 AS USED
IN THE EARLY "GREEN CARD RITE" OF THE ORDER OF SAINT LUKE

SENDING FORTH

180 A Commissioning Commendation

May we be made strong with strength coming from God,
and may we be prepared to endure everything with patience
as we joyfully give thanks to the One
who enables us to share in the inheritance of the saints in light,
rescuing us from the power of darkness,
 and transferring us to the realm of God's beloved Son.

[Adapted from Colossians 1:11-13, OSL]

181 A Commissioning Commendation

The God of all grace, who has called us to eternal glory in Christ, establish and strengthen you by the power of the Holy Spirit, that you may live in grace and peace.

[Adapted from I Peter 5:10, OSL]

182 A Commissioning Commendation

Rejoice in the Lord[2] always; again I say, rejoice.
May the peace of God, which goes beyond all our understanding,
guard our hearts and our minds in Christ Jesus.

[Adapted from Philippians 4:4,7, OSL]

---

[2] Or "Adonai" or "God."

THE GREAT LITANY   183

The Great Litany is the Church's most expansive prayer of supplication. Parts of it were used as early as the fifth century in Rome. It was the first English language rite prepared by Archbishop Thomas Cranmer, published in 1544. The form used here begins with an invocation of the Trinity, followed by a series of prayers which seek deliverance from evil, spiritual harm, and natural calamities, then a series of prayers which plead the power of Christ's incarnation, life, death, and resurrection for deliverance, wide-ranging prayers of intercession, and concludes with the Agnus Dei.

The Great Litany in its entirety is usually used at Festive Vespers or Evensong. It may also replace Mid-day Prayer or Compline, especially if a service of Word and Table is being held close in time. The Great Litany or portions thereof may replace the prayers of supplication at any office on Wednesdays or Fridays. Sections I and VI are always used; appropriate suffrages may be selected from sections II, III, IV, and V. The Great Litany may be spoken or chanted, and may be prayed in procession

When chanted, the community is encouraged to sing the responses in four-part harmony. Except in the first section, the cantor may improvise on the reciting chord. The organist is encouraged to vary the registration.

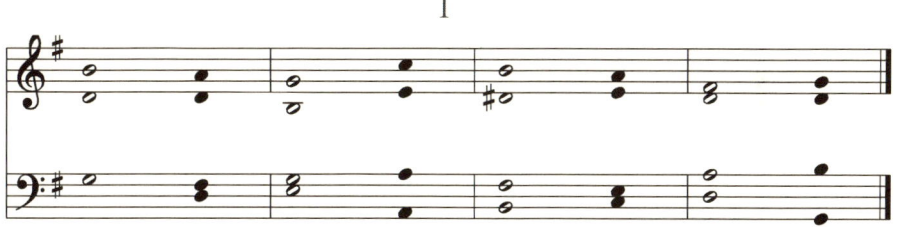

MUSIC: Stephen Elvey (1805 - 1860), alt.

    O God, creator of heaven and *earth*,
        have mercy up-*on us*.
    O God, redeemer of the *world*,
        have mercy up-*on us*.

    O God, sanctifier of the *faithful*,
        have mercy up-*on us*.
    O holy, blessed, and glorious Trinity, one *God*.
        have mercy up-*on us*.

THE GREAT LITANY

II

MUSIC: Jonathan Battishill (1738-1801), alt.

Remember not, Lord Christ, our *offenses*,
nor the offenses of our *forebearers*,
and do not re-*ward us*
according to our *sins*.
Spare us, good Lord, spare your *people*
whom you have redeemed with your most precious *blood*.
By your mercy preserve us for *ever*.
Spare us, good Lord.

From all evil and *wickedness*,
from alienation and sin
 and from the crafts and assaults of the *devil*;
and from despair and the loss of *hope*,
Good Lord, de-*liver us*.

From all blindness of *heart*;
from pride, vainglory, and hy-*pocrisy*;
from envy, hatred, and malice,
 and from all want of *charity*,
Good Lord, de-*liver us*.

From all inordinate and sinful affections,
 and from all the deceits of the world, the flesh, and the *devil*;
from all false doctrine, heresy, and *schism*;
from hardness of heart, and contempt of your Word and
 commandment,
Good Lord, de-*liver us*.

From lightning and tempest, earthquake, fire, and *flood*;
from plague, pestilence, and *famine*,
From all oppression, violence, battle, and murder,
 and from dying suddenly and unpre-*pared*,
Good Lord, de-*liver us*.

THE GREAT LITANY

III

MUSIC: Jonathan Battishill (1738-1801), alt.

By the mystery of your holy incar-*nation*,
by your holy na-*tivity*;
by your baptism, fasting, and temp-*tation*,
  Good Lord, de-*liver us*.

By your agony and bloody *sweat*;
by your cross and passion;
  by your precious death and *burial*;
by your glorious resurrection and ascension
  and by the coming of your Holy *Spirit*,
  Good Lord, de-*liver us*.

In all time of our tribu-*lation*;
in all time of our pros-*perity*;
in the hour of death
  and in the day of *judgment*,
  Good Lord, de-*liver us*.

IV

MUSIC: John Goss (1800-1880), alt.

We beseech you to hear us, Lord *God*,
  that your holy church universal
    might be governed by you in the right *way*.
  Illumine all bishops, priests and pastors, deacons and *ministers*,
    with true knowledge and understanding of your *Word*.

THE GREAT LITANY

MUSIC: John Goss (1800-1880), alt.

Both by their speaking and their *living*
may they set it *forth*
and show it ac-*cordingly*,
    Hear us, good *Lord*.

Bless and keep all your *people*.
Send forth laborers into your *harvest*
and draw all *people*
into your sovereign *realm*.

Give to all people increase of *grace*
to hear and receive your *Word*,
and to bring forth the fruits of the *Spirit*,
    Hear us, good *Lord*.

Bring into the way of truth all those who have erred and
  are de-*ceived*,
Give us a heart to love and *fear you*,
and to diligently live according to your com-*mandments*,
    Hear us, good *Lord*.

O God, rule the *hearts*
of all those in *authority*
that they may do justice and love *mercy*
and walk in the ways of *truth*.
Make wars cease in all the *world*;
give to all nations unity, peace and *concord*
and bestow freedom upon all *peoples*,
    Hear us, good *Lord*.

Show pity upon all prisoners and *captives*,
the homeless and the *hungry*,
and all who are desolate and op-*pressed*,
    Hear us, good *Lord*.

THE GREAT LITANY

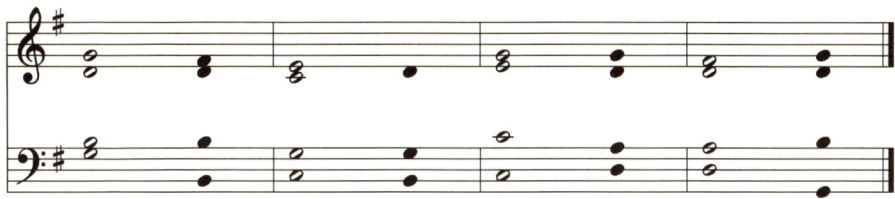

MUSIC: William Crotch (1775-1847), alt.

Preserve the bountiful fruits of the earth
   so that all may enjoy *them,*
 Inspire us in our several callings
   to do the work you give us to *do*
with singleness of heart as your servants
   and for the common *good,*
      Hear us, good *Lord*.

Preserve all who are in danger
   by reason of their labor or their *travel,*
Preserve and provide for all women in *childbirth,*
young children and orphans, the widows and *widowers,*
and all whose homes are broken or torn by *strife.*

Visit the *lonely,*
 strengthen all who suffer in mind, body and *spirit*;
  comfort with your presence those who are failing and in-*firm,*
      Hear us, good *Lord*.

Support, help, and comfort all who are in danger, and tribulation,
   and have mercy upon all *people.*
Give us true repentance,
   forgive us all our sins, negligence, and *ignorance,*
and endue us with the grace of your Holy Spirit
   to amend our lives according to your holy *Word,*
      Hear us, good *Lord*.

Forgive our enemies, persecutors, and slanderers,
   and turn their *hearts.*
Strengthen those who *stand*;
comfort and help the weak-hearted
   and raise up those who *fall.*
      Hear us, good *Lord*.

THE GREAT LITANY

MUSIC: William Crotch (1775-1847), alt.

Finally beat down Satan under our *feet*.
Grant to all the faithful departed eternal life and *peace*,
Grant that in the fellowship of *[Saint Luke or other saint(s) when appropriate and]* all the *saints*,
   we may enter your heavenly *realm*.

VI

MUSIC: Adapted from Stephen Elvey (1805 - 1860) and James Turle (1802 - 1882)

O Lamb of God, who takes away the sins of the *world*,
   have mercy up-*on us*.
O Lamb of God, who takes away the sins of the *world*,
   have mercy up-*on us*.
O Lamb of God who takes away the sins of the *world*,
   grant us your *peace*.

(When prayed apart from another service or office, The Great Litany is followed by The Lord's Prayer, spoken in unison, and is followed by a blessing. If prayed in procession, the procession stands in place during the Lord's Prayer and blessing).

[ADAPTED FROM THE 1544 LITANY OF THOMAS CRANMER, WHICH WAS BASED ON THE SARUM ROGATIONTIDE LITANY, LUTHER'S LATIN LITANY OF 1529, AND THE DEACON'S LITANY IN THE LITURGY OF CHRYSOSTOM; BY DWV]

CANTICLES

Canticle of Creation 184

(Benedicite, omnia opera Domini)

(May be used as the gathering hymn at any office or service; may be said or sung responsively, with cantor(s) singing the first part of each line and the community responding with "bless Ado-nai!", be sung antiphonally with the second voice taking the indented lines, or be sung together in unison or harmony throughout).

MUSIC: Adapted from Stephen Elvey (1805 - 1860) and James Turle (1802 - 1882)

All you works of the Most High, **bless ADO-*NAI*!**
Stars in the heaven, **bless ADO-*NAI*!**
Sun and moon, **bless ADO-*NAI*!**
Frost and cold, **bless ADO-*NAI*!**
Showers and dew, **bless ADO-*NAI*!**
Fire and heat, **bless ADO-*NAI*!**

    Night and day, **bless ADO-*NAI*!**
    Winter and summer, **bless ADO-*NAI*!**
    Shining light and enfolding dark, **bless ADO-*NAI*!**
    Wind and rain, **bless ADO-*NAI*!**
    Birds of the air, **bless ADO-*NAI*!**
    Beasts of the wild, **bless ADO-*NAI*!**

Servants of God, bless ADO-*NAI*!
Souls of the faithful departed, bless ADO-*NAI*!
Faithful men and women everywhere, bless ADO-*NAI*!
Children and youth, bless ADO-*NAI*!
Saints and the humble-hearted, bless ADO-*NAI*!
People of God, praise and exalt ADONAI for-*ever*!

[ADAPTED FROM "THE SONG OF THE THREE" (DANIEL 3:23 FF) OSL]

CANTICLES

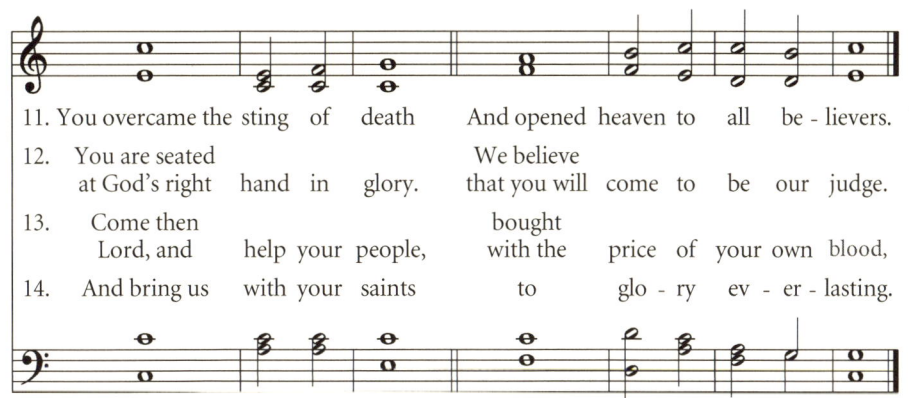

11. You overcame the sting of death   And opened heaven to all be-lievers.
12. You are seated   We believe
    at God's right hand in glory.   that you will come to be our judge.
13. Come then   bought
    Lord, and help your people,   with the price of your own blood,
14. And bring us with your saints   to glo-ry ev-er-lasting.

The following traditional versicles and responses may then be said:

Save your people, Lord, and bless your inheritance.
Govern and uphold them now and always.
Day be day we bless you.
We praise your name for ever.
Keep us today, Lord, from all sin.
Have mercy on us, Lord, have mercy.
Lord, show us your love and mercy,
for we have put our trust in you.
In you, Lord, is our hope:
let us never be put to shame.

[ELLC]

Gloria, Gloria 186

Glo-ri-a, glo-ri-a, in ex-cel-sis De-o!

Glo-ri-a, glo-ri-a! Al-le-lu-ia! Al-le-lu-ia!

May be sung as a canon

WORDS: Luke 2:14   GLORIA CANON
MUSIC: Jacques Berthier and the Community of Taizé, 1979   Irr.
Music © 1979 Les Presses de Taizé by permission of GIA Publications, Inc.

CANTICLES

187 Canticle of God's Glory
(*Gloria in Excelsis*)

Glory be to God on high and peace to God's people on earth.
We praise you, we bless you, we worship you, we glorify you, we give thanks to you for your great glory: O Lord God, heavenly King, God most blessed and holy. O Lord, Jesus Christ, Child of God; O Lord God, Lamb of God, chosen from on high,

WORDS: Luke 2:14; John 1:29. Adapted from canticles in Codex Alexandrinus, 5th cent.
MUSIC: Old Scottish chant
Adaptation © 1998, 2011 The Order of Saint Luke

CANTICLES
188 Canticle of Zechariah
(Benedictus, Luke 1:68-79 OSL)

(Sung at Morning Prayer; may be said or sung antiphonally, with the second voice taking the indented lines, or be sung together in unison or harmony throughout)

MUSIC: Heather Josselyn-Cranson, OSL, 2011   LYDIAN
© 2011 Order of Saint Luke

We bless you, ADONAI, God of *Israel*,
for you come to visit us and ransom us from *bondage*.
You have brought forth a strong De-*liverer*
in the house of your child *David*.

> This is what your holy prophets an-*nounced*:
> deliverance from enemies and from the hand of all who *hate us*;
> mercy a-mong our *ancestors*,
> and remembrance of your holy *covenant*.

This is the promise you swore to our ancestor, *Abraham*,
to make us una-*fraid*,
to rescue us from our *enemies*,
to serve before you, holy and just, all the days of our *lives*.

> And this, my little child, shall be called prophet of the Most *High*,
> going before you, ADONAI, to prepare your *paths*,
> making your people know de-*liverance*
> by the forgiveness of their *sins*.

[All:]
Through your merciful compassions, God our *God*,
the dawn from on high shall *visit us*,
to shine on those kept in dungeons and the shadows of *death*
and to guide our feet onto the path of *peace*.

[All:]
> Glory be to you,
> O Trinity most holy and blessed,
> who is now, ever was and ever shall be
> unto endless ages, A-men.

(On holy days:)
> Glory to God: Source of all, Eternal Word and Holy Spirit,
> one God, holy and blessed Trinity,
> who is now, ever was and ever shall be
> unto endless ages, A-men.

Canticle of Zechariah   189
(Benedictus, Luke 1:68-79 ELLC)

(Sung at Morning Prayer; may be said or sung antiphonally, with the second voice taking the indented lines with the final strophe and Gloria sung in unison, or be sung together in unison or harmony throughout)

MUSIC: Heather Josselyn-Cranson, OSL, 2011   LYDIAN
© 2011 Order of Saint Luke

> Blessed are you, Lord, the God of *Israel*,
> for you have come to your people and set them *free*.
> You have raised up for us a mighty *Savior*,
> born of the house of your servant *David*.
>> Through your holy *prophets*,
>> you promised of old to save us from our *enemies*,
>> from the hands of all who *hate us*,
>> to show mercy to our forebears
>>> and to remember your holy *covenant*.

CANTICLES

MUSIC: Heather Josselyn-Cranson, OSL, 2011   LYDIAN
© 2011 Order of Saint Luke

This was the oath you swore to our father *Abraham*:
to set us free from the hands of our *enemies*,
free to worship you without *fear*,
holy and righteous before you all the days of our *life*.

    And you, child, shall be called the prophet of the Most *High*,
    for you will go before the Lord to prepare the *way*,
    to give God's people knowledge of sal-*vation*
    by the forgiveness of their *sins*.

[All:]

    In the tender compassion of our *God*
    the dawn from on high shall break up-*on us*,
    to shine on those who dwell in darkness and the shadow of *death*,
    and to guide our feet into the way of *peace*.

                        [COPYRIGHT © 1988 ENGLISH LANGUAGE LITURGICAL CONSULTATION.
                                    ALL RIGHTS RESERVED. USED BY PERMISSION]

[All:]

    Glory be to *you*,
    O Trinity most holy and *blessed*,
    who is now, ever was and ever shall *be*
    unto endless ages, A-*men*.

(On holy days:)

    Glory to God: Source of all, Eternal Word and Holy *Spirit*,
    one God, holy and blessed *Trinity*,
    who is now, ever was and ever shall *be*
    unto endless ages, A-*men*.

CANTICLES
Canticle of Mary
190

(Magnificat; Luke 1:46-55 ELLC)

(Sung at Evening Prayer; may be said or sung antiphonally, with the second voice taking the indented lines, or be sung together in unison or harmony throughout)

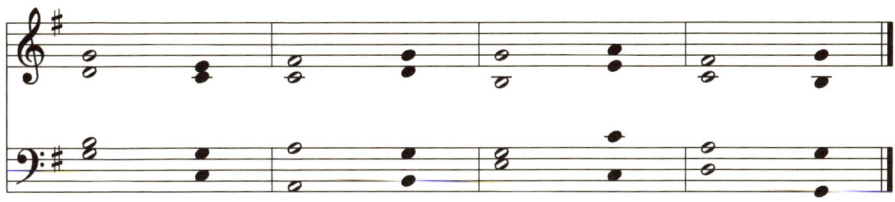

MUSIC: John Goss (1800-1880), alt.

My soul proclaims the greatness of the *Lord*,
my spirit rejoices in God my *Savior*,
for you, Lord, have looked with favor on your lowly *servant*.
From this day all generations will call me *blessed*.

> You, the Almighty, have done great things for *me*
> and holy is your *name*.
> You have mercy on those who fear *you*
> from generation to gener-*ation*.

You have shown strength with your *arm*
and scattered the proud in their con-*ceit*,
casting down the mighty from their *thrones*
and lifting up the *lowly*.

> You have filled the hungry with good things
>   and sent the rich away *empty*.
> You have come to the aid of your servant *Israel*,
> to remember the promise of mercy,
>   the promise made to our *forebears*,
> to Abraham and his children for *ever*.

[Copyright © 1988 English Language Liturgical Consultation.
All rights reserved. Used by permission.]

[*All:*]
> Glory be to *you*,
> O Trinity most holy and *blessed*,
> who is now, ever was and ever shall *be*
> unto endless ages, A-*men*.

CANTICLES

(On holy days:)

Glory to God: Source of all, Eternal Word and Holy *Spirit*,
one God, holy and blessed *Trinity*,
who is now, ever was and ever shall *be*
unto endless ages, A-*men*.

191   Canticle of Mary

(Magnificat; Luke 1:46-55 OSL)

(Sung at Evening Prayer; may be said or sung antiphonally, with the second voice taking the indented lines, or be sung together in unison or harmony throughout)

MUSIC: John Goss (1800-1880), alt.

My soul proclaims your greatness, *Lord*;
my spirit rejoices in you, my *Savior*;
for you have looked with favor on your lowly *servant*,
from this day all generations will call me *blessed*.

    You the Almighty have done great things for *me*,
        and Holy is your *Name*.
    Your have mercy on those who fear *you*
        in every gener-*ation*.

You have shown the strength of your *arm*;
you have scattered the proud in their con-*ceit*.
You have cast the mighty from their *thrones*;
you have lifted up the *lowly*.

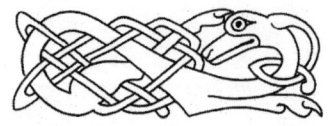

You have filled the hungry with good things;
>   and the rich have been sent away *empty*.
You have come to the help of your ser-vant *Israel*,
for you have remembered your promise of mercy,
>   the promise you made to our *forebears*,
to Abraham and his children for *ever*.

[TJC, OSL]

[All:]
>   Glory be to you,
>   O Trinity most holy and blessed,
>   who is now, ever was and ever shall be
>   unto endless ages, A-men.

(On holy days:)
>   Glory to God: Source of all, Eternal Word and Holy *Spirit*,
>   one God, holy and blessed *Trinity*,
>   who is now, ever was and ever shall *be*
>   unto endless ages, A-*men*.

Detail of the Madonna and Child from Folio 7 of the Book of Kells housed at Trinity College, Dubin, Ireland. This is the oldest image of Mary in a Western manuscript. *Public Domain Photo*

CANTICLES

192   The Canticle of Simeon
(Nunc Dimittis, Luke 2:29-32 ELLC)
(Sung at Compline)

MUSIC: Adapted from Stephen Elvey (1805-1860) and James Turle (1802 - 1882)

Now, Lord, you let your servant go in *peace*:
your word has been ful-*filled*.
My own eyes have seen the *salvation*
which you have prepared in the sight of every *people*:
a light to reveal you to the *nations*
and the glory of your people *Israel*.

[COPYRIGHT © 1988 ENGLISH LANGUAGE LITURGICAL CONSULTATION.
ALL RIGHTS RESERVED. USED BY PERMISSION]

Glory be to *you*,
O Trinity most holy and *blessed*,
who is now, ever was and ever shall *be*
  (move to the last measure)
unto endless ages, A-*men*.

(On holy days:)

Glory to God: Source of all,
  Eternal Word and Holy *Spirit*,
One God, holy and blessed *Trinity*,
who is now, ever was and ever shall *be*
  (move to the last measure)
unto endless ages, A-*men*.

CANTICLES

Canticle of the Resurrection   193
(Pascha nostrum)
(Sung at Saturday resurrection vigils and during the Great Fifty Days; may be spoken or sung together in unison or in four parts; for setting to psalm tone three, see p. 57; during Lent: spoken in unison, omitting the alleluias)

MUSIC: James Turle (1802-1882), alt.

[Alleluia!] Christ our Passover is sacrificed for *us*;
therefore let us keep the *feast*,
not with the old leaven of malice and *evil*,
but with the unleavened bread of sincerity and *truth*.

Christ being raised from the dead
   will never die a-*gain*;
death no longer has dominion over *him*.
The death he died, he died to sin, once for *all*,
but the life he lives, he lives to *God*.

So consider yourselves dead to *sin*
and alive to God in Jesus Christ our *Lord*.
For as in Adam all die,
   so also in Christ shall all be made a-*live*.
[Al-le-*luia*!]

[I Corinthians 5:7-8 and Romans 6:9-11,
Text adapted from BCP, DTB, DWV]

CANTICLES
194 Canticle of Redemption
(De profundis)

(Used at Vigils in Lent, at times of lamentation and distress, or at Services of Prayer for Reconciliation; may be said or sung ntiphonally, with the second voice taking the indented lines, or be sung together in unison or harmony throughout)

MUSIC: Heather Josselyn-Cranson, OSL, and William J. Beasley, OSL, 2011   PHRYGIAN
© 2011 Order of Saint Luke

Out of the depths have I called to *you*;
O God, hear my *voice*;
let your ears consider *well*
the voice of my suppli-*cation*.

> If you were to note what is done a-*miss*,
> O God, who could *stand*?
> For there is forgiveness with *you*;
> therefore you shall be *feared*.

I wait for you, O God; my soul waits for *you*;
in your word is my *hope*.
My soul waits for you, more than sentries for the *morning*,
more than sentries for the *morning*.

> O Israel, wait upon *God*,
> for with God there is *mercy*.
> With God there is plenteous re-*demption*;
> God shall redeem Israel from all their *sins*.

[Psalm 130 OSH Psalter]

[*All:*]

Glory be to you,
O Trinity most holy and blessed,
who is now, ever was and ever shall be
unto endless ages, A-men.

(On holy days:)
> Glory to God: Source of all, Eternal Word and Holy *Spirit*,
> one God, holy and blessed *Trinity*,
> who is now, ever was and ever shall *be*
> unto endless ages, A-*men*.

Canticle of the Redeemed 195
(Magna et mirabilia)

(Sung at Sunday Morning Prayer in Ordinary Time, on the Festivals of the Ascension and the Holy Trinity; may be said or sung antiphonally, with the second voice taking the indented lines, or be sung together in unison or harmony throughout)

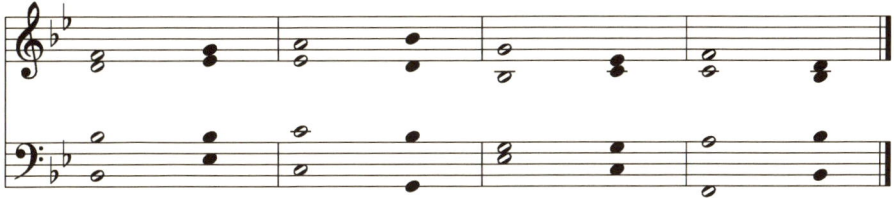

MUSIC: George A. MacFarren (1813-1887), alt.

Great and marvelous are your *works*,
mighty God of the *ages*;
just and true are your *ways*
among all *nations*.

> Who can fail to revere and glorify your name, Ado-*nai*,
> for you alone are *holy*?
> From nations throughout the world
>   we draw near and *worship you*,
> for your just and holy ways have been *revealed*.

[All:]

To you, O God, upon the *throne*,
to Christ the Lamb and to the Holy *Spirit*
be worship and praise, power and *glory*,
now and unto ages of ages, A-*men*.

[ADAPTED FROM REVELATION 15:3-4 AND 5:13
(EXCERPT FROM THE CANTICLE TO THE LAMB), OSL]

CANTICLES
196 Canticle of Thanksgiving
(Bonum est)

(May be sung at Vigils in Ordinary Time before Advent and at Monday Morning Prayer during Ordinary Time; may be said or sung antiphonally with the second voice singing the indented lines, the final strophe being in unison)

MUSIC: Jonathan Battishill (1738-1801), alt.

It is a good thing to give thanks to *God*
and to sing praises to your Name, O Most *High*;
to tell of your loving-kindness early in the *morning*
and of your faithfulness in the night *season*.

   It is a good thing to give thanks to *God*
   on the psaltery and on the *lyre*,
   and to the melody of the *harp*,
   for you have made me glad by your acts, O *God*,

(in unison)
I shout for *joy*
because of the works of your *hands*.
O God, how great are your *works*;
your thoughts are very *deep*.

[PSALM 92:1-5 OSH PSALTER]

[All:]
   Glory be to you,
   O Trinity most holy and blessed,
   who is now, ever was and ever shall be,
   unto endless ages, A-men.

(On holy days:)
   Glory to God, Source of All, Eternal Word and Holy *Spirit*,
   one God, holy and blessed *Trinity*,
   who is now, ever was, and ever shall *be*,
   unto endless ages, A-*men*.

CANTICLES

Canticle of Praise   197
(Venite Exultemus)
(Sung at Vigils and at Tuesday Morning Prayer in Ordinary Time; may be used as the gathering hymn at Services of Word and Table; may be said or sung antiphonally, with the second voice taking the indented lines, or be sung together in unison or harmony throughout)

MUSIC: Samuel Wesley (1766-1837), alt.

Come, let us sing to the Holy *One*;
let us shout for joy to the Rock of our sal-*vation*.
    Let us come before God's presence with thanks-*giving*,
    and raise a loud shout with *psalms*.

For you, O God, are a great *God*,
you are great above all *gods*.
    In your hand are the caverns of the *earth*,
    and the heights of the hills are yours *also*.

The sea is yours, for you *made it*,
and your hands have molded the dry *land*.
    Come, let us bow down and bend the *knee*,
    and kneel before God, our *Maker*.

[All:]
For you are our *God*;
we are the people of your *pasture*
and the sheep of your *hand*.
Oh, that today
    we would hearken to your *voice*

[PSALM 95:1-7 OSH PSALTER]

Glory be to *you*,
O Trinity most holy and *blessed*,
who is now, ever was and ever shall *be*
unto endless ages, A-*men*.

CANTICLES

(On holy days:)
  Glory to God: Source of all, Eternal Word and Holy *Spirit*,
  one God, holy and blessed *Trinity*,
  who is now, ever was and ever shall *be*
  unto endless ages, A-*men*.

198   Second Canticle of Isaiah

(Quaerite Dominum)
(Sung at Vigils in Advent and Wednesday Morning Prayer in Ordinary Time; may be said or sung antiphonally, with the second voice taking the indented lines, or be sung together in unison or harmony throughout)

MUSIC: Jonathan Battishill (1738-1801), alt.

"Seek me while I may be *found*;
call upon me while I am *near*.
Let wicked ones forsake their way of *life*
and sinners their ways of *thinking*.

  "Let them return to me so I may have mercy on *them*,
  to your God because I abundantly *pardon*.
  My thoughts are not your *thoughts*,
  neither are your ways my *ways*.

"As heaven is higher than *earth*,
my ways are higher than your *ways*;
so also are my *thoughts*
higher than your *thoughts*.

  "As rain and snow fall from heaven and do not return *there*,
  but water the earth, causing it to be *fruitful*–
  producing seed for the *sower*
  and food for the *eater*–

"so my word, which goes forth from my *mouth*,
does not return to me *empty*,
but accomplishes what I *will*
and succeeds in what I send it to *do.*"

[*All:*]
With joy you will go *out*,
and in peace you will be led *forth*.
Before you, the mountains and the hills will break out in joyous *praise*;
And all the trees of the field will clap their *hands*.

[Paraphrased from the Hebrew, Isaiah 55:6-12, CAB (OSL)]

[*All:*]
   Glory be to *you*,
   O Trinity most holy and *blessed*,
   who is now, ever was and ever shall *be*
   unto endless ages, A-*men*.

(*On holy days:*)
   Glory to God: Source of all, Eternal Word and Holy *Spirit*,
   one God, holy and blessed *Trinity*,
   who is now, ever was and ever shall *be*
   unto endless ages, A-*men*.

CANTICLES
199 Canticle of Joy
(Jubilate Deo)

(Sung at Vigils during Ordinary Time after Pentecost and at Thursday Morning Prayer in Ordinary Time; may be said or sung antiphonally, with the second voice taking the indented lines, or be sung together in unison or harmony throughout)

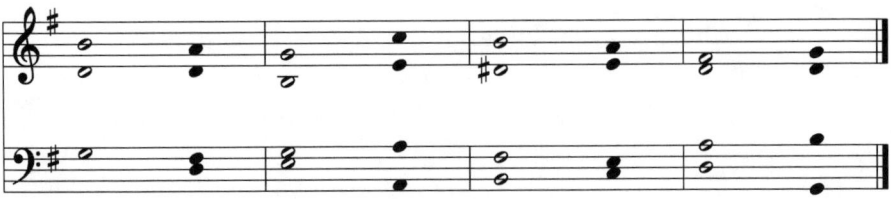

MUSIC: Stephen Elvey (1805-1860), alt.

May all lands be *joyful*
before you, O *God,*
serve you with *gladness*
and come before your presence with a *song.*

> For we know that you are *God;*
> you yourself have made us, and we are *yours;*
> we are your *people*
> and the sheep of your *pasture.*

We shall enter your gates with thanks-*giving,*
go into your courts with *praise,*
give thanks to *you*
and call upon your *Name.*

> For you are *good;*
> your mercy is ever-*lasting;*
> your faithfulness en-*dures*
> from age to *age.*

[PSALM 100, OSH PSALTER]

[All:]
> Glory be to *you,*
> O Trinity most holy and *blessed,*
> who is now, ever was and ever shall *be*
> unto endless ages, A-*men.*

CANTICLES

(On holy days:)
   Glory to God: Source of all, Eternal Word and Holy *Spirit*,
   one God, holy and blessed *Trinity*,
   who is now, ever was and ever shall *be*
   unto endless ages, A-*men*.

First Canticle of Isaiah 200
(Ecce Deus salvator)

(Sung at Friday Morning Prayer during Ordinary Time; may be said or sung antiphonally, with the second voice taking the indented lines, or be sung together in unison or harmony throughout)

MUSIC: James Turle (1802-1882), alt.

You, O God, are my sal-*vation*!
I am not afraid for I trust in *you*!
Indeed, you are my strength and my song, O *God*!
You have become my sal-*vation*!

   With joy you will draw water from the wells of sal-*vation*.
   On that day you will say,
      "Give thanks and call upon God's *name*!
   Make God's deeds known among the *nations*!
   Declare that God's name is ex-*alted*!"
[All:]
Sing to God, who has accomplished great *things*!
May this be made known throughout the whole *earth*!
Cry aloud and sing for joy, O Zion-*dweller*;
for the Holy One of Israel is great in your *midst*!

TRANSLATED FROM THE HEBREW: ISAIAH 12:2-6, CAB (OSL)

CANTICLES

[*All:*]

Glory be to you,
O Trinity most holy and blessed,
who is now, ever was and ever shall be
unto endless ages, A-men.

(*On holy days:*)

Glory to God: Source of all, Eternal Word and Holy Spirit,
one God, holy and blessed Trinity,
who is now, ever was and ever shall be
unto endless ages, A-men.

Note: *In this canticle, the use of the Hebrew YHWH is indicated by the word "God."*

201 Canticle of Wisdom

(*Sapientia aedificavit sibi donum*)

(*Sung for Saturday Morning Prayer in Ordinary Time; may be said or sung antiphonally, with the second voice taking the indented lines, or be sung together in unison or harmony throughout*)

MUSIC: William Crotch (1775-1847), alt.

Wisdom has built her house, setting up seven *pillars*.
She has prepared the food and wine and set her *table*.
    She has sent out her *servants*
        to call out from the heights above the *city*:

"Let those who want enlightenment *come*.
Come, taste my bread and drink my spiced *wine*.
    Give up your foolishness and *live*,
        And walk the path of under-*standing*."

If you are wise, your reward is *wisdom*;
if you teach the just, they grow in under-*standing*.
> Wisdom begins with reverence for *God*,
> and knowledge of the Holy One is *insight*.

[A PARAPHRASE ADAPTED FROM PROVERBS 9:1-6, 9-10, OSL]

[All:]
> Glory be to you,
> O Trinity most holy and blessed,
> who is now, ever was and ever shall be
> unto endless ages, A-men.

(On holy days:)
> Glory to God: Source of all, Eternal Word and Holy *Spirit*,
> one God, holy and blessed *Trinity*,
> who is now, ever was and ever shall *be*
> unto endless ages, A-*men*.

This 8th century Celtic cross from County Offaly, Ireland, depicts Christ below the Lamb of God surrounded by angels, along with scenes of Daniel and the Lion, David playing the harp, Abraham and Isaac, and a scene that seems to show the Trinity. Four Celtic knots may represent the four Gospels. Durrow Monastery was founded in the 6th century by St. Columba, one of the patron saints of Ireland, whose blessing is on page 59. The monastery also created the Book of Durrow, a sacred manuscript now housed at Trinity College, Dublin.

Public Domain Photo

PSALTER

On the Use of ADONAI

In recognition of the relational holiness of the divine name, the covenant name of God (YHWH in the text) is not pronounced. YHWH implies One whose "Isness" in the past, the present, and the future is actively and passionately present for us and all creation. No single name can embrace the rich meaning of the word. We have chosen to use ADONAI, a term of reverence, honor, and respect evoking both a sense of transcendence and personal relationship. ADONAI has been used from the time of post-exilic Judaism to replace YHWH. While the King James Version and subsequent versions and translations generally replaced YHWH with the word Lord, it is our hope that the use of ADONAI will remind us of richer and deeper meanings.

Litany Invoking ADONAI

The leader may read the first strophe, then all speak the boldfaced text with individuals taking turns reading the intervening lines for the remainder of the litany.

ADONAI—
  gathering up past, present and future
  in your presence for us and for all creation.

ADONAI—
  covenant maker,
  mighty deliverer,
  fire in the bush,
  wind over the deep.

ADONAI—
  water in the desert,
  ram in the thicket,
  promise under the terebinth,
  leaves for the healing of the nations,
  comforter of Jerusalem.

ADONAI—
  leveler of mountains,
  exalter of valleys,
  breath among the bones,
  shepherd in death's dark shadow,
  voice in the night,
  devouring fire.

ADONAI—
  liberator of slaves,
  judge of injustice,
  grieving for your people.
  Who is like you?
  Who is your equal?

ADONAI—
  strength of the weary,
  song of the redeemed,
  Holy of Holies,
  quail in the wilderness,
  "what is it" on the ground,
  mercy seat,
  name giver,
  "I am" with us.

ADONAI—
  yearning to be found,
  leading Israel like a flock,
  shutting the mouth of lions.

ADONAI—
  witness of misery,
  coming down among us,
  thrice holy,
  high and lifted up,
  calling us by name.

ADONAI! ADONAI!! ADONAI!!!

DTB

DIRECTIONS FOR USING THE PSALTER

When the psalm is spoken rather than sung:
- A liturgist may say the opening antiphon with the community repeating it.
- Then the liturgist may say the plainfaced lines with the community responding with the boldfaced lines, or
- The left side of the community may say the plainfaced lines with the right side of the community responding with the indented boldfaced lines.

When a psalm is sung to a psalm tone (see following page):
- The first note is a reciting note to which one or more syllables or words are sung; a slightly indented line indicates the reciting note is continuing on it.
- On the underlined syllable(s), move to the first black note.
- Sing the syllable(s) before the italicized syllable(s) on the second black note.
- Sing the italicized syllable(s) to the half note before the bar line.
- Follow the same directions for the second half of the psalm tone.
- The psalm tone is first played, then the cantor sings the antiphon with the community singing it in response.
- The cantor may then sing the plainfaced lines to the left with the community as a whole responding with the boldfaced lines, or
- The left side of the community may sing the plainfaced lines, with the right side of the community responding with the indented boldfaced lines.

At the conclusion of the psalm, the appropriate Gloria and the antiphon are said or sung by the community:

    Glory to you, O Trinity most <u>ho</u>ly and *blessed*
    one God, now and for-<u>ever</u>, A – *men*.

(on holy days:)
    Glory to God: Source of all, Eternal Word and <u>Ho</u>-ly *Spirit*,
    one God, holy and <u>bless</u>-ed *Trinity*,
    who is now, ever was and <u>ever</u> shall *be*
        unto endless <u>ages</u>, A-*men*.

The text for these psalms, a translation from the original languages, is that of the Priests for Equality in *The Inclusive Bible: The First Egalitarian translation* (Sheed & Word, 2007) and is used by permission.

Psalm tones one through five reprinted from *Lutheran Book of Worship*, © 1978 Augsburg Fortress. Used by permission.
Psalm tones six through eight by Dwight W. Vogel, OSL, 2011. © 2011 Order of Saint Luke.

Psalm 1 (see page 39)

Psalm 4 (see page 50)

Psalm 8

To the conductor: to be played on the Gittite harp
A psalm of David

Antiphon: When I behold your heavens, the work <u>of</u> your *fingers*,
who are we that you should <u>care</u> for *us*?

1 ADONAI, our Sovereign,
   how majestic is your Name in <u>all</u> the *earth*!
You have placed your glory a-<u>bove</u> the *heavens*!

2 **From the lips of infants and children**
   you bring forth words of <u>power</u> and *praise*,
   to answer your adversaries
   and to silence the <u>hostile</u> and *vengeful*.

3 When I behold your heavens,
   the work <u>of</u> your *fingers*,
the moon and the stars which you <u>set</u> in *place*,

4 **what is humanity that you should be <u>mindful</u> of *us*?**
   Who are we that you should <u>care</u> for *us*?

5 You have made us barely <u>less</u> than *God*,
and crowned us with <u>glory</u> and *honor*.

6 **You have made us responsible**
   for the works <u>of</u> your *hands*,
   putting all things <u>at</u> our *feet*,

7 all sheep and oxen, yes, even the beasts <u>of</u> the *field*,

8 the birds of the air, the fish of the sea,
   and whatever swims the paths <u>of</u> the *seas*.

9 **ADO-<u>NAI</u>, our *Sovereign*,**
   how majestic is your Name in <u>all</u> the *earth*!

Gloria and Antiphon

Psalm 23

A psalm of David

Antiphon: A<small>DONAI</small>, you <u>are</u> my *shepherd.*
you anoint my head with oil,
my cup <u>o</u>-ver-*flows!*

1   A<small>DONAI</small>, you <u>are</u> my *shepherd.*
    I want <u>no</u>-thing *more.*
2   **You let me lie down <u>in</u> green *meadows*;**
    you lead me beside <u>rest</u>-ful *waters*:
3   You re-<u>fresh</u> my *soul.*
    You guide me to lush pastures
       for the sake <u>of</u> your *Name.*
4   **Even if I'm surrounded by shadows of Death,**
    I fear no danger, for <u>you</u> are *with me*.
    Your rod and your staff,
       they <u>give</u> me *courage*.
5   You spread a table for me
       in the presence <u>of</u> my *enemies,*
    and you anoint my head with oil,
       my cup <u>o</u>-ver-*flows!*
6   **Only goodness and love will follow me**
       all the days <u>of</u> my *life*,
    and I will dwell in your house, A<small>DONAI</small>,
       for days <u>with</u>-out *end*.

Gloria and Antiphon

Psalm 27

By David

Antiphon: Teach me your way, <u>A</u>-*DO*-*NAI*,
   and lead me on <u>a</u> straight *path.*

1   A<small>DONAI</small>, you are my light, my salvation;
       whom <u>will</u> I *fear?*
    You are the fortress of my life;
       of whom will I <u>be</u> a-*fraid?*
2   **When my enemies attack me,**
       spreading vicious lies about me
          where-<u>ever</u> they *go*,

        they, my adversaries and foes,
           will <u>stum</u>ble and *fall*.

3   Though an army mounts a siege against me,
      my heart <u>will</u> not *fear*;
    though war break out against me,
      I will <u>still</u> be *confident*.

4   **One thing I ask of you, A<small>DONAI</small>,**
              one <u>thing</u> I *seek*:
          that I may dwell in your house
          all the days of my life,
          to gaze on your beauty
          and to meditate <u>in</u> your *Temple*.

5   You will keep me safe in your shelter
      when <u>trouble</u> a-*rises*,
    you will hide me under the cover of your Tabernacle;
      you will set me on a rock,
        high and <u>out</u> of *reach*.

6   **Then I'll be able to hold my head up,**
              even with my enemies sur-<u>round</u>-ing *me*.
          I will offer in your Tabernacle
            sacrifices of great joy;
            I will sing and make music to you, <u>A</u>-<small>DO-*NAI*</small>!

7   Hear me when I call, <u>A</u>-<small>DO-*NAI*</small>!
    Have mercy on me and <u>an</u>-swer *me*!

8   **Y<u>o</u>u say to my heart, "<u>Seek</u> my *face*,"**
          and so it is your <u>face</u> I *seek*!

9   Don't hide your face from me;
      don't turn your faithful one a-<u>way</u> in *anger*.
    Don't reject me, don't desert me,
      O God of my salvation,
      for you are my <u>on</u>-ly *help*.

10   **Even if my own <u>parents</u> re-*ject me*,**
          you, A<small>DONAI</small>, <u>will</u> ac-*cept me*.

11   Teach me your way, <u>A</u>-<small>DO-*NAI*</small>,
    and lead me on a straight path
      because <u>of</u> my *enemies*.

12   **Don't surrender me to the will <u>of</u> my *enemies*;**
          for defamers rise up against me <u>breath</u>-ing *violence*.

13 Even so I have *confidence*
       that I'll see the goodness of Adonai
          in the land of the *living*!
14   **Wait for God; stand tall**
          and let your heart take *courage*!
          Yes, wait for A-do-*nai*!

Gloria and Antiphon

Antiphon: Teach me your way, A-do-*nai*,
           and lead me on a straight *path*.

Psalm 46

For the conductor
By the disciples of Qorach: A song for soprano voices

Antiphon: Be still, and know that I am *God*!
           I will be exalted up-on the *earth*.

1 God is our refuge and our *strength*,
     who from of old has helped us in our dis-*tress*.
2   **Therefore we fear nothing,**
            even if the earth should open up in front of *us*
            and mountains plunge into the depths of the *sea*,
3 even if the earth's waters rage and *foam*
     and the mountains tumble with its *heaving*.
4   **There is a river whose streams**
            gladden the city of *God*,
         the holy dwelling of the Most High.
5 God is in its midst, it will nev-er *fall*;
   God will help it at *daybreak*.
6   Though nations are in turmoil and em-pires *crumble*,
            God's voice resounds, and it melts the *earth*.
7 Mighty Ado-*nai** is with *us*,
   our stronghold is the God of *Israel*!
8   **Come, see what Ado-*nai* has *done*;**
         God makes the earth *bounteous*!
9 God has put an end to war
     from one end of the earth to the *other*,
   breaking bows, splintering spears,
     and setting chariots on *fire*.

10   Be still, and know that I am *God*!
            I will be exalted among the nations;
            I will be exalted up-on the *earth*.

11   Mighty ADO-NAI* is *with us*
        our stronghold is the God of *Israel*!

Gloria and Antiphon
*Lit. YHWH Sabaoth (God of Hosts)

Psalm 51:1-17

For the conductor
A psalm of David
Written when the prophet Nathan came to him
after David had relations with Bathsheba

Antiphon: O God, create a clean heart in *me*,
                put into me a new and stead-fast *spirit*.

1   O God, have mercy on *me*!
      Because of your love and your great compassion,
         wipe a-way my *faults*;
2   **wash me clean of my *guilt*;**
           purify me of my *sin*.
3   For I am aware of my *faults*,
      and have my sin constant-ly in *mind*.
4   **I sinned against you alone,**
            and did what is evil in your *sight*.
         You are just when you pass sentence on me,
            blameless when you give *judgment*.
5   I was born in sin, con-ceived in *sin*
6   yet you want truth to live in my innermost being;
      teach me your *wisdom*!
7   **Purify me with hyssop until I am *clean*;**
           wash me until I am purer than new-fallen *snow*.
8   Instill some joy and gladness in-to *me*;
      let the bones you have crushed re-joice a-*gain*.
9   **Turn your face from my *sins*,**
           and wipe out all my *guilt*.
10   O God, create a clean heart in *me*,
      put into me a new and stead-fast *spirit*;

11	**do not banish me <u>from</u> your *presence*,**
	do not deprive me of your <u>ho</u>-ly *Spirit*!
12	Be my savior again, re-<u>new</u> my *joy*,
	keep my spirit <u>stead</u>y and *willing*;
13	**and I will teach trans-<u>gressors</u> your *ways*,**
	and sinners will re-<u>turn</u> to *you*.
14	Save me from bloodshed, O God, God of <u>my</u> sal-*vation*,
	and my tongue will ac-<u>claim</u> your *justice*.
15	**Open my lips, <u>A</u>-DO-NAI,**
	and my mouth will de-<u>clare</u> your *praise*.
16	Sacrifice gives <u>you</u> no *pleasure*;
	were I to present a burnt offering,
	you <u>would</u> not *have it*.
17	**My sacrifice, O God, is a <u>bro</u>-ken *spirit*;**
	you will not scorn this crushed and <u>bro</u>-ken *heart*.

Gloria and Antiphon

Antiphon: O God, create a clean <u>heart</u> in *me*,
             put into me a new and <u>stead</u>-fast *spirit*.

Psalm 62

To the conductor: for Jeduthun
A psalm of David

Antiphon: Trust in God <u>always</u>, my *people*;
             pour out your hearts before <u>God</u> our *refuge*.

1	In God alone my soul finds rest,
	for my deliverance <u>comes</u> from *God*,
2	who alone is my rock, my salvation, my fortress:
	I will <u>never</u> be *shaken*.
3	**How long will <u>you</u> be-*siege me***
	as though I were a crumbling wall
	or a <u>totter</u>-ing *fence*?
4	They connive to push me off a cliff;
	they delight in <u>tell</u>-ing *lies*.
	With their mouths they utter blessing,
	but in their <u>hearts</u> they *curse*. *Selah*
5	**In God alone my soul finds rest,**
	for my deliverance <u>comes</u> from *God*,
6	**who alone is my rock, my salvation, my fortress:**
	I will <u>never</u> be *shaken*.

7 Only in God—my deliverance, my glory—
    my <u>refuge</u> is *God*.
8 Trust in God always, my people;
    pour out your hearts before <u>God</u> our *refuge*.
9 **Humankind is but a breath,**
    mortals are <u>just</u> an il-*lusion*.
    Put them on the scales
    and the balance is thrown off:
    they weigh <u>less</u> than a *breath*.
10 Do not trust in extortion,
    or put false hopes in <u>sto</u>-len *goods*;
   do not set your heart on riches
    even when <u>they</u> in-*crease*.
11 **For God has said only one thing,**
    only two do I know:
    that to God a-<u>lone</u> be-longs *power*,
12 **and that you, ADONAI, are loving—**
    you repay all people according <u>to</u> their *deeds*.

Gloria and Antiphon

Psalm 67

To the conductor: for strings
A song of praise

Antiphon: Let the peoples shout and <u>sing</u> for *joy*;
           let all the <u>peo</u>-ples praise *you*!

1 O God, show us <u>kindness</u> and bless *us*,
   and make your face <u>smile</u> on *us*!   *Selah*
2 **For then the earth will ac-<u>knowledge</u> your *ways*,**
   and all the nations will know of your <u>power</u> to *save*.
3 Let the peoples <u>praise</u> you, O *God*,
   let all the <u>peo</u>-ples *praise you*!
4 **Let the nations shout and <u>sing</u> for *joy*,**
   for you dispense true justice to the world—
   you guide the nations <u>of</u> the *earth*!
5 Let the peoples shout and <u>sing</u> for *joy*;
   let all the <u>peo</u>-ples *praise you*!
6 **The land has <u>given</u> its *harvest*:**
   God, our <u>God</u>, has *blessed us*.

7 May God bless us, and may God <u>be</u> re-*vered*
even to the ends <u>of</u> the *earth*!

Gloria and Antiphon

Psalm 91

Antiphon: You will call upon me, and I will <u>an</u>-swer *you*;
I will be with <u>you</u> in *trouble*.

1 You who dwell in the shelter of <u>the</u> Most *High*
and pass the night in the shadow <u>of</u> Shad-*dai*,
2 **say: "A**DONAI**, my refuge and my <u>moun</u>-tain *fortress*,**
my God in <u>whom</u> I *trust*!"
3 For ADONAI says: "I will rescue you <u>from</u> the *snare*,
and shield you from <u>poi</u>-soned *arrows*.
4 **I will cover you <u>with</u> my *pinions*;**
under my wings you will take refuge;
my faithful-<u>ness</u> will *shield you*.
5 You have no need to fear the prowlers of the night
or the arrow that <u>flies</u> by *day*,
6 the plague that lurks in the shadows
or the scourge that <u>stalks</u> at *noon*.
7 **Though a thousand fall at <u>your</u> left *side***
and ten thousand at your right,
it will never <u>come</u> near *you*.
8 You will see it <u>pass</u> you *by*,
and witness the punishment of the corrupt
with <u>your</u> own *eyes*.
9 **Because you have made me your refuge**
and have me <u>as</u> your *stronghold*,
10 **no evil will befall you,**
and no disaster will come <u>near</u> your *tent*.
11 For I will command my angels
to guard you where-<u>ever</u> you *go*.
12 They'll carry you in their hands
so you don't hurt your foot <u>on</u> a *stone*.
13 **Y**o**u'll tread on the young lion**
as easily as one <u>does</u> a *cobra*;
you'll trample down both <u>lion</u> and *serpent*.
14 Because you love me, I <u>will</u> de-*liver you*;

I will rescue you
   because you ac-knowledge my *Name*.
15   **You will call upon me, and I will an-swer *you*;**
   I will be with you in trouble;
   I will deliver you and hon-or *you*.
16 I will satisfy you with a long *life*
   and show you my sal-*vation*.

Gloria and Antiphon

Psalm 92:1-5 *(Canticle of Thanksgiving, Worship Resources 196)*

Psalm 95:1-7 *(Canticle of Praise, Worship Resources 197)*

Psalm 96

Antiphon: Sing to Adonai, bless God's *Name*!
   Proclaim God's salvation day after *day*.

1 Sing to Adonai a new *song*!
   Sing to Adonai, all the *earth*!
2 **Sing to Adonai, bless God's *Name* —**
   God's salvation day after *day*.
3 Declare God's glory a-mong the *nations*,
   God's marvels to ev-ery *people*.
4   **Adonai is great, most worthy of *praise*,**
   Adonai is to be revered a-bove all *gods*.
5 The gods of the nations are *nothing*,
   they don't exist, but Adonai cre-ated the *universe*.
6   **In God's presence are splendor and *majesty*,**
   in God's sanctuary power and *beauty*.
7 Pay tribute to Adonai, you tribes of the *people*;
   pay tribute to the God of glory and *power*.
8   **Pay tribute to the glorious Name of A-do-*nai*;**
   bring out the offering, and carry it in-to God's *courts*.
9 Worship Adonai, ma-jestic in *holiness*;
   tremble in God's presence, all the *earth*!
10   **Say among the nations,**
     Adonai reigns su-*preme*!
   The world stands firm and unshakable:
     Adonai will judge each nation with strict *justice*.

11 Let the heavens be glad; let the <u>earth</u> re-*joice*;
   let the sea roar and all <u>that</u> it *holds*!
12 **Let the fields exult and all <u>that</u> is *in them*!**
   Let all the trees of the forest sing for joy
13   **at the presence of Adonai, for <u>God</u> is *coming*.**
   God is coming to <u>rule</u> the *earth*;
   to rule the world with justice
      and its <u>peoples</u> with *truth*!

Gloria and Antiphon

Antiphon: Sing to Adonai, <u>bless</u> God's *Name*!
      Proclaim God's salvation <u>day</u> after *day*.

Psalm 100 *(Canticle of Joy, Worship Resources 199)*

Psalm 103
(By David)

Antiphon: As high as heaven is a-<u>bove</u> the *earth*,
      so great is your love for those <u>who</u> re-*vere you*.

1 Bless Ado-<u>nai</u>, my *soul*!
   All that is in me, bless God's <u>ho</u>-ly *Name*!
2 **Bless Ado-<u>nai</u>, my *soul*,**
   and remember <u>all</u> God's *kindnesses*!
3 The One who forgives all your sins
   is the One who heals <u>all</u> your *dis-eases*;
4 the One who ransoms your life from the Pit
   is the One who crowns you
      with <u>love</u> and *tenderness*.
5 **The One who fills your years <u>with</u> pros-*perity***
   also gives you an eagle's <u>youth</u>-ful *energy*.
6 How you love justice, Adonai!
   You are always on the side of <u>the</u> op-*pressed*.
7 You revealed your intentions to Moses,
   your <u>deeds</u> to *Israel*.
8 **You are tender and compassionate, Adonai,**
      slow to anger, and <u>al</u>-ways *loving*;
9 **your indignation doesn't endure forever,**
      and your anger lasts only for <u>a</u> short *time*.
10 You never treat us as our <u>sins</u> de-*serve*;

you don't repay us in kind for the in-<u>jus</u>tices we *do*.
11   **For as high as heaven is a-<u>bove</u> the *earth*,**
           so great is [your] love for those <u>who</u> re-*vere you*.
12 As far away as the east is <u>from</u> the *west*,
    That's how far you remove our <u>sins</u> from *us*!
13   **As tenderly as parents <u>treat</u> their *children*,**
           that's how tenderly you treat your worshipers, <u>A</u>-DO-*NAI*!
14 For you know [of] what <u>we</u> are *made*;
    you remember that we're <u>nothing</u> but *dust*.
15   **We last no longer than *grass*,**
            live no longer <u>than</u> a *wildflower*;
16   **one gust of wind and we are *gone*,**
            never to be <u>seen</u> a-*gain*.
17 Yet your love lasts from age to *age*
     for those who revere you, <u>A</u>-DO-*NAI*,
    as does your goodness to our <u>child</u>-ren's *children*,
18   **to those who <u>keep</u> your *Covenant***
           and remember to o-<u>bey</u> your *precepts*.
19 You have established your throne <u>in</u> the *heavens*,
    and your reign extends over <u>ev</u>-ery-*thing*.
20   **Bless ADONAI, you *angels*,**
            you powers who <u>do</u> God's *bidding*,
           attentive to every <u>word</u> of com-*mand*!
21 Bless ADONAI, you <u>heaven</u>-ly *host*,
    you faithful ones who en-<u>force</u> God's *will*!
22   **Bless ADONAI, all *creation*,**
            to the far reaches <u>of</u> God's *reign*!
        Bless ADO-<u>NAI</u>, my *soul*!

Gloria and Antiphon

Psalm 104

Antiphon: I will sing to you <u>all</u> my *life*,
                I will make music for my God as long <u>as</u> I *live*.

1   Bless ADO-<u>NAI</u>, my *soul*!
     ADONAI, my God, how <u>great</u> you *are*!
        Clothed in majesty and *glory*,
2   **wrapped in a <u>robe</u> of *light*,**
        you stretch the heavens out <u>like</u> a *tent*.

3   You lay the beams for your palace
       on the <u>waters</u> a-*bove*;
    you use the clouds as your chariot
       and ride on the wings <u>of</u> the *wind*;
4   **you use the <u>winds</u> as *messengers***
         and fiery flames <u>as</u> at-*tendants*.
5   You fixed the earth on its foundations so it can <u>ne</u>-ver *totter*,
6   and wrapped it with the Deep as with a robe,
       the waters over-<u>topping</u> the *mountains*.
7   **At your rebuke the waters bolted,**
            fleeing at the sound <u>of</u> your *thunder*,
8   **cascading over the mountains, into the valleys,**
            down to the reservoir you <u>made</u> for *them*;
9   you imposed boundaries they must <u>ne</u>-ver *cross*
    so they would never again <u>flood</u> the *land*.
10   **You set springs gushing in ravines,**
            running down be-<u>tween</u> the *mountains*,
11   **supplying water for wild animals**
            and attracting the <u>thirsty</u> wild *donkeys*;
12 the birds of the air make their nests <u>by</u> these *waters*
    and sing a-<u>mong</u> the *branches*.
13   **From your palace you water the highlands**
            until the ground is sated by the fruit <u>of</u> your *work*;
14   **you make fresh grass grow for cattle**
            and plants for us to cultivate
            to get food <u>from</u> the *soil*,
15 wine to <u>cheer</u> our *hearts*,
    oil to make our faces shine,
       and bread to sus-<u>tain</u> our *life*.
16   **The trees of A**DONAI **drink their fill,**
            those cedars of Lebanon
17   **where birds <u>build</u> their *nests***
            and, on the highest branches,
            the stork <u>makes</u> its *home*.

18   For the wild goats there are <u>the</u> high *mountains*,
     and in the crags the rock <u>bad</u>-gers *hide*.
19   **You made the moon to <u>tell</u> the *seasons*,**
     and the sun knows <u>when</u> to *set*:
20   you bring darkness on, night falls,
     and all the forest <u>animals</u> come *out* –
21   savage lions roaring for their prey,
     claiming their <u>food</u> from *God*.
22   **The sun rises, they retire,**
     going back to lie down <u>in</u> their *lairs*,
23   **and people go out to work,**
     to labor again <u>un</u>-til *evening*.
24   A<small>DONAI</small>, what variety you have created,
     arranging every-<u>thing</u> so *wisely*!
  The earth is filled with your <u>cre</u>-a-*tivity*!
25   **There's the vast expanse of the Sea,**
     teeming with <u>count</u>-less *creatures*,
  living things large and small,
26   **with the ships going to and fro**
     and Leviathan whom you made to <u>fro</u>-lic *there*.
27   All creatures depend on you
     to feed them at the <u>prop</u>-er *time*.
28   Give it to them; they gather it up;
     open your hand; they <u>are</u> well *satisfied*.
29   **Hide your face; <u>they</u> are *terrified*.**
     Take away their breath; they die and re-<u>turn</u> to *dust*.
30   Send back your breath; fresh <u>life</u> be-*gins*
     and you renew the face <u>of</u> the *earth*.
31   **Glory forever to <u>A</u>-<small>DO</small>-*<small>NAI</small>*!**
     May you find joy in <u>your</u> cre-*ation*!
32   You glance at the earth <u>and</u> it *trembles*;
     you touch the mountains <u>and</u> they *smoke*!
33   **I will sing to you <u>all</u> my *life*,**
     I will make music for my God as long <u>as</u> I *live*.
34   May these re-<u>flections</u> of *mine*
     give as much pleasure as <u>God</u> gives *me*!
35   **May the corrupt vanish from the earth**
     and the violent ex-<u>ist</u> no *longer*!
  Bless A<small>DONAI</small>, my soul! <u>Al</u>-le-*luia*!

PSALTER

Gloria and Antiphon

Antiphon: I will sing to you <u>all</u> my *life*,
I will make music for my God as long <u>as</u> I *live*.

(In Lent replace the line with the following:

Bless ADO-<u>NAI</u>**, my** *soul*!)

Psalm 113

Antiphon: From the rising of the sun <u>to</u> its *setting*,
praised be the Name of <u>A</u>-DO-*NAI*!

1 [Alleluia!] You faithful of ADO-<u>NAI</u>, give *praise*,
praise the Name of <u>A</u>-DO-*NAI*!

2 **Blessed be the Name of <u>A</u>-**DO-***NAI*,**
from now and <u>for</u> all *times*!

3 From the rising of the sun <u>to</u> its setting,
praised be the Name of <u>A</u>-DO-*NAI*!

4 **You are high over all nations, <u>A</u>-**DO-***NAI*!**
Your glory tran-<u>scends</u> the *heavens*!

5 Who is like you, ADO-<u>NAI</u>, our *God*?
Enthroned so high,

6   you need to stoop
to see the sky <u>and</u> the *earth*!

7 **You raise the poor from the dust,**
and lift the needy <u>from</u> the *dung heap*,

8 **to give them a place at the table with rulers,**
with the leaders <u>of</u> your *people*.

9 You give the childless <u>couple</u> a *home*
filled with the joy of many children. <u>Al</u>-le-*luia*!

Gloria and Antiphon

(In Lent, replace the last line of the psalm with:
filled with the joy of <u>man</u>-y *children.*

Psalm 117 *(see p. 35)*

Psalm 130 *(see Canticle of Redemption, Worship Resources 194)*

Psalm 131
A Song of Ascents
By David

Antiphon: Israel, rely on ADONAI <u>like</u> a *child*,
now <u>and</u> for-*ever*!

1   ADONAI, my heart has no <u>lofty</u> am-*bitions*,
my eyes don't <u>look</u> too *high*.
   I am not concerned with <u>great</u> af-*fairs*
   or marvels be-<u>yond</u> my *scope*.
2   It's enough for me to keep my soul tranquil
and quiet like a child in its <u>moth</u>-er's *arms*;
my soul is as content as a <u>nurs</u>-ing *child*.
3   **Israel, rely on ADONAI <u>like</u> a *child*,**
   now <u>and</u> for-*ever*!

Gloria and Antiphon

Psalm 134 *(see page 50)*

Psalm 138
By David

Antiphon: I bow down and <u>praise</u> your *Name*
because of your <u>love</u> and *faithfulness*.

1   I thank you with <u>all</u> my *heart*;
I sing your praise be-<u>fore</u> the *gods*.
2   **I bow down in front of your holy Temple**
      and praise your Name
      because of your <u>love</u> and *faithfulness*,
      for you have put above everything else
      your Name <u>and</u> your *word*.
3   When I called, you <u>an</u>-swered *me*;
you made me bold and <u>strong</u> of *heart*.
4   **All the rulers of the earth will praise you, ADONAI,**
      when they hear the words <u>of</u> your *mouth*.
5   **They will sing about what you have done, ADONAI,**
      and about <u>your</u> great *glory*.

6 Even though you are so high above,
   you care <u>for</u> the *lowly*
   and see arrogant people from <u>far</u> a-*way*.
7 **Even when I'm surrounded by troubles,**
   you <u>keep</u> me *safe*;
   you oppose the anger of my enemies,
   and save me with <u>your</u> right *hand*.
8 You will do everything you have <u>prom</u>-ised *me*.
   ADONAI, your love is eternal;
   don't abandon the work <u>of</u> your *hands*.

Gloria and Antiphon

Psalm 139:1-11 *(see p. 51)*

Psalm 141 (selected) *(See Evening Prayer Canticle, Worship Resources 67 to 69)*

Psalm 146 *(See p. 5)*

Psalm 148

Antiphon: Praise the Name of <u>A</u>-DO-*NAI*
              whose Name a-<u>lone</u> is ex-*alted,*

1 [Alleluia!] Praise ADONAI <u>from</u> the *heavens*;
   praise God <u>in</u> the *heights*!
2 **Praise God, <u>all</u> you *angels*;**
   praise God, <u>all</u> you *hosts*!
3 Praise God, <u>sun</u> and *moon*;
   praise God, all you <u>shin</u>-ing *stars*!
4 **Praise God, you <u>high</u>-est *heavens*;**
   and you waters a-<u>bove</u> the *heavens*!
5 Let them praise the Name of <u>A</u>-DO-*NAI*,
   by whose command they <u>were</u> cre-*ated*.
6 **God established them for-<u>ever</u> and *ever***
   and gave a decree which <u>won't</u> pass a-*way*.
7 Praise ADONAI <u>from</u> the *earth*,
   you sea creatures and <u>o</u>-cean *depths*,
8 **lightning and hail, <u>snow</u> and *mist*,**
   and storm winds that ful-<u>fill</u> God's *word*,
9 mountains and all hills,
   fruit trees <u>and</u> all *cedars*,

10 wild animals and all cattle,
    small animals and <u>fly</u>-ing *birds*,
11 **rulers of the earth, leaders of all nations,**
   all the judges <u>in</u> the *world*,
12 **young men and young women,**
   old <u>people</u> and *children*;
13 let them all praise the Name of A<small>DONAI</small>
    whose Name a-<u>lone</u> is ex-*alted*,
14 whose majesty transcends heaven and earth,
    and who has raised up a Horn <u>for</u> God's *people*
        to the praise of the faithful, the <u>children</u> of *Israel*,
        the people dear to God! [<u>Al</u>-le-*luia*!]

Gloria and Antiphon

(In Lent, omit the Alleluias, and replace the last line with:
   the people <u>dear</u> to *God*!

Psalm 150

Antiphon: Let everything *that* has *breath*
            praise <u>A</u>-<small>DO</small>-*<small>NAI</small>*!

1 [Alleluia!] We praise you, A<small>DONAI</small>, <u>in</u> your *sanctuary*;
  we praise you in your <u>migh</u>-ty *skies*!
2 **We praise you for your <u>power</u>-ful *deeds*;**
  we praise you for your over-<u>whelm</u>-ing *glory*!
3 We praise you with the blast <u>of</u> the *trumpet*;
  we praise you with <u>lyre</u> and *harp*!
4 **We praise you with <u>timbrel</u> and *dance*;**
  we praise you with <u>strings</u> and *flute*!
5 We praise you with <u>clash</u>-ing *cymbals*;
  we praise you with re-<u>sound</u>-ing *cymbals*!
6 **Let everything *that* has *breath***
  praise A<small>DONAI</small>! [<u>Al</u>-le-*luia*!]

Gloria and Antiphon

In Lent, omit the Alleluias, and replace the last line with:
   Praise <u>A</u>-<small>DO</small>-*<small>NAI</small>*!

The Rule of Life and Service of the Order of Saint Luke

Chapters are encouraged to review the meaning of these vows from time to time, as well as to relate the topics which they study together to one or more of the vows. The ancient monastic practice of reading one of the vows and its commentary aloud when members of the Order break bread together is commended. All members are encouraged to review annually the way in which they are living the Rule of Life and Service with their confessor, spiritual director, spiritual companion, or another member of the Order. The vows are guides for our journey rather than markers of arrival at our destination.

Excerpts from 1.2.d-f of The Customary of The Order of Saint Luke

We affirm the apostolic hope:
> With the apostles and the Church through the ages, we affirm Jesus Christ, Sacrament of the presence of God, as the source of our hope. We take our name from Saint Luke the Evangelist, and seek to be incorporated into the paschal mystery he proclaims. We pray that we may be formed by the incarnation, life, death, resurrection, ascension, gift of the Holy Spirit, and coming again of Jesus Christ. We are sent forth to proclaim and to live the hope that good news brings.

We live for the Church of Jesus Christ:
> We believe that the Church is the Body of Christ and we are called to worship, learning, community, and service as members of that Body. We affirm our fidelity to oneness in Christ in the Church truly catholic, truly apostolic, truly evangelical, and truly reformed which supercedes all division by denomination, and which we believe God will gather from a broken Christendom. Our mission includes calling the Church to liturgical and sacramental renewal, and seeking to bring the healing grace of Christ to all Creation.

We seek the sacramental life:
> We are called to become aware of God's presence through eucharistic living. We seek to live out our baptism into Christ's death and resurrection. We receive with gratitude all that God has given us and offer it up to God. We receive it again from God, transformed to use for the sake of the world. We join the Church though the ages and around the world in recognizing that all time is in God's

hands. As we faithfully pray the Daily Office, and live so as to embody our prayers, we endeavor to live the sacramental life. By so doing, we seek to be formed as a means of grace for all those we meet and serve in Christ's name.

We promote the corporate worship of the Church:
We believe that the corporate worship of the Church is liturgy — the work of the people on behalf of all creation — which is our response to the revelation of God's grace. Through our collective memory and our shared hope, the Holy Spirit acts in Word and Sacrament making present to us the saving acts of God and transforming us so that we can be God's people. Through our worship, we seek the glorification of God and the sanctification of the Church. This worship is offered in the name of the community which claims it as the manifestation of its own identity and mission.

We seek to encourage the Church to worship with vitality and integrity, appropriating the rites and services of the Church, historically and ecumenically grounded, which enable us to worship together in the name of Jesus Christ. We honor the worship traditions of the past and seek to be open to new ways of expressing the heritage of faith they embody in ways that speak to us and for us in the present. We witness to the saving and transforming work of God which renews us in Christ's Body, the Church, through the continual offering up of our lives to God.

We magnify the sacraments:
We believe that the sacraments are Christ's gift to the Church. Individually and corporately we are called to lift up these mysteries in the life of the Church as means of grace through which we are formed as Christian disciples.

Through the baptismal covenant, we are incorporated into the death and resurrection of Jesus Christ. God calls us to live out the redemptive, liberating, justice-seeking ministry of Jesus. We seek to deepen our understanding of the Church, of the significance of the baptismal covenant, and the Eucharist for Christian discipleship and service.

We believe that the Eucharist re-presents the life-gift of Jesus Christ in which the living spirit of Christ is truly present to us, preserving and reforming Christ's Body, the Church. Frequent celebration of the

Eucharist forms us in the sacramental life empowering us to become Christ's healing presence in the world.

We accept the call to service:
By virtue of our baptism, God calls each of us to ministries which are a proclamation of Christ, seeking wholeness for Creation. Through sacramental, prophetic, and pastoral ministries we turn in openness and love to the world. We identify with the whole community of humankind, especially those who live on the margins, and invite people to touch our lives as we touch theirs. Thus may all know the perfect joy of being reconciled with God. In community with our brothers and sisters, we seek to discern ways in which we are called to serve God in the Order, the Church, and the world.

Adopted in its present form by the Council of The Order of Saint Luke, October, 2001

ACKNOWLEDGEMENTS AND INDICES

Metrical Index

(Numbers refer to Worship Resources)

(SM) 66.86
  CARLISLE, 135
  SUTTON COMMON, 100

(CM) 86.86
  MORNING SONG, 70
  ST. AGNES, 42
  ST. FLAVIAN, 118
  SERAPH, 48

(CMD) 86.86 D
  CAROL, 114
  ELLACOMBE, 73
  KINGSFOLD, 55, 120
  REMEMBER, 45
  VOX DILECTI, 102

(LM) 88.88
  CONDITOR ALME SIDERUM, 79, 89, 97
  EISENACH, 141
  HURSLEY, 23
  OLD 100th, 149
  ROCKINGHAM, 121
  SONG 34, 138
  SPLENDOR PATERNAE, 58
  TALLIS' CANON, 61, 81
  UFFINGHAM, 60
  VENI, CREATOR SPIRITUS, 127
  WHEN JESUS WEPT, 82

(LMD) 88.88 D
  CANDLER, 147
  SCHMÜCCKE DICH, 26

55.54 D
  BUNESSAN, 50

55.65
  SOUTHWELL, 103

55.76 D
  ST. LUKE, 76

667.667
  LE CANTIQUE DE SIMEON, 66

6.6.11 D
  DOWN AMPNEY, 84

76.76 D
  MERLE'S TUNE, 56
  MUNICH, 27

  ST. KEVIN, 122

7.7.6 D
  O WELT, ICH MUSS DICH LASSEN, 85

77.74
  TAKE ME AS I AM, 95

77.77
  CANTERBURY, 130

7.7.7.7 D
  ABERYSTWYTH, 92
  HOLLINGSIDE, 40

77.77.77
  DIX, 117
  PILOT, 22
  RATISBON, 57

78.77
  STAY WITH US, 74

84.84.888.4
  AR HYD Y NOS, 87

86.866
  LOBT GOTT, IHR CHRISTEN, 126

86.86 D
  ST. MATTHEW, 136

86.86.86
  MORNING SONG, 94

87.87
  MERTON, 111
  STUTTGART, 139

87.87 D
  BEECHER, 133
  HOLY MANNA, 28
  HYMN TO JOY, 131
  MUSICA MUNDANA, 30
  NETTLETON, 36, 132
  NEWPORT, 110
  PROMISE, 107

87.87.87
  ALLELUIA DULCE CARMEN, 123
  LAUDA ANIMA, 24, 93
  SICILIAN MARINERS, 31
  SOUTHWELL, 103

Metrical Index (continued)

88.44.88 with refrain
LASST UNS ERFREUEN, 134

88.63 with refrain
HEALER OF OUR EVERY ILL, 96

88.88 with refrain
GELOBT SIE GOTT, 140
VENI, VENI, EMMANUEL, 108

88.88.88
ST. PETERSBURG, 69

98.89
KEMPER, 46

98.98
EUCHARISTIC HYMN, 41
ST. CLEMENT, 77

9.9.9.11
PILGRIM, 49

10.7.10.7
GIFTS, 34

10.10.10.10
ADORO TE DEVOTE, 39
PENETENTIA, 37

10.11.10.12
NEW HOPE, 38

11.10.11.10
MORNING STAR, 115
STRENGTH AND STAY, 78

11.11.11.5
CHRISTE SANCTORUM, 86

11.11.11.11
ANNIVERSARY SONG, 29

12.9.12.9
WONDROUS LOVE, 148

Index of Tune Names
Numbers refer to Worship Resources

ABERYSTWYTH, 92
ADORO TE DEVOTE, 39
ALLELUIA DULCE CARMEN, 123
AMBROSIAN, 9
ANNIVERSARY SONG, 29
AR HYD Y NOS, 87
AS THE GRAINS, 35

BEECHER, 133
BUCKHANNON, 51
BUNESSAN, 50
BURLEIGH, 6

CANDLER, 147
CANTERBURY, 130
CARLISLE, 135
CAROL, 114
CHRISTE SANCTORUM, 86
CONDITOR ALME SIDERUM, 79, 89, 97
CRANHAM, 113

DIX, 117
DONA NOBIS PACEM, 106

DOWN AMPNEY, 84

EISENACH, 141
ELLACOMBE, 73
EUCHARISTIC HYMN, 41

GELOBT SIE GOTT, 140
GIFTS, 34

HEALER OF OUR EVERY ILL, 96
HOLLINGSIDE, 40
HOLY MANNA, 28
HYMN TO JOY, 131
HURSLEY, 23

KEMPER, 46
KINGSFOLD, 55, 120

LASST UNS ERFREUEN, 134
LAUDA ANIMA, 24, 93
LE CANTIQUE DE SIMEON, 66
LOBT GOTT, IHR CHRISTEN, 126

MERLE'S TUNE, 56, 142

Index of Tune Names (continued)

MERTON, 111
MEETING, 32
MICHAEL, 143
MORNING SONG (CM), 70
MORNING SONG (86.86.86), 94
MORNING STAR, 115
MUNICH, 27
MUSICA MUNDANA, 30

NETTLETON, 36, 132
NEW HOPE, 38
NEWPORT, 110

OLD 100th, 149
O WELT, ICH MUSS DICH LASSEN, 85
ONLY BREAD, 43
ORTHODOX KYRIE, 4

PEACE, 47
PENETENTIA, 37
PICARDY, 25
PILGRIM, 49
PILOT, 22
PROMISE, 107

RATISBON, 57
REMEMBER, 45
RHUDDLAN, 104
RISING, 124
ROCKINGHAM, 121

ST. AGNES, 42
ST. CLEMENT, 77
ST. FLAVIAN, 118

ST. KEVIN, 122
ST. LUKE, 76
ST. MATTHEW, 136
ST. PETERSBURG, 69
SCHMÜCCKE DICH, 26
SERAPH, 48
SICILIAN MARINERS, 31
SOMOS DEL SEÑOR, 52
SONG 34, 138
SOUTHWELL, 103
SPIRIT, 128
SPLENDOR PATERNAE, 58
STAR OF COUNTY DOWN, 71
STAY WITH US, 74
STUTTGART, 139
STRENGTH AND STAY, 78
SUTTON COMMON, 100

TAKE ME AS I AM, 95
TALLIS' CANON, 61, 81

UFFINGHAM, 60

VENEZ DIVIN MESSIE, 109
VENI, CREATOR SPIRITUS, 127
VENI, VENI, EMMANUEL, 108
VOX DILECTI, 102

WHEN JESUS WEPT, 82
WONDROUS LOVE, 148

Index of Authors, Composers, Arrangers, Translators and Sources

(Unless preceded by a "p," numbers refer to Worship Resources.)

Acts of the Apostles
  2:42-47, p. 95
  20:32, pp. 11, 97
Adam of St. Victor, 142
African American Spirituals, 6
Alcuin of York, p. 38
Aquinas, Thomas, 39
Ambrose of Milan, 58, 78, p. 35
Ambrosian Hymn, 185
Ambrosian Sacramentary, 98, p. 70
Amiel, Henri-Frederick, 88

Bach, J. S., 85, 141
Baker, Henry W., 112
Battishill, Jonathan, 183 II & III, 198
Beasley, William J., 15, 19, 144, 194, pp. 13-15
Beethoven, Ludwig von, 131
Benedict, Daniel T., 54, 80, 91, 119, 168, 177, pp. 5, 7, 12-15, 29, 31, 46, 54, 57, 58, 62, 294
Berthier, Jacques, 186
Billings, William, 82
Bianco of Sienna, 84
Bonor, Horatio, 37, 102
Book of Common Prayer, noted as BCP throughout
Bortniansky, Dimitri, 69
Bourgeous, Louis, 66, 149
Bridges, Robert S., 66, 85
Brokering, Herbert, 74
Brown, Cheryl A., 198, 200
Bruxvoort-Colligan, Richard, 34, 90
Burton-Edwards, Taylor, 188, pp. 30, 63

Caswall, E., 11, 173
Catholicum Hymnologicum Germanicum, 122
Chandler, John, 60, 126
Chatfield, Donald F., 129
Clark, Jeremiah, 60
Codex Alexandrinus, 187

Coffin, Henry Sloane, 108
Colossians 1:11-13
Cooney, Rory. 71
Corinthians, I
  5:7-8, p. 57
  11:25-26, p. 14
Corinthians, II
  4:6-7, pp. 51, 58
  5:17-19, 161
  13:14, 174, pp. 11, 78, 97
Cotter, Jim, 172, pp. 49, 54
Cranmer, Thomas, 183, pp. 74, 79
Crisp, George R.. 3, 21, 32, 76, 110, 145, pp. 16-18
Croft, William, 136, 185
Crotch, William, 183 V, 201
Crouch, Timothy J., 88, 171, pp. 31, 42, 45, 46, 64, 67, 68
Cruger, Johann, 26
Davis, Robert B., 49
Davis, Roby Furly, 112
Day's The Whole Book of Psalms, 118
Dearle, Edward, 37
Dix, William C., 117
Douglas, C. Winfred, 70
Duba, Arlo D., 67
Duck, Ruth, 27, 29, 38, 55, 73, 89, 94, 97, 103, p. 43
Dunstan, Sylvia G., 28
Dykes, J. B., 40, 42, 78, 102

Elkins, Heather Murray, 147, pp. 22-24
Eller, W. Vincent, 36
Ellerton, John, 77, 78
Elvey, Steven, 20, 63, 183 I & VI, 192, 199
Emerson, Luther Orlando, 87
Ephesians 3:16-19, p. 52
Erickson, John, 10
Eslinger, Elise, 12, 52
Ezekiel 36:24-28, p. 35
Fleischaker, Mary Frances, 139

Authors Index (continued)

Fleischner, Eva, 108
Flynn, Sarah, 69, 140, 150
Franck, Johann, 26
French Carol, 25

Gauntlett, Henry, 139
Gelasian Sacramentary, 83, p. 46
Gerhardt, Paul, 85
Gesangbuch, Meiningen, 27
Gesangbuch der Herzogl, 73
Gibbons, Orlando, 130, 138
Goodrich, David, 62
Goss, John, 24, 93, 183 IV, 190
Grant, John Webster, 127
Greek, 66
Grove, William Boyd, 24
Gould, John R., 22
Gulbert, Charles Mortimer, p. 42

Haas, David, 47
Harding, J. P., 115
Haugen, Marty, 35, 65, 96
Havergal, William H., 57
Heber. Reginald, 41, 87, 115, p. 54
Hebrews 13:20-21, 176, pp. 52
Helmore, Thomas, 108
Herbert, Petrus, 86
Hernaman, Claudia F. I., 118
Hermann, Nicholas, 126
Hodges, Edward, 131
Hodges, John S. B., 41
Holst, Gustav, 113
Hopkins, Gerhard Manley, 39
Hopson, Hal H., 56, 142
Hort, F. J. A., 78
Hosmer, Frederick Lucian, 87
Hutchings, Arthur, 109

Irish, 71
  see also Gaelic
Isaac, Heinrich, 85
Isaiah
   12:2-6, 200
   30:15, p. 31
   40:30-31, p. 37
   55:6-12, 198

J. G. Werner's Choralbuch, 57
James 5:13-14, p. 69
Jarboe, Robert S., 7, 45, 101
Jeremiah 3:15, p. 94
John 8:12, 63, pp. 41, 57
John, I
   1:5-7, 159
   1:8-9, p. 68
John of Damascus, 122
Josselyn-Cranson, Heather, 30, 48, 55,
   68, 86, 120, 141, 188-189, 194, pp. 8, 9
Julian of Norwich, 105

Kahn, Fred, 104
Katholisches Gesangbuch, 23
Keble, John, 61
Ken, Thomas, 81, 149
Kentucky Harmony, 70
Kimos, Constance, 124
Kocher, Conrad, 11

Langston, Archbishop Stephen, 173
Latin, 60, 79, 106, 108, 111, 112, 126,
   127, 138
LeCroy, Anne K., 138
Littledale, Richard F., 84
Liturgy of St. James, 25
Liturgy of St. Mark, 75
Lockhart, Charles, 135
Longfellow, Samuel, 130
Luke
   1:39-56, 70-71, 73, pp. 15, 45, 64
   1:68-79, 188-189, pp. 30, 63
   2:14, 186-187
   2:19, 178
   2:29-32, 89-90, 192, pp. 11, 55, 64, 84
   2:46-55, p. 14
   3:22, p. 16
   4:1-13, 118
   6:20-26, p. 74
   6:38, p. 9
   7:11-17, p. 14
   8:15, p. 18
   9:45, 47 p. 18
Luke (continued)

Authors Index (continued)

10:36-37, p. 18
13:30, p. 18
14:13,14,21, p. 18
15:1-32, pp. 9, 18
15:20-24, p. 8
16:25, p. 18
17:2, p. 18
18:16-17, p. 18
19:10, p. 18
21:3-4, p. 18
22:14-20, p. 13
22:24-28, pp. 14, 18
24:13-35, 74
24:29, 63, p. 41, 57
Lyte, Henry F., 93

MacFarren, George, 195, 196
Maclagan, William Dalrymple, 141
Manley, Jim, 1, 43, 44, 128
Mant, Richard, 135
Mark 1:12-13, 118
Marshall, Jane, 29
Martens, Mason, 9
Mason, Jackson, 142
Mason, John, 136
Maurus, Rabanus, 127
Mary of St. Philip, 109
Mattes, John Casper, 26
Matthew
  5:3-12, 99
  6:9-13, 8-12
  11:28-30, p. 52
Melkite Greek Catholic Church "Alleluia Press," p. 58
Mendelssohn, Felix, 27
Miller, Edward, 121
Montgomery, James, 42
Moore, William, 28
Monk, Edwin G., 185
Monk, William Henry, 111
Morse, Anna J., 46
Mother Thunder Mission, 12
Moultrie, Gerard, 25
Mozarabic Sacramentary, p. 46

Native American, 12

Neale, John Mason, 60, 108, 112, 122, 123, 138
Newman, John Henry, pp. 53, 83
New Zealand Prayer Book, pp. 53, 82
Niceta, Bishop, 185
Numbers 6:24-26, pp. 48, 71, 84

O'Donnell, Michael J., 178, pp. 5, 15-18, 68, 76

Paris Antiphoner 1681, 86
Parry, Joseph, 92
Patterson, Patricia, 31, 120, 124
Pellegrin, Abbe, 109
Pelz, Walter, 74
Perry, Michael, 56, 100
Peter, I
  1:3, p. 82
  2:14, 160,
  5:10, 181
Philippians
  2:6-11, p. 40
  4:4-7, 182, p. 77
Paget, Bishop Frances, p. 31
Playford, John L., 18
Power, David N., p. 44
Proulx, Richard, 94
Proverbs 9:1-6, 201
Prudentius, Aurelius Clemens, 112
Psalms
  see also PSALTER, pp. 297-313
  4:8, pp. 55, 61, 83
  23, p. 82
  30:5, pp. 55, 61, 83
  35:9, 63, pp. 41, 57
  46:10, 1
  51:15, 53, p. 27
  63:1-8, 62
  90:14, p. 28
  92:1-5, 196
  95:1-7, 197, pp. 28, 59
  100, 199
  103:1-4, pp. 67, 73, 78
  113:1-3, pp. 27, 37
  130, 194
  139:1-11, p. 51

Authors Index (continued)

Psalms (continued)
  141, 67-69
  145, 131
  146, p. 5

Rankin, Jeremiah E., 46
Revelation 5:13 & 15:3-4, 195
Riley, John Athelstan Laurie, 134
Robinson, Robert, 132
Roman Breviary, p. 53
Romans
  1:4-8, p. 82
  5:8. p. 77, 79
  6:8, p. 69
  6:9-11, p. 57
  12:2, p. 77, 80
  15:13, p. 43
Rossetti, Christiana G., 113
Russian Orthodox Liturgy, 4, 99

St. Columba, p. 59
Sarum, 64, pp. 55, 61, 74, 79, 83
Saliers, Don E., 51, pp. 18-21
Scanelli, Peter, 60
Schein, J. H., 141
Schönes Geistlichen Gesangbuch of 1609, 140
Scholefield, Clement Cottevill, 77
Scottish, 147, 187
Sears, Edmund H., 114
Second Supplement to Psalmody in Miniature, 121
Shanley, Aelred Seton, 82
Sleeth, Natalie, 107
Song of the Three, 184
Strathdee, Jim, 11, 116
Sutter, John W., p. 31

Tallis, Thomas, 53, 61, 81
Terstergen, Gerhard, 72
The European Magazine and Review 1792, 31
Theodoricus Petrus of Nyland, 112
Thomas a Kempis, p. 9
Timothy, I, 1:15, 160
Turle, James, 20, 63, 183 VI, 192, 193

United Church of Canada, 164, pp 69

van Dyke, Henry. 131
Vaughn Williams, Ralph, 84, 134
Vogel, Dwight W., 49, 105, 125, 137, 143, 146, 183, pp. 18-21, 39, 40, 42, 57
Vogel, Linda J., 157

Warren, Norman L., 100
Watts, Isaac, 121
Webbe the elder, Samuel, 123
Webber, Samuel, 121
Welsh, 87, 104
Wesley, Charles, 23, 40, 57, 92, 133
Wesley, Samuel, 197
William Damon's Psalms, 1579, 103
Willis, Richard Storrs, 114
Winkworth, Catherine, 26, 86
Winter, Miriam Therese, 70
Witt, C.F., 139
Woodford, James R., 39
Wyeth, John, 36, 132

Zechariah, Canticle of, 188-189, p. 30
Zimbabwe, 13
Zundel, John, 133

Topical Index

(Unless preceded by a "p," numbers refer to Worship Resources.)

Advent Hymns, 108-111
  Creator of the Stars, 79
Adonai
  Collect for Morning, 54
  Litany, p. 294
Affirmations of Faith, 162-165
Agnus Dei, 19-22
Alleluias, 8-12
Ascension Hymn, 126
Assurance of Pardon, 159-161; pp. 9, 43, 58
Awareness, Prayers of, 156-157, p. 43
  See also Confession, Prayers of

Beatitudes, 99
Benedictus, 55-56
Blessings
  Apostolic, 174
  Aaronic, 175
  Resurrection, 176
Canticles
  First of Isaiah, Ecce Deus Salvator, 200
  of Creation, Benedicte, omnia opera, 184
  of God's Glory, Gloria in Excelsis, 186, 187
  of Joy, Jubilate Deo, 199
  of the Holy Trinity, Te Deum Laudamus, 185
  of Mary, Magnificat,
    70-71, 73. 190-191, p. 45
  of Praise, Venite Exultemus, 197, p. 59
  of the Redeemed, Magna et Mirabilia, 195
  of Redemption, De Profundis, 194
  of the Resurrection, Pascha Nostrum, 193
  Second of Isaiah, Quaerite Dominum, 198
  of Simeon, Nunc Dimittis,
    89-90, 192, pp. 10, 55, 61, 64
  of Thanksgiving, Bonum est, 196
  of Wisdom, Sapientia Aedificavit, 201
  of Zechariah, Benedictus,
    55-58, 188-189, p. 30

Christmas Hymns, 112-114
  Let All Mortal Flesh, 25
  Creator of the Stars, 79
Commendations
  Good Shepherd, bless, 75
  Life is short, 88
  May the High God of Heaven, 177
  O God, the light of the minds, 83
  The God of all grace, 181
Commissions
  Life is short, 88
  May the High God of Heaven, 177
  May the word of Christ, 59
  May we be made strong, 180
  Rejoice in the Lord always, 182
  We have seen strange things, 178
  You are witnesses, p. 11
Communion, 37-45
Compline, pp. 48-55
  Hymns:
    God Who Made the Earth, 87
    Advent/Christmas, 79
    OT after Epiphany, 81
    Lent, 82
    Great 50 Days, 84
    OT after Pentecost, 85
    OT before Advent, 86
    Prayers, pp. 53-54
Confession, Prayers of, 154-158, pp. 8, 43
  in Eastertide, 125
  see also Awareness, Prayers of
Creeds, 162-165

Doxology, 149

Easter
  see The Great Fifty Days
Epiphany Hymns, 115-117
Evening Prayer
  Canticle of Mary, 70-71, 73, p. 45
  Entrance of the Light, 63, p. 41
  Evening Hymns, 74-78
    Hymn of Promise, 107
  Evening Prayer Canticle, 67-69

Topical Index (continued)

Hymn of Light, *Phos hilaron*, 65-66, p. 42
Prayers, 98, pp. 45-47
Thanksgiving for Light, 64, p. 42

Gathering Hymns
Be Still, 2
Christ Whose Glory, 57
Come Thou Fount, 132
God Whose Love, 24
Joyful, Joyful, We Adore, 131
Let All Mortal Flesh, 25
Maker of the Earth, 31
Planets Humming, 30
Gloria, 3 forms of the, p. 44
Going Forth, 174-179
  Hymns, 47-52
    All Shall Be Well, 105
    Dona Nobis Pacem, 106
    Hymn of Promise, 107
    Love Divine, All Loves Excelling, 133
    I Am the Light of the World, 116
Gospel Acclamations
  Alleluias, 8-12
  Gloria Christi, Gratia Tibi, 18
  in Lent, 17
Great Fifty Days Hymns, 122-124
  Come Down O Love Divine, 84
Great Litany, The, 183
Great Thanksgiving One, pp. 12-15
  Musical Responses, 144
  Alleluia, 15
  Agnus Dei, 19
  Kyrie, 5
  Lord's Prayer, 8 or 10
Great Thanksgiving Two, pp. 15-18
  Musical Responses, 145
  Alleluia, 16
  Agnus Dei, 21
  Kyrie, 3
  Lord's Prayer, 11
Great Thanksgiving Three, pp. 18-21
  Musical Responses, 146
  Alleluia, 14
  Agnus Dei, 20
  Kyrie, 4
  Lord's Prayer, 9

Great Thanksgiving Four, pp. 22-24
  Musical Responses, 147-149
  Alleluia, 13
  Agnus Dei, 22
  Kyrie, 6
  Lord's Prayer, 12

Healing, Service of Prayer for, pp. 67-71
  Hymns, 92-97
    For the Healing of the Nations, 104
    Heal Me, Hands of Jesus, 100
  Prayers, 98, pp. 70-71
Holy Spirit
  Hymns, 127-128, 130
    Come Down, O Love Divine, 84
    Maker of the Earth, 31
  Prayers, 129, 172
    Veni Sancte Spiritus, 173

Intercessions, 166-170
  Sung Intercessions, 166
Investiture of Officers, pp. 94-97

Kyrie eleison, 3-7

Lent
  Hymns, 118, 119-121
    What Wondrous Love, 148
  Prayer Anticipating Easter Vigil, 119
Lifelong Vows, Profession of, pp. 91-93
(St.) Luke, Feast of
  Hymns: 140-142
  Prayers, 150, p. 95

Marian Feasts
  Hymns, 138-139
    Creator of the Stars of Night, 79
    In the Bleak Midwinter 113
    Ye Watchers and Ye Holy Ones, st. 2, 134
  Thanksgiving for the Light, 137
Morning Prayer, pp 27-33
  Canticle of Zechariah, 55-56, 188-189, p. 30
  Hymns, 57-62
    see Gathering Hymns
    see also 109-142 for seasonal hymns
  Opening Sentence, 53
  Prayer, 54

Topical Index (continued)

Nunc Dimittis, 89-90, 192, pp. 10, 55, 61, 64

Order of Saint Luke, The
Affirmation of Vows, 53
Collect for the Order, 151
Hymns
    Go in Christ's Name, 49
    Life and Service, 143
Intercessions for the Order, 152
Investiture of Officers, pp. 94-97
Litany for the Order, 150
Profession of Vows, pp. 87-93

Pentecost
Hymns, 127-130
    Maker of the Earth and Ocean, 31
Prayers, 129, 173, p. 34

Phos Hilaron, 65-66, p. 42

Praise Hymns
Christ, Whose Glory Fills the Skies, 57
Come, Thou Fount of Every Blessing, 132
Joyful, Joyful We Adore You, 131
Love Divine, All Loves Excelling, 183
O Christ, Our Hope, 126
Of the Parent's Heart Begotten, 112
Praise God, From Whom All Blessings, 149
Praise, My Soul, the King of Heaven, 93
Salvation, Glory and Power, 147

Prayer Hymns
Christ, Whose Glory Fills the Skies, 57
Come Down, O Love Divine, 84
Come God and Hear My Cry, 103
Jesus, Lover of My Soul, 92
Maker of the Earth and Ocean, 31
Shepherd of Souls, 42
Spirit, Spirit of Gentleness, 128
Take, Oh Take Me As I Am, 95

Prayers
Evening, p. 46-47
for Healing, 98, pp. 70-71
for Illumination, p. 3
for Transformation, 72
Morning, 59, p. 31
Night, 80, 91
of Affirmation, 171
of the Day, p. 4
of the People, 166-173, pp. 7, 60

Presentation of the Gifts, 34-36
Profession of Vows, pp. 87-93
Reconciliation
Corporate Rite, pp. 72-77
Hymns, 99-104
    Be Still, 1
    Give Thanks to God, 94
    Have Mercy, 7
    Healer of Our Every Ill, 96
    Jesus, Lover of My Soul, 92
    Praise My Soul the King of Heaven, 93
    Take, O Take Me as I Am, 95
Individual Rite, pp. 78-80
Prayers
    for Reconciliation, 154-161
    for Transformation, 72
    9th Century Prayer, 98

Rule of Life and Service, p. 314
Saint Luke, 140-142
Saints, 134-138
Evangelists, 142

Sending Forth, 47-52
see also Going Forth, Commission, and Commendation

Silence, Invitation to, 1-2
Spirit, Holy
see Pentecost
Spirit Prayer, 172

Thanksgiving for the Light
Thanks be to You (Sarum), 64
Prayers, 64, 137, p. 42
Transitus
Hymns, 92, 105-107, 133, 135, 148
Rite, pp. 81-84

Word and Table, pp. 4-24
Gathering Hymns, 23-32
    O the Depth of Love, 40

Communion Hymns, 37-45
    As the Grains of Wheat, 35
    At this Table, 36

Topical Index (continued)

Invitation, Words of, 33, pp. 8, 10
Invitation, Sung, 45
Presentation of the Gifts, 34-36
   Jesus Took the Bread, 38
Great Thanksgivings
   (see Great Thanksgivings above)

Sending Forth Hymns, 46-52
Shepherd of Souls, 42
We Meet at His Table (with
   alternate words), 32

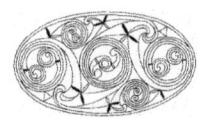

Index of First Lines and Common Titles

(Unless preceded by a "p," numbers refer to Worship Resources. Quotation marks signify the opening line of spoken acts of worship)

A thousand resurrections are happening, 124
"Adonai, give strength to the weary," 98
"Adonai, passionate presence," 54
"Adonai, gathering up past, present and future," p. 294
Affirmation of Vows, 153
Agnus Dei, 19-22, p. 82
All shall be well, 105
Alleluia, 13-16
Alleluia! Christ our Passover is sacrificed for us, 193
"All loving and all caring God," p. 68
All praise to thee, O God, this night, 81
All who hunger, gather gladly, 28
All you works of the Most High, 184
"Almighty God, send down your Holy Spirit upon," p. 90
"Almighty God, to whom all hearts are open," pp. 74, 79
Ambrosian Hymn, 185
Apostles' Creed, The, 162
"Arise, O Spirit of Life," 72
As the grains of wheat once scattered, 35
As the grain on scattered hillsides, 27
As the shadows deepen, 76
As with gladness those of old, 117
At this table bread is broken, 36
"Author of love," p. 75-76

Beatitudes, 99
"Be present, Spirit of God, within us," p. 53
Be still and know, 1-2

Index of First Lines and Common Titles (continued)

"Beginning and End of all things," p. 7
Benedicite, omnia opera Domini, 184
Benedictus, 55-56, 188-189, p. 30
Blessed are the poor in spirit, 99
"Blessed be the holy and blessed Trinity," 157
"Blessed are you, God of all grace," 137
"Blessed are you, O Holy One," p. 58
Blessed be the God of Israel, 56
Bonum est, 196
Bread of the world in mercy broken, 41
Breaking of the Bread, 44
"Bridegroom of Creation," p. 62
Brightest and best of the stars of the morning, 115
"By Word and water, God renews us this day," p. 27
Canticles (see Topical Index)
Christ beside us, Christ before us, 49
Christ, whose glory fills the skies, 57
Collect for The Order of Saint Luke, 151, p. 32
Colossians 3:16-17, 59
Come down, O Love Divine, 84
"Come from the east and the west", 33
Come, God, and hear my cry, 103
"Come, Holy Spirit, come, radiate your light," 173
Come, let us sing to the Holy One, 197
Come quickly, Lord, I call on you, 69
Come, sing ye choirs exultant, 142
Come, sinners, to the gospel feast, 23
Come, thou fount of every blessing, 132
Come, you faithful, raise the strain, 122
Creator of the stars of night, 79

"Dawn from on high," p. 28
"Dawn Treader, as light fades," p. 58
"Day dies away," p. 53
De Profundis, 194
Deck yourself, my soul, with gladness, 26
Divinum Mysterium, pp. 19-21
Dona nobis pacem, 106

Ecce Deum Salvator, 200
"Eternal Spirit, Life-Giver, Pain-Bearer," 172, p. 54
Evening Prayer Canticle, 67-69

Fast falls the night, 82
Fleeing from the city, 44
For all your saints, 135

Index of First Lines and Common Titles (continued)

For the healing of the nations, 104
For you shall go out in joy, 51

Gaelic, 50
Give ear, give ear, good Christians all, 123
Give thanks to the Source, 29
Give thanks to God who hears our cries, 94
Gloria, Gloria in excelsis Deo, 186
Gloria in Excelsis Deo, 187
Glory be to God on high, 187
Glory be to you, O Christ, 18
Go in Christ's name, 49
"God be in my head and in my understanding," 179
God, be merciful to us, 17
God be with you till we meet again, 46
"God of abundance" p. 31
"God of all mercy, we confess," 156
"God of life and light," p. 42
God calls us to forgive, 101
"God of mystery and mercy," p. 4
"God of tender compassion," p. 46
"God of the day and of the night," 80
God that made the earth and heaven, 89, p. 54
"God who sees us, sun sets," 91
God with Us, Emmanuel, 110
God whose love is reigning o'er us, 24
"Great Shepherd, bless your flock this night," 75
"Great Spirit, hear and help us as we pray," 129
 "Gracious God, who loves all and forgets none," 167
Great and marvelous are your works, 195
"Great God of power and love," 168
Great Litany, The, 183
Greek, 3-6, 66

Hark! A thrilling voice is sounding, 111
Heal me, hands of Jesus, 100
Healer of our every ill, 96
Here, O my Lord, I see thee face to face, 37
"Holy and gracious God, I have sinned," 158
Holy One, now let your servant go, 90
"Holy Spirit, come upon us this hour," p. 34
Holy Spirit, Truth divine, 130
"Holy Wisdom, in your lovingkindness, " p. 38
How shall I sing the majesty, 136
Hymn of Promise, 107

I am the Light of the world, 116

Index of First Lines and Common Titles (continued)

I heard the voice of Jesus say, 102
"Immersed in baptismal waters of God's grace," 119
In peace, let us pray to the Lord, 166
"In peace we will lie down and sleep," pp. 55, 61, 83
In the bleak midwinter, 113
In the bulb there is a flower, 107
In the morning I will sing glad songs of praise, 62
Intercessions for The Order of Saint Luke, 152, p. 47
It came upon a midnight clear, 114
It is a good thing to give thanks to God, 196

Jesus Christ, you are the light of the world, 63
Jesus, Lamb of God, 19-22
Jesus, lover of my soul, 92
Jesus took the bread, 38
Joyful, joyful, we adore you, 131
Joyous light of endless glory, 65
Jubilate Deo, 199

"Keep watch, dear Lord, with those," p. 53
"Kindle in our hearts, O God," p. 59
Kyrie eleison, 3-6

Let all mortal flesh keep silence, 25
"Life is short and we have never enough time," 88
Litany for The Order of Saint Luke, 150
Litany Invoking Adonai, p. 294
"Living God, make us conscious of your healing," 66
"Living, loving God," p. 39
Lord, have mercy, 7, p. 9
Lord Jesus, who through forty days, 118
"Lord Jesus Christ, who came to set us free," p. 40
Lord's Prayer, 8-11
Love divine, all loves excelling, 133
"Loving and merciful God, we offer you," p. 8
"Loving God, you abide with us," pp. 90, 93
"Loving God, you come to us with healing," p. 69

Maker of the earth and ocean, 31
Magna et mirabilia, 195
Magnificat, 70-71, 73, 190-191, p. 45
Mary, Canticle of, see Magnificat
Mary, woman of the promise, 139
May all lands be joyful before you, O God, 199
"May God bless us and keep us," 175
"May the God of peace," 176
"May the God whose mercy is from everlasting," 160

Index of First Lines and Common Titles (continued)

"May the High God of heaven refresh you," 177
"May the word of Christ dwell in you richly," 59
"May we be made strong," 180
"Merciful God, we have not loved you," 155
"Merciful God, we pray that all," p. 70
"Mighty and everlasting God," p. 32
"Mighty and merciful God, we have erred," 154
"Mighty and merciful God, your healing presence," p. 71
"Mighty God, from whom all thoughts of truth," p. 31
"Mighty God, through whom we come to know," p. 5
"Mighty God, we pray that all our brothers and sisters," p. 70
"Mighty God, who called your servant Luke," p. 95
"Most holy God, the source of all good desires," p. 46
"Most merciful God, we confess," p. 68
My heart sings out with joyful praise, 73
My prayers rise as incense, 67, 68
My soul cries out with a joyful shout, 71
My soul gives glory to my God, 70
My soul proclaims the greatness of the Lord, 190
My soul proclaims your greatness, Lord, 191

New every morning is the love, 61
"New every morning is your love," p. 29
Nicene Creed, The, 163
Now bless the God of Israel, 55
Now God be with us for the night is closing, 86
Now let your servant go in peace, 89
Now, Lord, you let your servant go in peace, 192
Now that daylight fills the skies, 60
Nunc Dimittis, 89-90, 192, pp. 10, 55, 61, 64

O blessed Luke whose sacred page, 141
O Christ, our hope, 126
O come, Divine Messiah, 109
O come, O come, Emmanuel, 108
O Creator Spirit, by whose breath, 127
O gladsome light, O grace of our Creator's face, 66
"O God, because you are the source of all life," 171
"O God, by whom we are guided in judgment," p. 31
"O God, in your servants you manifest the signs," p. 47
O God, open our lips, 53
"O God, save your people and bless your heritage," 170
"O God, the life of all who live," p. 46
"O God, the light of the minds that know you," 83
"O Lord, support us all the day long," pp. 53, 83
"O most Holy and Beloved," p. 49
O sisters, brothers, let us sing of Luke, 140

Index of First Lines and Common Titles (continued)

"O Shepherd of us all," 151, pp. 8, 90, 96
O splendor of God's glory bright, 58
O Strength and Stay, upholding all creation, 78
O the depth of love divine, 40
Of the Parent's heart begotten, 112
On the dark road to Jerusalem, 120
Our Father, 8-11
Out of the depths have I called, 194

Pascha nostrum, 193
Peace before us, 47
Phos Hilaron, 65, 66, p. 42
Planets humming as they wander. 30
Praise God from whom all blessings flow, 149
Praise, my soul, the king of heaven, 93
Pues Si Vivimos, 52
Quaerite Doniminum, 198

"Rejoice in the Lord always," 182
Remember, 45
"Remove all the stains of sin," p. 9
"Risen Savior, at this hour," p. 37
"Risen Son, day dies away," p. 62

Saint Patrick's Breastplate, 50
Salvation, glory and power to God, 147
Sapientia Aedificavit Sibi Donum, 201
Seek me while I may be found, 198
Shepherd of souls, refresh and bless, 42
"Show us your mercy, O Lord," 169
Simeon, Canticle of
    see *Nunc Dimittis*
Somos del Señor, 52
Spirit Prayer, 172
Spirit, Spirit of Gentleness, 128
Stay with us till night has come, 74

Take, O take me as I am, 95
Te Deum Laudamus, 185
"Thanks be to you, O God, author of eternal light," 63
The beauteous day now closes, 85
The broken bread, the outpoured wine, 45
The day you gave, O Lord, is ended, 77
The gifts of God for the people of God, 34
"The God of all grace who has called us," 181
"The grace of our Lord Jesus Christ," 174
"The message we have heard from Jesus," 159

Index of First Lines and Common Titles (continued)

The Word whom earth and sky and sea, 138
Thee we adore, O Savior, 39
This is only bread, you know, 42
"Triune God, Giver of grace," p. 43

Veni, Creator Spiritus, 127
Veni, Sancte Spiritus, 173
Venite Exultemus, 197, p. 59
"Visit this place, O Lord," p. 53
"We are not alone, we live in God's world," 164
"We believe in God, eternal yet ever-moving One," 165
We bless you, Adonai, God of Israel, 188
We cannot know what worship is, 48
"We have this assurance from God," 161
"We have seen strange things today," 178
We meet at his table, 32
What wondrous love is this, 148
When I survey the wondrous cross, 121
When we are living, it is in Christ Jesus, 52
When we must bear consistent pain, 97
When we struggle in confusion, 110
"When we turn our feet toward home," p. 8
Wisdom has built her house, 201
With Luke the Evangelist we proclaim, 143

Ye watchers and ye holy ones, 134
You are God, we praise you, 185
You, O God, are my salvation, 200
Your light has filled our lives, 125
Zechariah, Canticle of
   see *Benedictus*

Acknowledgements

Responsible efforts have been made to trace the owner(s) and/or administrator(s) of each copyright. We regret any omission and will, upon written notice, make the necessary correction(s) in subsequent printings.

ANZPB/NKMOA, A New Zealand Prayer Book – Ne Karatha Mihinare o Aotearoa, Anglican Church in Aotearoa, New Zealand and Polynesia, P O Box 87188, Meadowbank, Auckland 1742

BCP, The Book of Common Prayer (1979), The Church Hymnal Corporation; see Church Publishing, Inc.

ELLC, English Language Liturgical Consultation, www.englishtexts.org

LTP (Liturgical Training Publications), Archdiocese of Chicago: Liturgy Training Publications; 1-800-933-1800. www.LTP.org

Acknowledgements (continued)

NRSV, *New Revised Standard Version of the Bible*, Division of Christian Education of the National Council of the Churches of Christ in the United States of America; publisher: Thomas Nelson, Inc., Nashville, TN 37214

OSH, (Psalms in The Daily Office), The Order of Saint Helena, 3042 Eagle Drive, Augusta, GA 30906-3346

TEV *Today's English Version of the Bible* from The American Bible Society, 1965 Broadway, New York, NY 100223

TIB (Psalter), *The Inclusive Bible* by Priests for Equality, Sheed and Ward (imprint of Rowman & Littlefield Publishers, Inc.), 4501 Forbes Blvd., Suite 200, Lanham, MD 20706

Alleluia Press, Melkite Greek Catholic Church, Baron and Baroness Jose De Vinck, 627 Franklin Turnpike, P. O. Box 103, Allendale, NJ 07401-351

Augsburg Fortress Publishers, 100 @. Fifth Street, Suite 600, Minneapolis, MN 55402

Cairns Publications (Jim Cotter), www.CotterCairns.co.uk

Church Publishing Inc. 445 5th Ave., New York, NY 10016

Concordia Publishing House, 3558 South Jefferson Ave., St. Louis, MO 63118-3968; www.cph.org

Desert Flower Music (Jim and Jean Strathdee)

General Commission on the Status and Role of Women of The United Methodist Church, Chicago, IL; gcsrw@gcsrw.org.

GIA Publications, Inc., 7404 S. Mason Ave., Chicago, IL 60638; www.giamusic.com 800.442.1358

Hope Publishing Company, Carol Stream, Il 60188,

The Jubilate Group (admin. Hope Publishing Company, Carol Stream, IL 60188)

Medical Mission Sisters, 8400 Pine Road, Philadelphia, PA 19111

Selah Publishing Inc., 4055 Cloverlea St., Pittsburgh, PA 15227-3443

United Church of Canada; www.united-church.ca/sales/ucph/order

Upper Room, General Board of Discipleship, 1008 Grand Ave., Nashville, TN 372112-2104

The United Methodist Publishing House, 201 Eighth St. South, Nashville, TN 37202

Westminster John Knox Press, 100 Witherspoon St., Louisville, KN, 40202-1396

Wood Lake Publishing, 9590 Jim Bailey Rd, Kelowna, BC V4V 1R2, Canada

WCC Publications, World Council of Churches, Geneva 2, Switzerland

worldmaking.net, P. O. Box 190, Strawberry Point, IA 52076 (Richard Bruxvoort-Colligan)

Contributors

(In addition to those in sources listed under ackowledgments)

BBT	Barbara Troxell, OSL
CAB	Cheryl A. Brown, OSL
DTB	Daniel T. Benedict, OSL
GRC	George R. Crisp, OSL
HJC	Heather Josselyn-Cranson, OSL
HME	Heather Murray Elkins, OSL
LJV	Linda J. Vogel, OSL
MJO'D	Michael J. O'Donnell, OSL
OFB	O French Ball, OSL
SF	Sarah Flynn, OSL
TAR	Thomas A. Rand, OSL
TBE	Taylor Burton-Edwards, OSL
TJC	Timothy J. Crouch, OSL
DES	Donald E. Saliers, OSL
DWV	Dwight W. Vogel, OSL

Cynthia Astle, OSL
William J. Beasley, OSL
Donald F. Chatfield
Jim Cotter
Ruth Duck
Elise Eslinger
George R. Crisp, OSL
David Goodrich
Bishop William Boyd Grove, OSL
Robert Jarboe, OSL
Constance E. Kimos
Vince McGlothin-Eller, OSL
James K. Manley
Patricia J. Patterson
David N. Power
Jim and Jean Strathdee

Made in the USA
San Bernardino, CA
21 March 2014